SUPPLEMENT TO MAX FARRAND'S
THE RECORDS OF THE FEDERAL
CONVENTION OF 1787

SUPPLEMENT TO MAX FARRAND'S
THE RECORDS OF THE FEDERAL CONVENTION OF 1787

JAMES H. HUTSON, *editor*

with the assistance of
LEONARD RAPPORT

YALE UNIVERSITY PRESS   NEW HAVEN AND LONDON

Introduction and annotations copyright © 1987 by Yale University.
All rights reserved.

Set in Caslon Olde Style type by
Brevis Press, Bethany, Connecticut.
Printed in the United States of America by
The Murray Printing Company, Westford, Massachusetts.

Library of Congress catalog card number: 86–51340
International standard book numbers: 0–300–03903–4
0–300–03904–2 (pbk.)

The paper in this book meets the guidelines for permanence
and durability of the Committee on Production Guidelines
for Book Longevity of the Council on Library Resources.

10   9   8   7   6   5   4   3   2   1

CONTENTS

INTRODUCTION

In 1911 the Yale University Press published, in three volumes, *The Records of the Federal Convention of 1787*, edited by Max Farrand. The press reissued the *Records* in 1923, 1927, and 1934. In 1937 it reprinted them again with the addition of what Farrand called a "fourth, supplementary volume." This volume was a potpourri: it contained a list of errata discovered and corrected in volumes 1–3, additional information about the location of documents appearing in these volumes, the texts of the first twenty-one amendments to the Constitution, two revised indexes, and the texts of documents related to the creation of the Constitution that had been uncovered since the first printing of the *Records* in 1911.

The organization of the supplement was eccentric. New documentary material was sandwiched between errata and amendments and was keyed to the page numbers at which it should have appeared in the earlier volumes. At the same time a double chronological scheme was used. Materials that would have appeared in volumes 1 and 2 were arranged chronologically and then a new chronology was established for materials that would have appeared in volume 3. Because of its peculiar arrangement and its medley of diverse material, the supplementary volume is not, in the opinion of many scholars, easy to use; its revision has been frequently suggested.

As Farrand anticipated, a substantial amount of new documentary material, illuminating the creation of the Constitution, has come to light since 1937. In 1980 the Permanent Committee for the Oliver Wendell Holmes Devise, as its contribution to the Bicentennial of the United States Constitution, resolved to sponsor a revised supplement to Farrand's *Records*, which would incorporate this new material and whatever additional documentation could be discovered by a diligent search of the nation's manuscript repositories. The Yale University Press agreed to publish the new volume. The Librarian of Congress, chairman ex-officio of the Holmes Devise, warmly endorsed its initiative and encouraged the Chief of the Library's Manuscript Division to serve as editor of the supplement. The American Historical Association and Project 87 offered their assistance in raising the necessary funds. The National Endowment for the Humanities, under the auspices of its own program to celebrate the Bicentennial of the Constitution, generously granted the money requested. Leonard Rapport, long a senior staff member at the National Archives and Records Administration, who for years has collected documents on the Federal Convention, generously put his research at the editor's disposal and agreed to assist him in an intensive search for new manuscript material.

This volume is being issued simultaneously in hardcover and paperbound. In paperbound it will be a companion to Farrand's first three volumes, which have been reissued in that format. The volume supplants Farrand's "fourth, supplementary volume" of 1937, which is not being reprinted. The new supplement contains the fresh manuscript material discovered by Leonard Rapport and the editor in their search of the nation's repositories and it incorporates all of the documents in Farrand's 1937 supplement that were generated at Philadelphia in the summer of 1787; that is, all documents printed by Farrand in that volume which relate to the framing of the Constitution. The editor has chosen to omit those documents which are not records of the Federal Convention of 1787: the first twenty-one amendments to the Constitution, Farrand's discussion of the merits of rival editions of Madison's notes, and information about the acquisition of constitutional documents by various repositories, principally by the Library of Congress.

The editors of the Yale University Press decided that Farrand's 1937 supplement, though supplanted, should not be treated as a "non-volume"; copies of it are still being sold and it is on the shelves of libraries. Therefore, in the two indexes at the end of this volume, both incorporated from Farrand's 1937 supplement, that volume's existence is acknowledged by reference to it as volume 4. The present volume is identified in the indexes as volume "S" (for "Supplement"). Although index entries 4 and S will refer, in most cases, to the same documents, the duplication was considered by the editors to be a small enough price to pay to serve the convenience of scholars and libraries that still hold Farrand's 1937 supplement.

In choosing for publication documents discovered since the appearance of the 1937 supplement, the editor has adhered to Farrand's principles of documentary selection. Though nowhere explicitly stated, they are clear enough. Farrand confined himself, as rigorously as possible, in selecting his documents to those that illustrated what occurred in Philadelphia between May 14, the day the Convention was called to meet, and September 17, the day it adjourned. Except for the delegates' credentials and instructions he published little from the pre-Convention period. Gaillard Hunt's new multivolume edition of Madison's writings was, for example, available to Farrand but he included none of what might be called Madison's Constitution-planning letters—those of March and April to Randolph, Jefferson, and Washington—nor did he include Madison's "Vices of the Political System." It became apparent, during the preparation of this volume, that Farrand published little pre-Convention material because, aside from the familiar Madison documents, little survives that reveals the delegates' thinking about the task before them in Philadelphia. There are, to be sure, pre-Convention resolves of state legislatures relating to the appointment of delegates as well as letters written by delegates to friends and family as they traveled to Philadelphia, but these reveal nothing about the writing of the Constitution. Following Farrand's practices, they will not be included. The editor had hoped that letters written in transit as well as vouchers for reimbursement of travel and subsistence expenses, submitted to state legislatures after the delegates returned from Philadelphia, would permit the compilation of a more accurate attendance log than Farrand published (at 3:586–90). But such vouchers as exist are imprecise, reckoning attendance only by months or total days present, and do not improve Farrand's statistics. When these can be corrected, footnotes or other editorial devices are employed to do so.

During the Convention various delegates copied for their own use plans of government submitted by their colleagues. To establish the most authoritative text of each of these plans, Farrand collated as many of them as he could locate. The results of his investigations of the Virginia plan, the New Jersey plan, and Hamilton's plan of June 18 are published in appendixes in volume 3 (593–630). In preparing the present volume a few additional holograph copies of Convention plans and reports were discovered, that is, a copy of the Virginia plan in Lansing's notes, a copy of the Committee of the Whole House report of June 13 in Charles Cotesworth Pinckney's papers, and one or two more. These plans and reports were compared with those published in Farrand and were discovered to contain an occasional trifling difference, what Farrand called the "inevitable slight variations in wording, spelling, and punctuation" (3: 593). Since these documents compel no revision in Farrand's conclusions about the best texts of the Convention plans, they are, following Farrand's own practices with regard to slightly variant versions of the Virginia and other plans, not printed in this volume.

Farrand approached the post-Convention years with the same discrimination as he did the pre-Convention period. He was interested in documents generated by the ratification debates only insofar as a member of the Convention, participating in those exchanges, revealed something about what had occurred at Philadelphia. These revelations he published; exhortations and polemics he omitted. Farrand also published reminiscences about the Convention by delegates in private correspondence and public debate, in some cases decades after 1787, but he was careful to ascertain the credibility of these remarks before including them. This volume contains a considerable amount of retrospective material that meets Farrand's criterion for inclusion. For the post-Convention period today's student has a resource unavailable to Farrand: Merrill Jensen's edition of *The Documentary History of the Ratification of the Constitution* (Madison, 1976–), now carried forward by Jensen's colleagues, John P. Kaminski and Gaspare J. Saladino. The *Documentary History* is a continuation of the story told in Farrand's *Records* and should be consulted by everyone interested in the framing of the Constitution.

WHAT IS AND IS NOT INCLUDED

The new supplement contains, as mentioned above, the relevant documentary material from Farrand's 1937 supplementary volume. In his preface to that supplement Farrand mentioned two recently discovered collections of Convention documents, those of John Lansing, Jr., and Charles Cotesworth Pinckney, which were unavailable to him but which he assumed would become accessible to scholars "in the course of a few years." Farrand was correct about Lansing's notes, for they were published by Joseph R. Strayer in 1939 under the title *The Delegate from New York*. They are included in their entirety in the present volume with the permission of their publisher, Princeton University Press. Pinckney's papers were given, in due course, to the Library of Congress. They comprise, principally, working documents of the Convention such as the Committee of Detail report and some notes of proceedings in the South Carolina Ratifying Convention. Only one document met the requirements for publication in this volume. Convention papers—notes of debates, draft speeches, resolutions, and plans—of several other delegates have been discovered and are printed here. Some are copious, others consist of only a single document. Delegates represented by newly discovered documents are: John Dickinson, Pierce Butler, Gunning Bedford, George Mason, James Wilson, and Elbridge Gerry.

Scores of letters, written by delegates during the Convention and touching on its business, have been found and appear for the first time in this volume. A far greater number of delegate letters written at Philadelphia were excluded because they dealt with personal business and family matters. The temptation to include some of these letters was strong and in certain cases the editor succumbed to it, thus violating in these instances Farrand's selection guidelines. Letters from Elbridge Gerry to his wife are included, for example, because they so graphically convey the flavor of the summer of 1787 in Philadelphia and illustrate the context in which the Constitution was written. A few communications written by "outside" groups to the membership of the Convention, for example, an antislavery petition from a society of Pennsylvanians and a letter from Rhode Island merchants to an "unofficial" delegate at the Convention, have been included to illustrate the variety of interests that confronted the delegates.

Research has disclosed a number of what appear to be relevant letters that the editor has been unable to locate, that is, Nicholas Gilman to John Gilman, July 28, 1787 (mentioned in Nicholas Gilman to Joseph Gilman, July 31, 1787), Connecticut delegates to Samuel Huntington, June 20, 1787 (mentioned in Huntington to delegates, July 9, 1787), and others. A more regrettable omission is Robert Yates's Convention notes which Evarts B. Greene and Richard B. Morris, in *A Guide to the Principal Sources of Early American History (1600–1800) in the City of New York* (New York, 1929), p. 187, identified at the New York Public Library. A search in that repository by Leonard Rapport did not discover these notes nor has the staff of the library been successful in finding them. The editor hoped to find Convention Secretary William Jackson's notes of debates, which he took in addition to keeping the "official" records that were published in 1819 at Congress's direction, as the *Journal, Acts, and Proceedings of the Convention* (printed in full by Farrand). Jackson informed Timothy Pickering on August 11, 1827 (see below) that he took notes of the debates in a form of shorthand and was at that moment transcribing them. Although some scholars have presumed that the notes may be extant, the editor has not located them.

The present supplement does not, then, include all Convention documents that may exist. Perhaps no compilation of eighteenth-century documents can be considered definitive, because even after two centuries new manuscripts continue to surface with surprising regularity. Farrand recognized that his own work might require revision; at some time in the future this supplement may need to be merged into a newer, more comprehensive volume. The editor would not regret such an event, because it would mean that new material had been discovered that would enhance our understanding of the Constitution.

EDITORIAL METHOD

Because this supplementary volume will be issued, in paperbound, as a set with the first three Farrand volumes and because it contains copious material from Farrand's fourth volume, it appeared to be self-evident that its format and editorial apparatus should conform to Farrand's style. The editor was comfortable with this decision, because Farrand, though publishing the *Records* in 1911, was a "modern" editor in the most crucial sense: he recognized and insisted that documents be printed with fidelity to the original texts. Farrand, it has been said, was oldfashioned in his economical, even parsimonious, use of footnotes. There now appears to be a reaction against the luxuriant editorial styles of the 1950s and 1960s on financial as well as scholarly grounds, and Farrand's spare style of footnoting, his preference for letting the documents speak for themselves, appears to be anything but antiquated and unenlightened.

The editor has followed, as far as the requirement of being consistent with Farrand permitted, the practices that have become standard in modern documentary editions sponsored by the National Historical Publications and Records Commission.

Documents are reproduced with fidelity to the originals. Eighteenth-century spelling and grammar are retained, as is punctuation, with the exception that thorns and tildes are expanded and missing periods are added at what are obviously the ends of sentences; all new sentences begin with capital letters. Arcane or incomprehensible abbreviations are also expanded. Badly misspelled words that may be misleading are correctly spelled in brackets inserted after the word. Conjectural readings are also inserted in brackets. Obvious slips of the pen and inadvertent repetitions are silently corrected.

At the bottom, left, of each document the repository in which it is found or the publication in which it appears is indicated. The state of the document is described by the following abbreviations: ALS (autograph letter signed), AD (autograph document), DS (document signed), TR (transcript).

A NOTE ON THE INTEGRITY OF THE DOCUMENTARY RECORD

The two principal documentary accounts of proceedings in the Federal Convention are James Madison's and Robert Yates's notes of debates, printed by Farrand in volumes 1 and 2. The integrity of both sets of notes—the faithfulness with which they record what was said on the floor of the Convention—has been challenged in recent years. In preparing this volume, the editor discovered documents and pursued lines of investigation that shed additional light on the question of the reliability of Madison's and Yates's notes. Since these notes are such indispensable parts of the records of the Federal Convention, the results of this research are presented below.

Madison's notes, indisputably the most important account of events at the Convention, were published posthumously in 1840. Although most readers immediately accepted them as authoritative, partisans of Alexander Hamilton challenged their veracity, and there has been an undercurrent of skepticism about their accuracy ever since. Gaillard Hunt, for example, in a preface to an edition of Madison's notes, published in 1920, commented on "the suspicious investigator, who thinks that Madison may have made alterations in his original record so as to suppress or distort the truth or give a coloring to the facts."[1]

---

1. Gaillard Hunt and John M. Scott, *The Debates in the Federal Convention of 1787* (New York, 1920), xxi.

Hunt, it appears, had a premonition of Crosskey—Professor William Winslow Crosskey of the University of Chicago Law School, perhaps the most suspicious investigator ever to write about Madison's notes. Crosskey's true feelings about Madison and his notes were revealed in his constitutional law classes, which he began, according to the reminiscences of a student, by slamming Farrand's *Records* on his desk and promising "to demonstrate to you that Madison was a forger—he tampered with the notes he kept of the debates at the federal constitutional convention in order to suit his own political advantage and that of his party."[2] Crosskey was more circumspect in his opus, *Politics and the Constitution in the History of the United States*, the first two volumes of which were published in 1953. There he merely suggested "the possibility that his [Madison's] testimony may have been, not inadvertently, but deliberately false and misleading" as to what the various members had said, although elsewhere in the volume he became more explicit, declaring that Madison "presented falsely the sentiments of other men" and inserted "spurious dialogue" in his notes.[3] What were Madison's motives in doctoring his manuscript? To create an appearance of political consistency, Crosskey argued; to obscure the difference between political positions he espoused in 1787 and contrasting views he adopted later in his career.

Crosskey's volumes aroused conflicting passions. Admirers praised them extravagantly; detractors accused the author of McCarthyism on the grounds that Crosskey made unproven charges and innuendos against Madison (Crosskey promised to present his proof in later volumes).[4] Mixed reviews did not discourage Professor Crosskey. He completed most of a third volume, bringing his account up to the eve of the Convention, which was published posthumously by a disciple, William Jeffery, in 1980, and he finished some sections on the Convention itself, one of which on the ex-post-facto clause was published posthumously in 1968.[5] It characteristically charged Madison with fabricating passages in his notes and further distorting them by deliberately omitting relevant information.

Crosskey's conclusions were endorsed in 1970 by Paul Clarkson and Samuel Jett, biographers of *Luther Martin of Maryland* (Baltimore, 1970), who charged that "scores of . . . serious (and often demonstrably inaccurate) 'corrections,' alterations, and additions, made over a period of fifty

2. Abe Krash, "William Winslow Crosskey," *University of Chicago Law Review* 35 (1968): 232.

3. *Politics and the Constitution*, 1: 313, 2: 1009, 1012, 1020.

4. For the charge of McCarthyism, see Henry Hart, Jr., "Professor Crosskey and Judicial Review," *Harvard Law Review* 67 (June 1954): 1475.

5. William W. Crosskey, "The Ex-Post-Facto and the Contracts Clause in the Federal Convention: A Note on the Editorial Ingenuity of James Madison," *University of Chicago Law Review* 35 (1968): 248–54.

years . . . raise a serious question as to accuracy of his [Madison's] record."[6] That Crosskey's influence persists is demonstrated by the treatment Madison's notes receive in Christopher and James Collier, *Decision in Philadelphia: The Constitutional Convention of 1787* (New York, 1986). The Colliers employ the work of S. Sidney Ulmer, himself a partisan of Crosskey, who in 1958 charged that Madison's "objectivity" as a reporter of the Convention debates was "corrupted beyond repair,"[7] to assert that "Charles Pinckney of South Carolina was cheated of credit for his role in modeling the Constitution" by Madison's having "suppressed" evidence of his activities in Philadelphia.[8] And, in a passage of pure Crosskey, the Colliers charge that after 1800 Madison became interested in "controlling as much as he could the history" of the creation of the Constitution and "altered his own speeches" to accomplish his objective. Madison, they concluded, "improved his own arguments and abbreviated those of his opponents."[9]

That Madison made some changes in his notes after the Convention concluded has been known for decades and was discussed by Farrand in his introduction to the 1911 edition of the *Records*. When the journal of the Convention was published in 1819, Madison collated it with his notes and made changes. When Yates's notes were published two years later by Citizen Genet, Madison collated his and Yates's notes and made additional changes. In fact, as scholars discovered in 1930, and as Farrand related in his 1937 supplement, Madison collated his notes with a copy of the journal shortly after the Convention adjourned. Washington, it appears, lent him Jackson's holograph version of the journal in 1789; Madison copied it, collated the copy with his notes, and made at least a score of changes.

Crosskey was aware of these various revisions, the great majority of which involved establishing the exact texts of motions and resolutions and ascertaining accurate vote tallies, and does not appear to have intended to make them the foundation of his conviction that Madison "forged" his notes. Rather, Crosskey's position, insofar as it is accessible, seems to be that Madison invented dialogue at the Convention exactly as a writer of fiction would have done. Thus, John Dickinson's speech on August 29, explaining Blackstone's definition of the scope of ex-post-facto laws, was "a later Madisonian fabrication";[10] debates on August 21 on the imports

6. 95.

7. Ulmer, "Charles Pinckney: Father of the Constitution," *South Carolina Law Quarterly* 10 (1958): 227, 245.

8. Collier, 64, 69.

9. Ibid., 66–67, 81.

10. Crosskey, "The Ex-Post-Facto and the Contracts Clause," 252.

and exports clause contained "certain spurious passages";[11] a colloquy between Dickinson and Gouverneur Morris on August 15 had "very much the appearance of a later interpolation."[12]

There is no visual evidence to support these charges; an examination of the relevant manuscript pages of Madison's notes reveals no significant alteration of the text on any of these dates. Crosskey's allegations must be based, then, on a theory that Madison completely rewrote his notes (or parts of them) at a later date using a fresh supply of paper and substituted the newly composed sheets for the ones he had prepared earlier. Does an examination of the paper used in Madison's manuscript support such a theory?

Watermarks on the pages of Madison's manuscript notes reveal that he used British papers, predominantly those of the celebrated Kentish manufacturer James Whatman, whose family has been called the "most eminent British paper makers of the eighteenth century."[13] On all but seven days of the Convention Madison used Whatman paper, recognized by three watermarks: (1) "J Whatman"; (2) crown and post horn with a pendant cursive "W"; (3) crown and post horn with a pendant "GR." The only days Madison did not use Whatman paper were June 26, June 29, July 17, and July 18 when he employed paper with the watermark "T French" and September 7, 15, and 17, when he used paper marked "Budgen." All of this paper must have been manufactured before 1794, because none of it is dated, and a British law of 1794 required all paper to be dated to obtain a rebate on the excise tax on exportation.[14]

A comparison of Madison's notes with letters he wrote during the Convention demonstrates that on every date on which a comparison can be made the paper used for the notes and letters was identical. For example, on July 18 Madison wrote Jefferson a letter on paper with Whatman's crown, post horn, and cursive "W" watermark; the July 18 pages in the notes bear the same watermark. When chain lines and laid lines are compared, the letter and note sheets prove to be identical. Similar results are obtained by comparing other letters written during the summer, for example, Madison to Pendleton, May 27, to Jefferson, June 6, to Monroe, June 10, to Madison, Sr., July 28, September 4, to the notes composed on each of these days. Paper studies appear to indicate that Madison's notes were written in the summer of 1787, not later.

Also militating against the theory of a massive adulteration of Madison's notes is the recent discovery of the "Eppes copy" of those notes. In the summer of 1791, possibly as late as 1793, Jefferson's nephew, John Wayles

11. *Politics and the Constitution,* 1: 313.

12. Ibid., 2: 1021.

13. Thomas Balston, *James Whatman Father & Son* (London, 1957), 1.

14. Ibid., 157.

Eppes, living at the time with his uncle in Philadelphia, transcribed Madison's notes.[15] Eppes's transcription, minus the pages from June 21 to July 18, has been found in the Edward Everett papers at the Massachusetts Historical Society. Comparing it with Madison's notes on August 15, 21, and 29, the dates on which Professor Crosskey claimed fabrications and interpolations, demonstrates that the two documents are identical, which means that no changes were made in Madison's notes (on these dates, at least) after Eppes executed his copy in 1791 or 1793. It appears, then, that Madison did not rewrite the story of the Constitutional Convention late in life.

What of the claim of Crosskey and his followers that Madison distorted his notes by willful omissions? Did Madison, in fact, "cheat" Charles Pinckney out of his place in the Convention pantheon by "suppressing" his plan of government? Madison's usual practice in taking notes at the Convention was to refrain from recording long motions, reports, and plans in the expectation that he could obtain copies of them later and enter them in his notes at his convenience. The "length" of Pinckney's plan, he claimed in a memorandum written after the Convention, "prevented the taking of a copy" when it was introduced.[16] After the Convention ended had Madison (as seems likely) attempted to obtain a copy of Pinckney's plan, none would have been available, as Pinckney informed Matthew Carey on August 10, 1788.[17] That Madison was not conducting a vendetta against Pinckney with the object of concealing his contributions at the Convention is shown by his having obtained from the South Carolinian an autograph copy of his June 25 speech, which was duly published in his notes.

Crosskey's charges that Madison did not fully explain certain proceedings in the Convention, as, for example, Rutledge's motion of August 27 on the jurisdiction of the Supreme Court,[18] or that he failed to record the scores of unsuccessful motions made on the last days of the Convention amount to a complaint that Madison failed to provide a verbatim account of the proceedings, as a contemporary reporter, armed with electronic recording gear, might have done. No one knew the shortcomings of his notes better than Madison himself; it was to improve their accuracy and completeness that he painstakingly copied the Convention journal in 1789, collating it and later the printed copy of the journal with his notes and making additions and corrections as required. In making these changes his

15. For a discussion of Eppes's transcription, see Julian P. Boyd, ed., *The Papers of Thomas Jefferson*, 19 (Princeton, 1974), 549–51, and Robert A. Rutland, et al., eds., *The Papers of James Madison*, 10 (Chicago, 1977), 8–9.

16. Farrand, 3: 504.

17. Ulmer, "James Madison and the Pinckney Plan," *South Carolina Law Quarterly* 9 (1957): 420.

18. *Politics and the Constitution*, 1: 621–22.

intention, insofar as the present editor can judge, was the laudable one of giving the American people as thorough a record as he could of a seminal event in their history. A heavy burden of proof rests upon those who would contend that Madison, as editor, progressively corrupted his notes after 1787.

Until the last decade the integrity of Yates's notes was not challenged by scholars, although Madison himself, as soon as he examined the publication of the notes in 1821, protested its "extreme incorrectness."[19] In 1978, however, the present editor discovered a document in the Edmond C. Genet papers in the Library of Congress that demonstrates that Professor Crosskey's suspicions, apparently misplaced as they relate to Madison's notes, would apply with full force to Yates's notes. The original manuscript of Yates's notes, as indicated above, has disappeared, although it may be extant. Genet published Yates's notes in 1821 from a copy made by John Lansing, Jr., who along with Yates and Alexander Hamilton represented New York at the Philadelphia Convention.[20] Yates's widow lent Lansing her husband's notes sometime after his death in 1801. Lansing, as he wrote Genet on July 6, 1821 (below), made a copy with dispatch—in a month, as stipulated by Mrs. Yates. Although tempted to annotate Yates's material, Lansing "made the transcript verbatim, without the least mutilation or other alteration." The copy, Lansing stressed on this and other occasions, was literally correct. Apparently keeping the original, he returned the copy to Mrs. Yates from whom Genet obtained it by 1808. In 1821 Genet published the Lansing copy, with such other Convention documents as he could procure, as *Secret Proceedings and Debates of the Convention Assembled at Philadelphia in the year 1787.*

One sheet of Lansing's copy of Yates's notes, dated July 5, has been discovered in Genet's papers. Comparing it to the published version of Yates's notes for that date (see below) reveals that Genet deleted half of the sheet and paraphrased much of the remainder. If Genet inflicted the same editorial depredations on the remainder of his edition, Yates's notes, as we now have them in print, cannot be considered a reliable source for documentary proceedings at the Federal Convention.

Genet may have exercised a lighter editorial hand on other parts of the Lansing copy, specifically, the notes for the first week of the Convention. Lansing first attended the Convention on June 2. In his own notes of June 1 he asserted that he copied Yates's notes up to that point (and on June 5 as well, when he was ill). We do not know when Lansing made this copy. He could have done it on the spot in Philadelphia or years later when

19. Farrand, 3: 446.

20. For a discussion of Genet's edition of Yates, see James H. Hutson, "Robert Yates's Notes on the Constitutional Convention of 1787: Citizen Genet's Edition," *Quarterly Journal of the Library of Congress* 35 (July 1978): 173–82.

Yates's widow turned her husband's notes over to him for copying. If Lansing incorporated an accurate transcription of Yates's notes for May 25–June 1 into his own notes and if the copy of Yates's notes that he returned to Mrs. Yates—and that eventually came into Genet's possession—was equally accurate, then Lansing's notes for May 25–June 1 and his copy of those notes which Genet used for his publication should have been identical or close to it. By comparing Genet's edition of Yates's notes for May 25–June 1 to Lansing's notes for the same dates we should, therefore, be able to ascertain the extent of the editorial changes Genet made. This comparison has been made in this edition and readers will find footnotes in Lansing's notes showing the changes presumably made by Genet. These changes, though numerous, are far less drastic than the surgery performed by Genet on the July 5 sheet of Lansing's copy and may indicate that Genet's edition is not as corrupt as the editorial carnage of July 5 would suggest. On the other hand, so many assumptions must be made to permit inferences to be drawn about Genet's editorial practices on the May 25–June 1 material that the suggestions offered here are speculative, at best. What can be said with certainty is that until Yates's original manuscript notes are found readers can have far less confidence in the integrity of Genet's edition of his notes than they can in Madison's notes.

ACKNOWLEDGMENTS

The following institutions generously permitted the publication in this volume of documents in their possession; their assistance is gratefully acknowledged: American Antiquarian Society, American Philosophical Society, John Carter Brown Library, Columbia University, Connecticut Historical Society, Connecticut State Library, Delaware Hall of Records, Duke University, Hagley Museum and Library, Harvard University, the Huntington Library, Independence National Historical Park, Library Company of Philadelphia, Maryland Historical Society, Massachusetts Historical Society, Morristown National Historical Park, New England Historic Genealogical Society, New Hampshire Division of Records, New Hampshire Historical Society, New Jersey Archives, New-York Historical Society, New York Public Library, North Carolina Division of Archives and Records, Northumberland County Record Office, Historical Society of Pennsylvania, Rutgers University, John Rylands Library, Virginia State Library, Wadsworth Atheneum, College of William and Mary, Yale University.

SUPPLEMENT TO MAX FARRAND'S
THE RECORDS OF THE FEDERAL
CONVENTION OF 1787

MONDAY, MAY 14, 1787

GEORGE WASHINGTON: DIARY[1]

Monday 14th.   This being the day appointed for the Convention to meet, such Members as were in town assembled at the State Ho[use]; but only two States being represented—viz.—Virginia and Pennsylvania—agreed to attend at the same place at 11 'Oclock to morrow.

Dined in a family way at Mr. Morris's.

WILLIAM SHIPPEN TO THOMAS SHIPPEN

. . . May 14. Eight members of Convention met this morning, old Franklin first on the ground tho' a bad day and he cant attend the Council of this State once in 3 Weeks. He is pushing to make Temple Franklin Secretary of the Convention. Jackson is a Candidate.[2] . . .

ALS (Library of Congress)

1. Farrand published only selected entries from Washington's laconic Convention diary. All entries will be published here, although many of them reveal nothing about what was happening in the Convention. Some, however, describe the social context in which the delegates moved, a subject which did not interest Farrand and which caused him to delete passages about Washington's and other delegates' recreations and amusements in Philadelphia.

Washington left two sets of diary entries for the period of the Convention, his "Philadelphia journal" and his "regular Mount Vernon diaries." The "Philadelphia journal" was written on the spot at the Convention. When Washington returned home, he copied and expanded its entries in his "regular" diary. The editors of the contemporary edition of Washington's papers print both sets of entries but prefer the "second and more complete (revised) version" that Washington prepared at Mount Vernon. That version is the source of the entries printed here; Farrand published selections from both versions. See Donald Jackson and Dorothy Twohig, eds., *The Diaries of George Washington*, 6 vols. (Charlottesville, 1976–79), 5:152–85, 237–46.

2. As was John Beckley, clerk of the Virginia House of Delegates, who arrived in Philadelphia with Virginia governor Edmund Randolph on May 15. "I find," wrote Jonathan Williams, Jr., to his cousin, William Temple Franklin, from Richmond, April 9, 1787, "that Mr. Beckley the Clerk of this Assembly is gone on to the Convention with Governor Randolph with the express view of getting himself chosen secretary to that Body and he no doubt has secured the Virginia Interest" (Library Company of Philadelphia). Reporting Jackson's election on May 25, William Shippen informed his son Thomas on May 27 that "Old Dr. F. [was] much mortified that he had not Interest enough to procure the place for his Grandson" (Shippen Papers, Library of Congress).

I

RHODE ISLAND COMMITTEE TO JAMES VARNUM

Providence May 14, 1787

Sir

By request of the merchants and Tradesmen of this Town we inclose to your care a letter addressed to the National Convention now convened at Philadelphia,[3] which we desire you to deliver in such way as you may think best, and if the Convention shou'd be so condescending as to permit you to take a seat with them, when the Commercial affairs of the Nation are discussed we shall think ourselves highly favor'd, to have you there to speak for us.

Our Opinions are that all Goods etc. the produce or Manufacture of the United States or any of them may be Transported to any or all of them, free of any Duty or Excise,

That all Goods Imported from any Foreign Nation that pays the National Impost at the first port of Entry may be Transported to any of the United States free of any further Duty or Import.

That the carrying Trade shou'd be Insured to the Ships and Vessels that belong to the subjects of the United States on reasonable terms.

And we hope the Consideration of a General Currency throughout the United States will not be forgot by the Convention, As it is so nearly Connected with Trade and Commerce.

If you find that you can be of service to the Mercantile Interest of this State by tarrying in Philadelphia after you have finish'd your other business we shall be ready to reimburse the Extra Expense You may be at.

We heartily wish a Recommendation may go from the Convention for the Comprehending of Vermont In the Number of the United States.

P.S. Least you should have left the City before this reaches you we have thought expedient to transmit a duplicate to Tench Francis Esq. to be by him delivered.

ALS (John Carter Brown Library)

3. For this letter, dated May 11, 1787, see Farrand, 3:18–19.

TUESDAY, MAY 15, 1787

GEORGE WASHINGTON: DIARY

Tuesday 15th.   Repaired, at the hour appointed to the State Ho[use], but no more States being represented than were yesterday (tho' several more members had come in) we agreed to meet again to morrow. Govr. Randolph from Virginia came in to day.

Dined with the Members, to the Genl. Meeting of the Society of the Cincinnati.

ERASTUS WOLCOTT TO THE GOVERNOR AND GENERAL ASSEMBLY OF CONNECTICUT

Hartford, May 15

The Subscriber, impressed with a lively Sense of the Honour done him in an Appointment he has received from your Honours in your present Session as a Delegate to a general Convention of the States to be held at the City of Philadelphia on the 2d Monday of May instant, takes Liberty on this Occasion to return his grateful Acknowledgement.

He has ever made it a principle to serve the public with Alacrity in every Appointment he has had the Honour to receive and in the present Instance would freely counteract his private Wishes to domestic Enjoyment natural to one in his advanced Period of Life to serve the public under his present Appointment were it consistant with his personal Safety.

But having never had the Small Pox a Disorder to which he would be greatly exposed in the City to which he is appointed to repair, he cannot suppose it would be prudent for him to hazzard his Life without the most pressing Necessity and as there are many Gentlemen in the State who are at least equally capable to execute the business of such a Commission to the Satisfaction of the public as himself, that would not be exposed to the Effects of that fatal Disorder, such a Necessity cannot exist. This Consideration when duly weighed, he is confident, will be his sufficient Apology

3

to the Honorable Assembly in declining the Appointment he has had Honour to receive[1]

And is with every Sentiment of Respect
Your Honours most obed. and most humble Servant
Erastus Wolcott

ALS (Connecticut State Library)

1. Roger Sherman was appointed to replace Wolcott. Wolcott's apprehensions about smallpox were not chimerical. In an account submitted to the officers of the Connecticut Pay Table, April 29, 1788, for reimbursement of Convention expenses, Oliver Ellsworth claimed £2 8s. for "Cash paid a Physician for my servant in the small pox—my self when sick" (Connecticut State Library). The claim was disallowed.

WEDNESDAY, MAY 16, 1787

GEORGE WASHINGTON: DIARY

Wednesday 16th.   No more than two States being yet represented, agreed till a quoram of them should be formed to alter the hour of Meeting at the State house to One oclock.

Dined at the President Doctr. Franklins and drank Tea, and spent the evening at Mr. Jno. Penns.

THURSDAY, MAY 17, 1787

GEORGE WASHINGTON: DIARY

Thursday 17th.   Mr. Rutledge from Charleston and Mr. Chs. Pinkney from Congress having arrived gave a representation to So: Carolina and Colo. Mason getting in this Evening placed all the Delegates from Virginia on the floor of Convention.

Dined at Mr. Powells and drk. Tea there.

GEORGE WASHINGTON TO GEORGE AUGUSTINE WASHINGTON

Dear George   Philadelphia May 17th 1787

After short stages and easy driving, I reached this city on Sunday afternoon. Only 4 states, viz. Virginia, South Carolina, New York and the state we are in are as yet represented, which is highly vexatious to those who are idly and expensively spending their time here.

I hope that the fine rains which have watered this part of the Country were not confined to it; or rather, that the clouds which produced them, were not unproductive as they hovered over you. All nature seems alive from the effect of them, about this City; and the Grain appears very differently from ours.

As we have not commenced the business yet, it is impossible to say when it will end. I have not even a hope that it will meet with dispatch. . . .

ALS (Morristown National Historical Park)

FRIDAY, MAY 18, 1787

GEORGE WASHINGTON: DIARY

Friday 18th.   The representation from New York appeared on the floor
to day.

Dined at Greys ferry, and drank Tea at Mr. Morris's—after which
accompanied Mrs. [Morris] and some other Ladies to hear a Mrs. O'Con-
nell read (a charity affair). The lady being reduced in circumstances had
had recourse to this expedient to obtain a little money. Her performe. was
tolerable—at the College-Hall.

JARED INGERSOLL TO THOMAS SHIPPEN

Philadelphia, May 18, 1787

Dear Sir.

. . . We have no news to communicate, unless that our prospects appear
to become more gloomy. I look with much anxiety. I fear confusion, if
nothing worse. Our federal Government seems to be expiring. What will
be the substitute, whether better or worse or how soon any other System
may get established, it is impossible to predict. . . .

ALS (Library of Congress)

SATURDAY, MAY 19, 1787

George Washington: Diary

Saturday 19th.   No more States represented.

Dined at Mr. Ingersolls. Spent the evening at my lodgings—& retird. to my room soon.

William Livingston to David Brearley

Burlington 19 May 1787

Dear Sir

The State has added to our Delegates in Convention, Mr. Clark and myself. I suspect that by the middle of next week at farthest we shall have a full representation by the attendance of Mr. Clark and Mr. Patterson. Mr. Houston's ill state of health which I sincerely regret will I fear prevent his going tho' he told me that he intended it. It will be more agreeable to me, and what is of more consequence more useful to the State in my opinion that I should remain here during the sitting of the Legislature which I imagine will not be protracted beyond three weeks. After the rising of the Assembly, I will upon sufficient notice prepare for the journey chearfully take the place of any one of you that shall choose to return home and if our Delegation should during the sitting be unavoidably reduced to two I will leave the Legislature and go to the Convention rather than that the State should for a single day be unrepresented in it, but in that case I should wish to have notice sufficient to enable me first to go to Elizabeth Town where I should want two or three days to arrange my own affairs and prepare for the Journey.

TR (Massachusetts Historical Society)

WILLIAM PIERCE TO GEORGE TURNER[1]

New York, May 19, 1787

. . . I wish much to be with you, but Schemmerhorn has not yet made his appearance; and untill he arrives with my credentials, it will be in vain for me to go on. Pray are there any Members with you in my predicament?

The Convention is much talked of here, and various are the conjectures about the alterations that will probably take place in the federal government. You are, I find, for having matters *highly toned*. I am for powers equal to a prompt and certain execution, but tempered with a proper respect for the liberties of the People. I am for securing their happiness, not by the will of a few, but by the direction of the Law.

Upon whatever principles a Government is founded, whethers rights are equally distributed among the People at large or among a few, some respect ought to be paid to the temper of the People, as produced by one or the other of these rights. To depart from the general freedom of our Governments [indecipherable phrase] and to step into a Monarchy, which will at times be despotic, would plunge the States into a tumult infinitely worse than anarchy itself: torrents of blood would follow the confusion.

I maintain that it would be even dangerous too suddenly to abolish the State inquisition of Venice. Mankind may be fashioned in some measure to any kind of Government, and when changes are necessary, they should be brought about gradually, keeping in view some of the original principles to which they have been accustomed. From this you may learn, that I am not for a total change of the Commonwealth.

Fortunate indeed would be that People who could live under a Government that would operate only by fixed and established Laws, and not be made liable to obey the will of a Body independent of the Government itself. It is a matter of doubt with me whether any expedient by which I would be understood to mean anything that is extraneous ought ever to be practiced by a People desirous of living under a well regulated system of Laws. The creation of power not recognized by the constitution is ever

1. Major George Turner of South Carolina was secretary of the second general meeting of the Society of the Cincinnati, convened at this time in Philadelphia. On May 12 he wrote a former comrade-in-arms that he anticipated a "Revolution" in which the Cincinnati "must, se defendendo, become active and important." George Washington, Turner reported, was expected "among us in a few Hours more," an event which Turner did not altogether relish because the general's "extreme Prudence and Circumspection (having himself much Fame to lose) may cool our laudable and necessary Ebullition with a few drops, if not a Torrent, of cold water. Let us never lose sight of the rational Liberties of the People. But let us remember that energetic Government is essential to their Security" (Turner to "my dear General," May 12, 1787, Maine Historical Society).

dangerous to liberty. The exercise of the dictatorial power in Rome was inconsistent with their commonwealth; the creation of Prators, of Tribunes, of the Decemvirs etc. gave such an unsettled Spirit to the People, that they were never satisfied but when they were in pursuit of expedients to suit the various situations to which they were constantly shifting. Unless *we* can settle down into some permanent System very shortly, our condition will be as fickle and inconstant, as that of the Romans; and our political schemes be nothing more than chimeras and disorders.

Now Sir the great point—shall we be three confederate Republics or not? I leave you to examine the interrogatory.

Mrs. Pierce joins me in the most respectful compliments to Mrs. Turner.

> I am dear Sir
> Yours very affectionately
> Wm. Pierce

The Statesman and the Phylosopher have their attention turned towards us: the oppressed and wretched look to America.

ALS (Connecticut State Library)

SUNDAY, MAY 20, 1787

GEORGE WASHINGTON: DIARY

Sunday 20th.   Dined with Mr. & Mrs. Morris and other Company at their farm (called the Hills). Returned in the afternoon & drank Tea at Mr. Powells.

MONDAY, MAY 21, 1787

GEORGE WASHINGTON: DIARY

Monday 21st.   Delaware State was represented.
   Dined, and drank Tea at Mr. Binghams in great Splender.

OLIVER ELLSWORTH: RECEIPT

Hartford, May 21, 1787

Received from the Committee of Pay Table their Order on Treasury for Two Hundred pounds payable out of the Interest of the Monies arising on the taxes of one shilling and three pence on the pound payable in April and July 1782 to enable me to defray my expenses as Delegate to the Convention to be held at Philadelphia and for which I am to account with the state of Connecticut £200.[1]

Oliver Ellsworth

ALS (Connecticut State Library)

HENRY KNOX TO JOHN SULLIVAN

Philadelphia, 21 May, 1787

(Private)
To His Excellency President Sullivan:
   My dear sir,
   As an old friend, a number of Gentlemen members of the convention have pressed me to write you soliciting that you urge the departure of the delegates from New-Hampshire. Impressed most fully with the belief that

   1. Virtually identical receipts for the same sums were executed on this date by Connecticut's two other delegates, William Samuel Johnson and Roger Sherman (Ellsworth signing for Sherman). Ellsworth also executed a receipt, May 16, for "Sixteen pounds lawful Money" to defray Convention expenses. On December 1, 1787, Sherman submitted an account to the Pay Table Office, claiming reimbursement of £181 10s. for 121 days' attendance at the Convention; on January 6, 1788, Johnson claimed £220 10s. for 147 days, May 22–October 17, at the Convention and Congress; on April 29, 1788, Ellsworth claimed £159 for 106 days, May 18–August 31, at the Convention (Connecticut State Library).

we are verging fast to anarchy and that the present convention is the only means to avoid the most flagitious evils that ever afflicted three millions of freemen, I have cheerfully consented to their request and beg leave to have recourse to your kind friendship for an excuse if any is necessary.

There are here a number of the most respectable characters from the several states, among whom is our illustrious friend Genl. Washington, who is extremely anxious on the subject of the New-Hampshire delegates.

A number of states sufficiently for organization and to commence business will assemble this week. If the delegates come on, all the states excepting Rhode-Island will be shortly represented. Endeavour then my dear Sir to press this matter with all your powers. I am persuaded from the present complexion of opinions, that the issue will prove that you have highly served your Country in promoting the measures.

I am etc.

H. Knox

ALS (New Hampshire Historical Society)

TUESDAY, MAY 22, 1787

Tuesday 22d. The Representation from No. Carolina was compleated which made a representation for five States.

Dined and drank Tea at Mr. Morris's.

William Blount to John Gray Blount

New York May 22d 1787

I have before informed you that I was confined to the House with the blind piles and so I am yet but they are much mended. The Complaint is hardly called Sickness but it is undoubtedly the most painful teasing Complaint that I have ever experienced and I have had great Use for what I have none of when in pain namely Patience. I am this day informed that Williamson, Spaight and Martin are at Philadelphia or I should have sat out for that place on tomorrow or next day intolerable as traveling certainly would have proved to my Breeches. At present it is uncertain when I shall go but certainly not till I am quite well unless my Colleagues should inform me of a greater Necessity for my joining than I at present conceive. . . .

ALS (North Carolina Division of Archives and History)

Nathaniel Gorham to Caleb Davis

N. York May 22d 1787

. . . Upon examining our Commission for the Convention we find that three are required as the number to represent the state. And no Gentleman having come forward but Mr. King and myself he is gone to Philadelphia and I continued here in order if possible to keep a Congress. I have been daily in hope of seeing Mr. Dana or Mr. Gerry or both. However as Congress cannot be kept up at present I shall set off for Phila. tomorrow or next day in hopes that some of the other Gentm. will soon be after me. The business of the Convention is of the last importance for if the meeting or its doings should prove abortive the present phantom of a Government must soon expire. If those Gentm. have not set off do speak to them and let them know that by the Commission three are necessary. I am extreamly desirous of attending the Legislature at least some part of the next Session. I have therefore to beg you to get a resolve impowering two to represent the State in the convention and if any of the Gentm. in the present Commission cannot attend to get others appointed in their room. I must beg your pardon for all this trouble and remain your Friend

and Humble Servant
Nathaniel Gorham

ALS (Massachusetts Historical Society)

WEDNESDAY, MAY 23, 1787

GEORGE WASHINGTON: DIARY

Wednesday 23d.   No more States being represented I rid to Genl. Mif-
flins to breakfast—after which in Company with him Mr. Madison, Mr.
Rutledge and others I crossed the Schuylkill above the Falls. Visited Mr.
Peters—Mr. Penns Seat, and Mr. Wm. Hamiltons.

Dined at Mr. Chews—with the Wedding guests (Colo. Howard of
Baltimore having married his daughter Peggy). Drank Tea there in a very
large Circle of Ladies.

JACOB BROOM TO THOMAS COLLINS

Philada. 23 May 1787

Sir,

I take the liberty to inform you, that Mr. Read and myself are the only
Deputies who have attended from our State until Monday evening last,
when Mr. Bassett arrived. Mr. Dickinson is not yet come on.

The Gentlemen who have been present from the different States have
daily attended at the State House, and as often have been in expectation of
meeting a competent number of States to proceed to business, but as yet
only six are represented by a quorum, viz. New York, Pennsylvania,
Delaware, Virginia, North and South Carolina. There are Members also
from Massachusetts, Georgia, Maryland, and Jersey and one Gentleman
from the latter would form a quorum; he is hourly expected; when he shall
arrive it is probable that the business will be entered upon. All the States
have now appointed except Rhode Island and no good is to be expected
from her. I have enclosed you a News Paper which will give you an account
of some of their proceedings. Very little has yet been said upon the subject
of the present meeting, therefore 'tis difficult to gather any thing whereon
to form an opinion of their views. It is universally agreed that something
ought to be done to establish the Government of the United States upon a
more respectable footing than the present system. The Members of the
Convention being fully impressed with a sense of this, do not talk of
separating, but intend (at least) to attempt some plan. Two Legislative
Branches and one Executive seems to be a prevailing sentiment; but how
extensive their powers will be a weighty subject of consideration. One Plan

16

has made its appearance introduced by a Mr. Pinckney of S. Carolina. It appears to me to be a Compound, abstracted from the several Constitutions and the Articles of Confederation, except in a few particulars; one of them is a proposed Consolidation of the States and Members to be sent to the Federal Councils in proportion to the Number of Inhabitants; this will by no means be agreeable to the Citizens of the lesser States, tho it will be an object with the larger ones. We have no powers given us to treat on that tender subject and tho I am convinced there is not a Member from our State who could be draged into a Measure of the kind, yet I am well pleased that the Legislature shewed their disapprobation to it in the Act appointing their Deputies.

If a Quorum should be present from our State, in about a fortnight, or less, I intend to have the Honor of visiting you at Dover; by that time I expect our Legislature will be convened; and in the meantime, if opportunity should present, and any thing transpire worth communicating, I will do myself the Honor to write again to your Excellency.

I am with the greatest respect and esteem your Excellencys most obedient and most Humble Servant.

Jacob Broom

ALS (Historical Society of Pennsylvania)

THURSDAY, MAY 24, 1787

GEORGE WASHINGTON: DIARY

Thursday 24th.   No more States represented.

Dined and drank Tea at Mr. John Ross's.

One of my Postilion boys (Paris) being sick, requested Doctr. Jones to attend him.

WILLIAM PIERCE TO JOHN SULLIVAN

My dear Sir   New York, May 24th. 1787.

I wrote you several Weeks ago, and informed you the reason why I did not procure for you the Epaulets you wrote to me for. At that time there was not a good pair to be purchased, nor is there a pair yet to be had here that will suit you. Colo. Fish and myself have enquired through the City, but none that are elegant can be found.

In a day or two I shall set off for Philadelphia, at which place it is probable I shall be able to accommodate you. Nothing will give me more pleasure than to serve you at any Time.

The military spirit prevails here so much that all the fashionable gold Epaulets are purchased up to adorn the Shoulders of our *young Bucks*.

I will thank you sir to have my Certificate dated at Pumpton Plains in New Jersey, Decr. 1st. 1779. It shall be preserved to be handed down from one generation to another.

When I get to Philadelphia I will write you more fully. The Convention, I suppose, will proceed to business sometime next Week. Virginia, Pennsylvania, New Jersey, Maryland, New York, Delaware, Georgia, South Carolina, North Carolina and Massachusetts, will be on the floor, Monday next. Connecticut and New Hampshire will it is hoped, be on in a few Days. As for Rhode Island we shall pay no attention to her whether she sends on Deputies or not.

Please to make my respectful compliments to your Lady and Family, in which Mrs. Pierce joins, altho' a perfect stranger.

I am my dear sir, with great esteem and affection,

Wm. Pierce

ALS (New Hampshire Historical Society)

FRIDAY, MAY 25, 1787

John Lansing: Notes on Debates

Attended the Convention of the States at the State House in Philadelphia when the following States were represented.[1]

New York—by Col. Hamilton and myself.

Jersey—by Judge Brearsley, Mr. Houston, and Mr. Paterson

Pennsylvania—by Robert Morris, James Wilson, G. Morris, Mr. Fitzsimmons.

Deleware—Judge Reed, Mr. Broome, and Mr. Basset.

Virginia—General Washington, Governor Randolph, Mr. Wyth, Mr. Mason, Mr. Matthewson.

North Carolina—

South Carolina—Mr. Rutledge, C. Pinkney, C. C. Pinkney, Mr. Butler.

A Motion by R. Morris[2] that General Washington take the Chair unanimously agreed to.

When seated he[3] declared that as he never had been in a similar Situation[4]

---

1. Lansing's notes are published, as mentioned above, from the text presented by Joseph Strayer in *The Delegate from New York* (Princeton, 1939). Just before this volume went to press, the editor learned that the original manuscript of Lansing's notes was held by the James S. Copley Library, La Jolla, California.

The relationship between Lansing's notes, his copy of Yates's notes, and Genet's edition of Yates's notes has also been discussed above (pp. xxv–xxvi). Lansing copied and incorporated Yates's notes into his own notes from May 25 to June 1, when he was absent from the Convention, on June 2, and on June 5, when he was ill. On these days the differences between his notes and Genet's edition of Yates's notes are identified to illuminate Genet's editorial practices and to suggest the extent to which he may have altered Yates's notes.

In listing the delegates on this day, Genet probably consulted the printed *Journal*; he gave full, correctly spelled names of all delegates mentioned by Lansing, added Blair and McClurg to the Virginia delegation, and inserted the names of four North Carolina delegates.

2. Yates: "and seconded."

3. Yates: "(General Washington)."

4. Yates: "such a situation."

he felt himself embarrassed—that he hoped his Errors as they were[5] unintentional would be excused.

Mr. Hamilton in behalf of the State of New York moved that Major Jackson be appointed Secretary—The Delegates from[6] Pennsylvania moved for Temple Franklin—Carried for Jackson[7] who was[8] called in and took his Seat.

After which the respective Credentials of the seven States were read— N.B. That of Deleware restrained its Delegates from assenting to an Abolition of the 5*th* Section[9] of the Confederation which directed[10] that each State shall have a vote.[11]

Door-keepers and Messengers being appointed the House adjourned to Monday the 28*th* Day of May at 10 o'Clock.

GEORGE WASHINGTON: DIARY

Friday 25th.   Another Delegate coming in from the State of New Jersey gave it a representation and encreased the number to Seven which forming a quoram of the 13 the Members present resolved to organize the body; when, by a unanimous vote I was called up to the Chair as President of the body. Majr. William Jackson was appointed Secretary and a Comee. was chosen consisting of 3 Members to prepare rules & regulations for conducting the business and after [ap]pointing door keepers the Convention adjourned till Monday, to give time to the Comee. to report the matters referred to them.

Returned many visits to day. Dined at Mr. Thos. Willings and sp[en]t the evening at my lodgings.[12]

GEORGE READ TO JOHN DICKINSON

Philada. May 25th. 1787.

Being told last Evening by Govr. Randolph of his having engaged a couple of rooms in a House at a small distance from our present lodgings

5. Yates: "would be."

6. Yates: "for."

7. Yates: "by a majority Mr. Jackson carried it."

8. Yates: "who was" omitted.

9. Yates: "article."

10. Yates: "by which it is declared."

11. Yates: "one vote."

12. On May 26 Mrs. Samuel Meredith reported to her husband that "General Washington invited himself to breakfast with me Yesterday. Tom and the 3 Girls were at Table and behaved extremely well. It is observed that the General is very grave. I do not wonder at it. A Man of his reflection must feel strongly our present unhappy situation" (Read Papers, Historical Society of Pennsylvania).

and that he will move to them to morrow Evening I renewed my application on your behalf this Morning and am told that the room here which Mr. Randolph leaves you may have—it is on the first floor, up one pair of Stairs, on 5th. Street—the same which I used theretofore and you have seen me in—my present lodging room is behind it and there are doors which form a Communication between the two—As Mr. Randolph expects his lady his Situation is too Confined in this House. He is to dine at our Table—Since my Application on your behalf here on Monday last—another has been made for Mr. Gerry who is expected daily—but mine being first I now have the Offer for you—I wish you cou'd be here on the Sunday Evening. We make our Quorum today two additional So. Carolina Deputies came in Allibone's-Packet yesterday—and there is intelligence of the Arrival of two Georgia Deputies at N: York making four in the whole but one from Maryland yesterday—none as yet from Connecticut N Hampshire or Rhode Island tho the first of these three are hourly expected—You shou'd be here at the first opening of the Budget—

Let me hear from you speedily ⎫
if any Accident prevents ⎬
your Coming soon— ⎭

Farrand 4:61–62

DANIEL CARROLL TO MICHAEL MORGAN O'BRIEN

My dear friend,   Annapolis, May 25th. 1787

Yesterday the General Assembly appointed me one of the Deputies for this State to attend the foederal Convention in Phila. As this appointment was neither wished for, or expected by me, and I have been detained from home all last Winter and 6 weeks this Spring, it will be some time before I can enter on the execution of this Trust. I dare not think of residing in Philada. during the Summer months.[13] My health, thank God, is much better, than I have been for several years past. Moderate (but constant dayly) exercise, temperance and attention, have in great measure conquered my nervous complaints without the aid of Medicine. I request the favor of you to look out for a convenient and economical situation where I can board in a small family somewhere near my former temporary residence near German Town. I would prefer the Situation from it being High, healthy, and at a suitable distance. You may perhaps think of some other Situation which may answer better under all circumstances. Make no positive agreement. Communicate to me what occurs by post to Georgetown.

13. Farrand chose not to print the remainder of this letter.

You will receive my answer in time before I can possibly set off. I shall have a servant and two Horses. It is necessary to attend to economy in this business. . . .

ALS (Historical Society of Pennsylvania)

SATURDAY, MAY 26, 1787

GEORGE WASHINGTON: DIARY

Saturday 26th.   Returned all my visits this forenoon. Dined with a club at the City Tavern and spent the evening at my quarters writing letters.

SUNDAY, MAY 27, 1787

GEORGE WASHINGTON: DIARY

Sunday 27th.   Went to the Romish Church—to high Mass. Dined, drank Tea, and spent the evening at my lodgings.

RUFUS KING TO HENRY KNOX

Philadelphia 27. May 87

Seven states assembled on the 25th. and appointed Genl. Washington President & Majr. Jackson Secretary of the Convention. If Connecticut, Georgia & Massachusetts are represented tomorrow, we shall have Ten States—I hope this will be the case but the event is uncertain—no proposition has been agitated except in private conversation, and excepting the mere organization of the convention we are as when you left us.

Farrand, 4:63

RUFUS KING TO NATHAN DANE

Philadelphia 27 May 87

Dear Sir

New York, New Jersey, Pennsylvania, Delaware Virginia North and South Carolina were represented on Friday; and the Convention proceeded to appoint Genl. Washington their President and Major Jackson their secretary. We are adjourned until Tomorrow and flatter ourselves that Massachusetts Connecticut and Georgia will be then represented. Maryland has one Delegate present, but it is uncertain when his Colleagues will arrive. Nothing has transpired in the present unopened condition of the business of this meeting which furnishes reasonable Grounds even to conjecture the Result of their Deliberations. . . .

ALS (Yale University)

MONDAY, MAY 28, 1787

JOHN LANSING: NOTES ON DEBATES

Met pursuant to Adjourenment. A Committee of three Members (whose Appointment I omitted in the Entry of the Proceedings on Friday last) reported a Set of Rules for the Order of the Convention which being considered by Articles were agreed to and additional ones proposed and referred to the same Committee. The Representation was this Day encreased to nine States—Massachusetts and Connecticut became[1] represented.

Adjourned to next Day.

GEORGE WASHINGTON: DIARY

Monday 28th.   Met in Convention at 10 Oclock. Two States more— viz.—Massachusetts, and Connecticut were on the floor to day.

Established Rules—agreeably to the plan brot. in by the Comee. for the governmt. of the Convention & adjourned. No com[municatio]ns without doors.

Dined at home, and drank Tea, in a large circle at Mr. Francis's.

1. Yates: "becoming."

TUESDAY, MAY 29, 1787

John Lansing: Notes on Debates

Met pursuant to Adjournm't.[1]
The additional Rules agreed to.

His Excellency Governor Randolph, a Member from Virginia,[2] in a long and elaborate Speech shewed the Defects in the System of the present foederal Government as totally inadequate to the Peace, Safety and Security of the Confederation and the absolute Necessity of a more energetic Government. He closed his[3] Remarks with a Set of Resolutions[4] which he proposed to the Convention for their Adoption and as leading Principles whereon to form a new Government—he candidly confessed that they were not intended for a foederal Government—he meant a strong, *consolidated* Union in which the Idea of States should be nearly annihilated—(Copy of these Resolutions is marked a.)[5]

He then moved that they should be taken up in a[6] Committee of the whole House.

Mr. C. Pinkney, a Member from South Carolina[7] added that he had reduced his Ideas of a new Government to a System which he read and confessed that it was grounded on Principles similar to those in the Resolutions.[8]

The House then resolved that they would[9] next Day form themselves into a Committee of the whole to take into Consideration the State of the Union.

Adjourned to next Day.

1. Yates omits this phrase.
2. Yates adds "got up, and."
3. Yates: "these."
4. Yates: "fifteen in number."
5. Yates: "I have taken a copy of these resolutions, which are hereto annexed."
6. Yates omits "a."
7. Yates: "then."
8. Yates: "on the same principle as of the above Resolutions."
9. Yates: "the."

GUNNING BEDFORD: NOTES ON DEBATES

Mr. Randolph

1. Congress unable to prevent War
2. Not able to support war
3. Not able to prevent internal Sedition or rebellion
4. Cant prevent dissentions of one state with another, except as to territory
5. No power to prevent encroachments of the several states on Confederacy Answer

1st To prevent war Congress must possess wealth and men. Must dispose of her wealth in fortifying herself and must be able to command money and hire men to put herself at all times in a defenceable situation. Cant these objects be attained by a compulsory power in Congress to command money and men from the several States?

2d To support war. Money and men answer this purpose. A compulsory power in Congress will command

3. Cant prevent sedition or insurrection and rebellion. Vest Congress with power to call for troops and to send them into the states where insurrection or rebellion exists. Who to determine which party in the right rebels or the state? Vest Congress with power to determine this question on notice given to the parties.

4. Cant prevent dissentions of one state with another save as to territory. Vest them with this power in all cases either immediately or thro their judiciary.

5. Congress not able to prevent encroachments of the states. Let the boundary be ascertained with precision and let it be determined by the judiciary.

6. Congress cant avail themselves of imposts. Let the general regulation of trade be vested in them.

7. Congress ought to be enabled to prevent emissions of paper money. Let them be vested with such power.

8. No power to erect great works, improve navigation promote agriculture etc. They ought not to have such powers. A state has the right to avail herself of all natural advantages. To erect great works would enable them to draw money independent of the states and would end in aristocracy oligarchy and tyranny.

9. Congress ought to be paramount to state legislatures. Let Congress be empowered to negative all laws that interfere with confederation and if appeal by the state, let the question be determined in the judiciary.

AD (American Antiquarian Society)

JOHN DICKINSON:[10] REVISION OF VIRGINIA PLAN

Dickinson entered two substantive revisions on his copy of the Virginia Plan, introduced this day by Randolph. He changed the second article to read (his revisions in italics):

Resolved therefore that the rights of suffrage in the *first Branch of the* national legislative ought to be proportioned to the *Taxes and contributions respectively collected in each state and paid into the common Treasury*.

To the seventh article Dickinson added (his additions in italics):

Resolved that a National Executive be instituted; to be chosen by the national Legislature for the term of *seven* years: to receive punctually at stated times a fixed compensation for services rendered, in which no increase or diminution shall be made so as to affect the Magistracy, existing at the time of the increase or diminution; and to be ineligible a second time and that besides a general authority to execute the National Laws it ought to enjoy the executive rights vested in Congress by the Confederation *with power to carry into Execution the national Laws* [and] *to appoint officers in cases not otherwise provided for*.

AD (Historical Society of Pennsylvania)

GEORGE WASHINGTON: DIARY

Tuesday 29th.   Attended Convention and dined at home—after wch. accompanied Mrs. Morris to the benifit Concert of a Mr. Juhan.

JOHN DICKINSON TO POLLY DICKINSON

Tuesday Evening

My dear Polly,

I had a very pleasant Journey and am very well. My hopes of something good for our Country are strong. Virtue and Wisdom must be employed. May Heaven bless our Endeavours.

The tenderest Love to our precious Children. Tell them to be very good.

Your truely affectionate

ALS (Historical Society of Pennsylvania)

10. The Dickinson documents are published from texts established by the editor of this volume in "John Dickinson at the Federal Constitutional Convention," 3 *William and Mary Quarterly* 40 (April 1983): 256–82.

JAMES MCHENRY TO PEGGY MCHENRY

Philadelphia 29 May 1787

. . . We are beginning to enter seriously upon the business of the convention, so that I shall have but little leisure to give my Peggy, except the
reading of your letters. . . .

PHOTOSTAT (Library of Congress)

WEDNESDAY, MAY 30, 1787

Met[1] pursuant to adjournm't.

The Convention pursuant to order resolved itself into a Committee of the whole.

Mr. Gorham (a member of[2] Massachusetts) appointed Chairman.

Mr. Randolph then moved his *first Resolution*[3]—b.

Mr. G. Morris observed that it was an unnecessary Resolution as the subsequent Resolutions would not square with it.

It was then withdrawn by the Proposer and in Lieu thereof the following were proposed—here Resolutions Q.

In considering the Question on the first Resolve various Modifications were proposed when Mr. C.[4] Pinkney observed at last that if the Convention agreed to it it appeared to him the[5] Business was at an End for as the Powers of the House in general were to revise the present Confederation and to alter and[6] amend it as the Case might require, and[7] to determine its Inefficacy[8] or Incapability of Amendment or Improvement must End in a[9] Dissolution of the Powers.

This Remark had its Weight and in Consequence of it the *1st* and *2nd* Resolve was droped and the Question agitated on the third.

This last resolve had also its Difficulties—the Term *Supreme* required Explanation—it was asked whether it was intended to annihilate State Governments. It was answered only so far as the Powers intended to be granted

---

1. Yates adds "Convention met."

2. Yates: "from."

3. Lansing copied Randolph's "first Resolution," i.e., the first proposition of the Virginia plan, as well as the three substitute resolutions introduced after the "first Resolution" was withdrawn and which he called Resolutions Q, in the back of his notebook. His version of them is similar to that which appears in Madison's notes; Farrand, 1:33.

4. Yates omits "C."

5. Yates: "that their."

6. Yates: "or."

7. Yates omits "and."

8. Yates: "insufficiency."

9. Yates: "the."

to the new Government should clash with the states,[10] the latter was to yield. The Question was then put[11]—

for the Resolve	Against it
Massachusetts	Connecticut
Pennsylvania	New York—divided
Deleware	The other States unrepresented[12]
Virginia	
North Carolina	
South Carolina	

The next Question was on the following Resolve[13]—

In Substance, that the Mode of the present Representation in Congress[14] was unjust—the Suffrage ought to be in Proportion of[15] Numbers or Property.

To this Deleware objected in Consequence of the Instructions[16] in their Credentials and moved for postponing it which was agreed to.[17] Adjourned till to Morrow.

Pierce Butler: Notes on Debates

May the 30th 1787

Resolved therefore that a National Government ought to be established, consisting of a supreme legislature, judiciary & executive
• Resolved that the Representation in the National Legislature be not according to the present system
• Not agreed to

PHOTOSTAT (Library of Congress)

John Dickinson: Draft Motions[18]

I.

1. That an union of the States merely federal cannot accomplish the Objects of the Confederation, namely "Common Defense Security of Liberty and General Wellfare."

10. Yates: "when."
11. Yates omits this phrase.
12. Yates: "Jersey and."
13. Yates: "resolution."
14. Yates omits "in Congress."
15. Yates: "to."
16. Yates: "restrictions."

17. Yates: "to have the consideration thereof postponed to which the house agreed."

18. Motion I shows Dickinson tinkering with the tripartite substitute for the first resolution in the Virginia Plan, motion II with the resolution introduced by his Delaware colleague, George Read.

2. That no Treaty or Treaties between any of the states as individual Sovereigns can accomplish the Objects proposed by their Institution; namely "Common Defense Security of Liberty and General Wellfare."

3. Resolved therefore that a National Government ought to be established consisting of a supreme Legislature Judiciary and Executive

instead of "accomplishing the Object, of the Confederation" say securing the Liberty and promoting the Happiness of the People of

II.

Resolved, 2—That to accomplish the Objects proposed by the Confederation, a more effective Government, consisting of a Legislative, Judiciary and Executive ought to be established

Resolved 1—That the Confederation is so defective that it cannot accomplish the Objects proposed by it, namely "Common Defense security of Liberty and general Wellfare."

AD (Historical Society of Pennsylvania)

Draft Motion[19]

Resolved that it is the opinion of this Convention that the strictest friendship and Alliance, as well offensive as defensive should subsist between the states of America. Resolved that it is the opinion of this Convention that the Territory of the States is too extensive to consist of one Republic only Resolved therefore that it is the opinion of this Convention that the security of equal Liberty and general Welfare will be best preserved and continued by forming the States into three Republicks distinct in their Governments but United by a Common League Offensive and Defensive.

PHOTOSTAT (Library of Congress)

19. Found in Pierce Butler's papers in a hand resembling Butler's but not indisputably his. A Butler holograph would not answer the question of whether Butler composed the resolutions himself or copied them from someone else. The resolutions are undated; they are assigned this date because they address a common problem and share a common vocabulary—"equal Liberty and general Welfare"—with other resolutions introduced on May 30. They seem to relate, in some way, to Hamilton's remark of May 29, recorded by McHenry, that "it struck him as a necessary and preliminary inquiry to the propositions of Virginia whether the united States were susceptible of one government, or required a seperate existence connected only by leagues offensive and defensive and treaties of commerce" (Farrand, 1:17).

GEORGE WASHINGTON: DIARY

Wednesday 30th.   Attended Convention.
    Dined with Mr. Vaughan. Drank Tea, and spent the evening at a
Wednesday evenings party at Mr. & Mrs. Lawrence's.

ELBRIDGE GERRY TO ANN GERRY

Philadelphia 30th May 1787
I have received my dearest Life, six of your Letters, the two last of which
have given me inconceivable pleasure. I am in the same Family in which
I have lived, when here, since the year 1778. Doctor Jones has long resided
in it, and is frequently called on by his patients in the Night. Notwithstanding this I have been alarmed, whenever awoke by persons who wanted
him, and have dreaded to hear their Business, lest it should respect my
dearest Girl or our lovely Babe: after your next Letter I shall feel easy on
that score but my Love, I must request You to guard against the Effects
of the excessive Rains we have had, by avoiding carefully the Evening
Air, and indeed the early morning Air. Perhaps you will say there is no
Danger of taking the latter, but I thot it best to give the Caution. These
Rains have made the Earth so moist, that the uplands are like Meadows,
and at this Season when the Sun has such power, they will produce such
Exhalations as will make the atmosphere very damp and unhealthy.
Checked perspirations, Color and Fever will I am apprehensive be the
prevalent Consequence; and the frequent use of porter with Exercise when
the Weather is clear and moderate, will perhaps be the best preventatives.
The heavy, inelastic air of this city has given me a Head-Ache at Times,
accompanyed with a Loss of appetite but I am otherwise very well. Indeed
I am sometimes restless, but impute this to the Use of Tea which I propose
to omit. I have not Occasion for the Care of any Females, except of my
dearest love, to preserve Health; but if I had, every attention would be
paid me here which I could wish or require. . . .
    Much inquiry has been made for you my love, but Mrs. Morris has
not been amongst those who made it. I dined at her table as I informed
you with an elegant Circle, but I have not called on her since, & I shall
not again till you arrive. Perhaps the Curiosity of many may be of the
Nature you mention, it's utmost object may be to see you on some public
Occasion; for private Interviews would require Hospitality which does not
flourish much in this Govt. Indeed my love there is and always has been
as much difference between the Hospitality of this City and that of New
York, as between the Sociability of a quaker and of a military Society. The
Members of the first are like Monks and Nuns cloistered in a monastery,

and the others are like Citizens of the World who have neither Attachments nor prejudices from professions or local Circumstances. Whenever you arrive then, You much not expect the attention of New York, and whether you receive many or none, it will not to me be a Matter of Consequence: to be independent, is my Determination. . . .

Mrs. King is very friendly whenever I meet her, but I have lost my visiting Relish. I am happy to hear the attentions of your Friends, pray remember me in the most friendly Terms to all of them. . . .

ALS (Sang Collection, Southern Illinois University)[20]

WILLIAM BLOUNT TO JOHN GRAY BLOUNT

New York May 30th 1787

I have before informed that an Indisposition had detained me here. I am I believe over the pain of it unless I bring it on by too much Exercise say by traveling. On the 25th seven states assembled in Convention and chose a President and Secretary and by this Time I think there are eleven States represented only New Hampshire and Rhode Island being unrepresented. I can not suppose anything definitive will be done in Convention in less than a Month and most people suppose not in less than two or three Months and I shall certainly be in Philadelphia in less than a Week. . . .

ALS (North Carolina Division of Archives and History)

RICHARD DOBBS SPAIGHT TO JOHN GRAY BLOUNT

Philadelphia, 30th May 1787

Dear Sir:

. . . A Convention was not formed untill friday last, and then only by seven states; at present we have nine; Genl. Washington was of course unanimously elected President. The business being only just begun, it is a difficult point to say when we shall make a finish. Indeed I fear that much time will be expended in this business, much more than I expected when I came from home, and of course another supply of cash must take place to enable us to stay here. Should that article be deemed necessary and the Govt. grant warrants for a farther advance of salary would it be agreeable to you to remit mine to me? . . .

ALS (North Carolina Division of Archives and History)

20. Copies of the Gerry documents that appear in this edition were acquired from the Sang Collection at Southern Illinois University, but the collection has since been sold at auction and dispersed. The present ownership of the Gerry documents is impossible to ascertain.

WILLIAM SAMUEL JOHNSON TO SAMUEL WILLIAM JOHNSON

New York, May 30 1787

My Dear Son:

. . . I go on tomorrow Morning to Philadelphia where Delegates are assembling from all the States in the Union, except Rhode Island, in a special convention for the purpose of reforming and strengthening our federal government. An arduous task! Gen. Washington presides and my colleagues from Connecticut are Mr. Sherman and Mr. Ellsworth. It is an affair of high and agitated expectation throughout the continent, but what will be the Issue of it no man can yet foresee. . . .

ALS (Yale University Library)

ROBERT BURTON[21] TO JOHN GRAY BLOUNT

Philadelphia May 30 1787

. . . the Convention sitting here are so very private that there is no telling what business they are on . . .

ALS (North Carolina Division of Archives and History)

WILLIAM DAVIE TO JAMES IREDELL[22]

Philadelphia, May 30, 1787

Dear Sir:

After a very fatiguing but rapid journey I arrived here on the 22nd. The Gentlemen of the Convention had been meeting from day to day waiting for the presence of seven States; on the 25th the members from Jersey attended, and General Washington was chosen president.

Yesterday nine States were represented, and the great business of the meeting was brought forward by Virginia, with whom the proposition for a Convention had originated.

As no progress can yet be expected in a business so weighty and at the same time so complicated, you will not look for anything new from this quarter.

Be so good as to favor me, by the next post, with your opinion how far the *introduction* of judicial and executive powers derived from Congress would be politic or practicable in the States and whether *absolute* or *limited* powers for the regulation of trade both as [to] the *exports* and *imports*. I

21. Burton was a North Carolina delegate to Congress.
22. Farrand (3:31) omitted the final paragraph of this letter.

trouble you frequently and I expect your opinion without reserve. Make my compliments to Mr. Johnston and believe me with

>great respect
>your mo. obd.
>W. R. Davie

ALS (Duke University)

THURSDAY, MAY 31, 1787

Met pursuant to Adjournment.

This Day the State of Georgia[1] was represented[2] so that there were now ten States represented.

The House[3] again in[4] a Committee of the whole.[5]

The third Resolve[6] "that the national Legislature ought to consist of two Branches" was taken into Consideration and without any Debate agreed to.[7]

The *4th Resolve* "that the Members of the first Branch of the national Legislature ought to be elected by the People of the several States" was opposed[8] by Massachusetts and Connecticut who supposed they ought to be elected[9] by the Legislature[10] and Virginia supported the Resolve, alledging that this ought to be the democratic Branch[11] and as such immediately vested in the People.

The[12] Question was carried but the remaining Part of the Resolve detailing the Powers was postponed.

The *5th* Resolve[13]—postponed.

The *6th* Resolved detailed—.[14]

1. Yates: "Jersey."

2. Yates: "in convention."

3. Yates: "went."

4. Yates: "into."

5. Yates: "Mr. Gorham in the chair."

6. Yates: "to wit."

7. Yates: "(N. B. As a previous resolution had already been agreed to, to have a supreme legislature, I could not see any objection to its being in two branches.)"

8. Yates: "and strange to tell."

9. Yates: "chosen."

10. Yates: "legislatures."

11. Yates: "of government."

12. Yates: "This."

13. Yates: "That the members of the second branch of the national legislature ought to be elected by those of the first out of a proper number of persons nominated by the individual legislatures, and the detail of the mode of election and duration of office was postponed."

14. Yates: "is taken in detail."

That each Branch ought to possess the Right of originating Acts. Agreed.

That the National Legislature ought to be empowered to enjoy the Legislative Rights vested in Congress by the Confederation. *Agreed*.

[15]to legislate in all Cases in[16] which[17] seperate States are incompetent. *Agreed*.

Adjourned.[18]

GEORGE MASON: NOTES

In the Choice of the Senate, there is a material Difference between classing different Districts of the same State for the choice of Deputies or sub-electors, to appoint the Senators for their State; & classing together different States for that purpose—in the latter mode, there wou'd be Confusion, by blending together, in the choice, the Representations of different States.—The principal objection to each State's choosing separately, seems to be in the Danger of making the Senate too numerous; as the smallest State must have an Integral Vote in the Senate & the larger States in proportion.—

Might not this objection be obviated, by apportioning duly the Representation to each State, giving the smaller States an Integer, & confining the larger States to sending a smaller number of Senators than their proportion, to deliver their due number of votes? This method wou'd perhaps be exceptionable in the first Branch of the Legislature; but the objections do not apply, with equal Force, to the Senate.

Farrand, 4:14–15.

GEORGE WASHINGTON: DIARY

The State of Georgia came on the Floor of the Convention to day which made a representation of ten States.

Dined at Mr. Francis's and drank Tea with Mrs. Meredith.

GEORGE WASHINGTON TO HENRY KNOX

Philadelphia, May 31, 1787.

My dear Sir: It gave me great pleasure to find by your letter of the 29th. that you were freed from all apprehension on acct. of Miss Lucys eye, and that we might flatter ourselves with the expectation of seeing Mrs.

15. Yates: "And, moreover."
16. Yates: "to."
17. Yates: "the."
18. Yates omits.

Knox and you at this place. It was not untill Friday last that Seven States Assembled in Convention. By these I was, much against my wish, unanimously placed in the Chair. Ten States are now represented, and Maryland probably will be so in the course of a few days. Should New Hampshire come forward, Rhode Island will then stand very *singularly* alone.

As it is not even certain that this letter will get to New York before you shall have left it I will only add Compliments to Mrs. Knox and assurances of the sincerest friendship of Yr.etc.

John C. Fitzpatrick, ed., *The Writings of George Washington*, 39 vols. (Washington, D.C., 1931–44), 29:224–25.

FRIDAY, JUNE 1, 1787

Met pursuant to Adjournm't.

[1]7*th* Resolve. That a national Executive be instituted. *Agreed.*
to continue in Office[2] 7 Years. *Agreed.*
a general Authority to execute the Laws. *Agreed.*
to appoint all Officers not otherwise provided for. Agreed.

Adjourned to[3] next Day.

Thus far Judge Yates—I have been prevented from attending the Convention at an earlier Day.

GEORGE WASHINGTON: DIARY

Friday 1st. June.   Attending in Convention and nothing being suffered to transpire no minutes of the proceedings has been, or will be inserted in this diary.

Dined with Mr. John Penn, and spent the evening at a superb entertainment at Bush-hill given by Mr. Hamilton—at which were more than an hundred guests.

DAVID BREARLEY, WILLIAM HOUSTON, WILLIAM PATERSON TO THE
COUNCIL AND GENERAL ASSEMBLY OF NEW JERSEY

That the Convention now sitting in Philadelphia, of which they are Members on the Part of New Jersey, have found it indispensibly necessary to employ a Secretary, a Messenger, and a Doorkeeper.

That to defray the Wages of these Persons and the Expence of Stationary etc. some Funds will be requisite and the Convention possess none of any Kind.

That as Congress have recommended the Meeting, they will no Doubt ultimately discharge the necessary Expenses attending it, but that there is little or no Prospect that they will be again in Session until sometime after the Convention rises.

1. Yates: "The."
2. Yates: "for."
3. Yates: "the."

That the Proportion of New Jersey will be, upon a rough Estimate, about five Shillings a Day, and, to Appearances the Convention will sit about two or three Months.

The Subscribers therefore pray, that the Honourable the Legislature will authorize them to draw on the Treasury, not exceeding a certain Amount, of which they, in their wisdom, will determine, for the Purpose of paying the Wages and Expenses aforesaid as far as the Proportion of the State shall require; the Account to be settled on proper Vouchers to be taken for what is paid and disbursed.[4]

David Brearley
William Paterson
William Houston

ALS (New Jersey Archives)

JOHN LANSING TO WILLIAM COXE

Sir   Bristol June 1st 1787
I am now on my Way to Philadelphia at which place I shall probably remain for some Weeks. As it is inconvenient for me to wait on you at present I shall do myself that pleasure when I return as I wish to have some Conversation with you on the Subject of your Affairs entrusted to my Care. If [in] the meantime you should be in Philadelphia I shall be happy to see you at the City Tavern where I intend to lodge.

I am sir your most obedient
and very humble Servant
J. Lansing Junior

ALS (Historical Society of Pennsylvania)

ROBERT YATES TO ABRAHAM YATES

Philadelphia June 1 1787

Sir
Mr. Lansing who this day arrived here informs me that you are sur-prized you have not heard from me.

I answered yours on the 20 ult. and sent it by the post, and I presume that you are now in possession of it.

Alas sir! my forebodings there are too much realized, and to prevent any member from communicating the future proceedings of Convention

4. On June 4 the New Jersey General Assembly authorized the delegates to draw upon the Treasurer for any sum not to exceed £30 "to defray this State's Quota of the general Expenses which may accrue in the Course of the Convention" (*Votes and Proceedings of the eleventh General Assembly of the State of New-Jersey,* 35).

additional Rules have since been entered into, one of which strictly prohibits the communication of its business until the final close of it. While I remain a sitting member these rules must be obligatory. How long I shall remain future events must determine. I keep in the meanwhile an exact journal of all its proceedings. This communication is in the most perfect confidence, in which only one other Person beside yourself can participate. My respectful compliments to the Governor and remain Sir

Your most obedient humble Servant
Robert Yates

ALS (New York Public Library)

SATURDAY, JUNE 2, 1787

JOHN LANSING: NOTES ON DEBATES

Attended Convention.

Present eleven States.

Mr. Pinkney called for the Order of the Day—Resolved into a Committee of the whole.

Mr. Wilson moved that the States should be divided into Districts consisting of one or more States and each District to elect a Number of Senators to form the second Branch of the national Legislature—the Senators to be elected and a certain Proportion to be annually dismissed—avowedly on the Plan of the *New York Senate.*

Question put—rejected.

In the 7*th* Resolve the words *to be chosen by the national Legislature* agreed to.

President Franklin moved that the Consideration of that Part of the 7*th* Resolve which had in Object the making Provision for a Commpensation for the Service of the executive be postponed for the Purpose of considering a Motion that the *Executive should receive no Salary Stipend or Emolument for the Devotion of his Time to the public Services but that its Expences should be paid.*

Postponed Consideration.

Mr. Dickenson moved that in the 7*th* Resolve the words *and removeable on Impeachment and Conviction for malconduct or Neglect in the Execution of the Duties of the Office* should be inserted after the words *ineligible a second Time.* Agreed.

The Remainder postponed.

Mr. Butler moved to fix the Number of which the Executive should consist. Ent[ere]d on Consideration.

Mr. Randolph—Sentiments of the People ought to be consulted—they will not bear the Semblance of Monarchy—he prefered three Divisions of the States and one Executive to be taken from each—this Division obvious—it had been marked for other Purposes—If a single Executive Persons remote from him neglected—Local Views would be attributed to him, frequently well founded—often without Reason—this would excite Disatisfaction—he was therefore for an *Executive of three.*

Butler—Delays, Divisions, and Dissentions arise from an Executive

43

consisting of many—Instance Holland distracted State occasioned by her many Councellors.

Further Consideration postponed.

Mr. C. Pinkney—Notice for Reconsideration of Mode of Election of the first Branch of the Legislature.

Adjourned till Monday next.

GEORGE WASHINGTON: DIARY

Saturday 2d.   Majr. Jenifer coming in with sufficient powers for the purpose, gave a representation to Maryland; which brought all the States in Union into Convention except Rhode Island which had refused to send delegates thereto.

Dined at the City Tavern with the Club & spent the evening at my own quarters.

PENNSYLVANIA SOCIETY FOR THE ABOLITION OF SLAVERY: ADDRESS[1]

To the honorable the Convention of the United States of America now assembled in the City of Philadelphia. The memorial of the Pennsylvania Society for promoting the Abolition of Slavery and the releif of free Negroes unlawfully held in bondage.

The Pennsylvania Society for promoting the Abolition of Slavery and the releif of free Negroes unlawfully held in Bondage rejoice with their fellow Citizens in beholding a Convention of the States assembled for the purpose of amending the federal Constitution.

They recollect with pleasure, that among the first Acts of the illustrious Congress of the Year 1774 was a resolution for prohibiting the Importation of African Slaves.

It is with deep distress they are forced to observe that the peace was scarcely concluded before the African Trade was revived and American Vessels employed in transporting the Inhabitants of Africa to cultivate as Slaves the soil of America before it had drank in all the blood which had been shed in her struggle for liberty.

To the revival of this trade the Society ascribe part of the Obloquy with which foreign Nations have branded our infant States. In vain will be their Pretentions to a love of liberty or a regard for national Character, while they share in the profits of a Commerce that can only be conducted upon Rivers of human tears and Blood.

1. This address was submitted to the Society's president, Benjamin Franklin, for presentation to the Convention. At a meeting on July 2, 1787, the Society was informed that Franklin had not presented the address and other documents, because he "had thought it advisable to let them lie over for the present."

By all the Attributes, therefore, of the Deity which are offended by this inhuman traffic—by the Union of our whole species in a common Ancestor and by all the Obligations which result from it—by the apprehensions and terror of the righteous Vengeance of God in national Judgements—by the certainty of the great and awful day of retribution—by the efficacy of the Prayers of good Men, which would only insult the Majesty of Heaven, if offered up in behalf of our Country while the Iniquity we deplore continues among us—by the sanctity of the Christian Name—by the Pleasures of domestic Connections and the pangs which attend there Dissolutions—by the Captivity and Sufferings of our *American* bretheren in Algiers which seem to be intended by divine Providence to awaken us to a Sense of the Injustice and Cruelty of dooming our *African* Bretheren to perpetual Slavery and Misery—by a regard to the consistency of principles and Conduct which should mark the Citizens of Republics—by the magnitude and intensity of our desires to promote the happiness of those millions of intelligent beings who will probably cover this immense Continent with rational life—and by every other consideration that religion Reason Policy and Humanity can suggest the Society implore the present Convention to make the Suppression of the African trade in the United States, a part of their important deliberations.

Signed by order of the Society

June the 2 1787

Jonathan Penrose Vice President

AD (Historical Society of Pennsylvania)

SUNDAY, JUNE 3, 1787

Sunday, 3d. Dined at Mr. Clymers and drank Tea there also.

GEORGE WASHINGTON TO GEORGE AUGUSTINE WASHINGTON

Philadelphia, June 3, 1787

. . . It is painful to hear that the fine rains which are constantly watering this Country and which have given a vigour and verdure to the grain and grass about this City which is hardly to be described, should not have extended to you. The coolness of the weather is common to both, and the complaint of too much rain here, is now accompanied with apprehensions and indeed reports of damage from frost.[1]

As there is not the smallest prospect of my return before harvest and God knows how long it may be after it, I enclose you observations I made at last harvest. . . .

The sentiments of the different members seem to accord more than I expected they would, as far as we have yet gone. There are now 11 states represented and not much hope of another as Rhode Island refused to send and New Hampshire seems unable by some reason or another to come on. . . .

ALS (Huntington Library)

NATHANIEL GORHAM TO NATHAN DANE

Philadelphia June 3 1787

We have now eleaven States—and have been every day last week in a Committee of the whole—in which to sound the sentiments of each other several propositions relative to a general Government have been submitted—the business was opened by Govr. Randolph of Virginia in an able manner—& I think there is a prospect that the Convention will agree in a pretty good plan—. . . I do not know that I am at liberty to mention in

1. "This 9th of June is the first day of this Spring that a Fire would be disagreeable so cold and wet has been the Season" (William Shippen to Thomas Lee Shippen, June 4–9, 1787, Shippen Papers, Library of Congress).

any manner what the Convention has done—but to you in confidence I can say that they have agreed I believe unanimously that there ought to be a National Legislative Executive & Judiciary—

Farrand, 4:63–64

RUFUS KING TO HENRY KNOX

Philadelphia 3 June 87

Mr. Jennifer has arrived from Maryland. Mr. Danl. Carrol, and Mr. Mercer, who was formerly in Congress from Virginia, are in the Maryland Deputation and are expected in a few days—Eleven States are represented, but we proceed slowly—I am unable to form any precise Opinion of the Results—Nothing however very important has turned up and issued unfavorably . . . the weather has been, and continues, very cold for the season; we have now a Fire in our Chamber and find it extremely pleasant—

Farrand, 4:64

MONDAY, JUNE 4, 1787

Mr. Pinkney moved that the Blank in the 7*th* Resolution fixing the Number of the Executive be filled with the Word *one*.

Mr. Wilson—It is congenial to the Feelings of the People to have a single Executive—they have been accustomed to it—Every State has a single Person as Executive—three may divide and adopt distinct Propositions.

Mr. Sherman—ought to have a single Executive but a Council to aid him.

Question whether Blank shall be filled with the Word *one*.

Affirm.		Neg.	
Massachusetts	I	New York	I
Connecticut	I	Deleware	I
Pennsylvania	I	Maryland	I
Virginia	I	—	
North Carolina	I		3
South Carolina	I		
Georgia	I		
	7		

The 8*th* Clause was then considered.—Mr. Gerry moved its Postponement to take up the following "that a national Executive shall have a Right to negative every national Act *which shall not be afterward past unless by— Part of each Branch of the National Legislature.*"

Mr. Wilson and Mr. King spoke in its Favor.

Question carried for postponing *6 Ayes—4 Noes.*

Next Question on Motion by Mr. Wilson that the Executive have an uncontrolled Negative by expunging the Words scored. Dr. Franklin— Mr. Maddison and Mr. Bedford against expunging.

Carried unanimously against it.

Motion by Mr. Butler that the Executive be vested with a Power to suspend all Act of national Legislature for   Days.

Unanimously carried in the Negative.

9*th* Resolve—that a national Judiciary be established. Agreed *8 States to 2*—Connecticut and Maryland negative.

Adjourned till to Morrow.

GEORGE MASON: DRAFT SPEECH[1]

It is not yet determined how the Executive is to be regulated whether it is to act solely from its own Judgment, or with the Advice of others whether there is, or is not to be a Council annexed to it; and if a Council, how far their Advice shall operate in controuling the Judgment of the supreme magistracy—If there is no Council of State, and the executive power be vested in a single Person; what are the Provisions for its proper Operation, upon casual Disability by sickness, or otherwise.—These are Subjects which must come under our Consideration; and perhaps some of the most important Objections would be obviated by placing the executive Power in the hands of three, instead of one Person.

There is also to be a Council of Revision; invested, in a great Measure, with a Power of Negative upon the Laws; and an Idea has been suggested, either within or without doors, that this Council should be formed of the principal Officers of the State,—I presume of the members of the Treasury Board, the Board of War, the Navy Board, and the Department for foreign Affairs: it is unnecessary, if not improper, to examine this part of the Subject now, but I will venture to hazard an Opinion, when it comes to be thoroughly investigated, that we can hardly find worse Materials out of which to create a Council of Revision; or more improper or unsafe Hands, in which to place the Power of a Negative upon our Laws.—It is proposed, I think, Sir, in the Plan upon your Table, that this Council of Revision shall be formed out of the Members of the Judiciary Departments joined with the Executive; and I am inclined to think, when the Subject shall be taken up, it may be demonstrated, that this will be the wisest and safest mode of constituting this important Council of Revision.—But the foederal inferior Courts of Justice must, I presume, be fixed in the several respective States, and consequently most of them at a great Distance from the Seat of the foederal Government: the almost continual Operation of the Council of Revision upon the Acts of the national Parliament, and upon their Negative of the Acts of the several State legislatures, will require that this

1. Farrand printed this draft speech in volume 4 from the holograph copy, which was not available when he prepared volumes 1–3. In volume 1 (110–14) he printed the draft from a version contained in a biography of Mason. The wording of the two versions is identical (with the exception of what are evidently typographical errors), although there are differences in punctuation and spelling, caused by Mason's biographer's efforts to "modernize" the text.

Council should be easily and speedily convened; and consequently, that only the Judges of the Supreme foederal Court, fixed near the Seat of Government, can be Members of it; their Number will be small: by placing the Executive Power in three Persons, instead of one, we shall not only increase the Number of the Council of Revision (which I have endeavoured to show will want increasing), but by giving to each of the three a Vote in the Council of Revision, we shall increase the Strength of the Executive, in that particular Circumstance, in which it will most want Strength—in the Power of defending itself against the Encroachments of the Legislature.—These, I must acknowledge, are with me, weighty Considerations for vesting the Executive rather in three than in one Person.

The chief Advantages which have been urged in favour of Unity in the Executive, are the Secrecy, the Dispatch, the Vigour and Energy, which the Government will derive from it; especially in time of war.—That these are great Advantages, I shall most readily allow—They have been strongly insisted on by all monarchical Writers—they have been acknowledged by the ablest and most candid Defenders of Republican Government; and it can not be denied that a Monarchy possesses them in a much greater Degree than a Republic.—Yet perhaps a little Reflection may incline us to doubt whether these Advantages are not greater in Theory than in Practice—or lead us to enquire whether there is not some pervading Principle in Republican Governments which sets at Naught, and tramples upon this boasted Superiority—as hath been experienced, to their cost, by most Monarchys, which have been imprudent enough to invade or attack their republican Neighbors. This invincible Principle is to be found in the Love the Affection the Attachment of the Citizens to their Laws, to their Freedom, and to their Country—Every Husbandman will be quickly converted into a Soldier, when he knows and feels that he is to fight not in Defence of the Rights of a particular Family, or a Prince; but for his own. This is the true Construction of the pro Aris & focis which has, in all Ages, performed such Wonders—It was this which, in ancient times, enabled the little Cluster of Grecian Republics to resist, and almost constantly to defeat the Persian Monarch—It was this which supported the States of Holland against a Body of veteran Troops thro' a thirty Years War with Spain, then the greatest Monarchy in Europe, and finally rendered them victorious.—It is this which preserves the Freedom and Independence of the Swiss Cantons in the midst of the most powerful Nations—And who that reflects seriously upon the Situation of America, in the Beginning of the late War—without Arms—without Soldiers—without Trade, Money, or Credit—in a Manner destitute of all Resources, but must ascribe our Success to this pervading, all-powerful Principle?

We have not yet been able to define the Powers of the Executive; and however moderately some Gentlemen may talk or think upon the Subject,

I believe there is a general Tendency to a strong Executive and I am inclined to think a strong Executive necessary—If strong and extensive Powers are vested in the Executive, and that Executive consists only of one Person; the Government will of course degenerate (for I will call it degeneracy) into a Monarchy—a Government so contrary to the Genius of the People that they will reject even the Appearance of it—I consider the federal Government as in some Measure dissolved by the Meeting of this Convention—Are there no Dangers to be apprehended from procrastinating the time between the breaking up of this Assembly and the adoption of a new System of Government—I dread the Interval—If it should not be brought to an Issue in the Course of the first Year the Consequences may be fatal—Has not the different Parts of this extensive Government, the several States of which it is composed a Right to expect an equal Participation in the Executive, as the best means of securing an equal Attention to their Interests? Should an Insurrection, a Rebellion or Invasion happen in New Hampshire when the single supreme Magistrate is a Citizen of Georgia, would not the People of New Hampshire naturally ascribe any Delay in defending them to such a Circumstance and so vice versa— If the Executive is vested in three Persons, one chosen from the northern, one from the middle, and one from the Southern States, will it not contribute to quiet the Minds of the People, and convince them that there will be proper attention paid to their respective Concerns? Will not three Men so chosen bring with them, into Office, a more perfect and extensive Knowledge of the real Interests of this great Union? Will not such a mode of Appointment be the most effectual means of preventing Cabals and Intrigues between the Legislature and the Candidates for this Office, especially with those Candidates who from their local Situation, near the Seat of the federal Government, will have the greatest Temptations and the greatest Opportunitys? Will it not be the most effectual means of checking and counteracting the aspiring Views of dangerous and ambitious Men, and consequently the best Security for the Stability and Duration of our Government upon the invaluable Principles of Liberty? These, Sir, are some of my motives for preferring an Executive consisting of three Persons rather than of one.

Farrand, 4:15–20

GEORGE WASHINGTON: DIARY

Monday 4th.   Attended Convention. Representation as on Saturday.

Reviewed (at the importunity of Genl. Mifflin and the officers) the Light Infantry—Cavalry—and part of the Artillery, of the City.[2]

Dined with Genl. Mifflin & drk. Tea with Miss Cadwallader.

2. "In the Evening my wife and I went to Market Street Gate, to see the great and good Man General Washington. We had a full View of him and Major Jackson who walked with him, but the Number of People that followed him, on all Sides, was astonishing. He has been out on the Field to view Capt. S. Miles with his Troop of Horse, the Light Infantry, and Artillery" (Jacob Hiltzheimer, diary, American Philosophical Society).

TUESDAY, JUNE 5, 1787

JOHN LANSING: NOTES ON DEBATES[1]

Met pursuant to Adjournment.

Being indisposed I did not attend but Judge Yates gave me the following Account of their Proceedings.

The 9*th* Resolve. *That a national Judicial be established to consist of one Supreme Tribunal and of Inferior Tribunals*—agreed to—unanimously.

Mr. Wilson moved that the Judicial be appointed by the Executive instead of *the national Legislature*. Mr. Maddison opposed—the Judges ought to be appointed by the Senetorial Branch of the Legislature. Moves *that* the words *the national Legislature* be struck out.

Carried 8 for and 2 against.

Good Behaviour and fixed Salaries carried unanimously.

The remainder of the Clause postponed.

10. Resolve—Read and agreed to.

11. Resolve—Read and postponed.

12. Resolve—Read and agreed to.

13. Resolve—Read and postponed.

14. Resolve—Same.

15. Resolve—Mr. Maddison enforced the Necessity of this Resolve for that the new Constitution ought to have the highest Source of Authority—at least paramount to the several Constitutions—points out the Mischiefs arising from the present Confederation depending on ordinary State Authorities—Instance the Effect of Treaties when contrasted with antecedent Acts of Legislature.

Mr. King—the People have tacitly agreed to the Confederation and that the Legislature have a Right to confirm any Alterations in it. A Convention of the States however the most eligible to confirm new Government.

Mr. Wilson—People must ratify—all will not come in soon—but as the States do they will confederate.

Postponed 7 States to 3.

Question on 9*th* Resolve to strike out *Inferior Tribunals*. Carried by 5 States against 4. 2 States divided—New York of that Number.

1. Lansing's transcription of Yates's notes and the version of those same notes printed by Genet in 1821 differ substantially on this day; both are presented for the reader's consideration.

Mr. Wilson—in Addition to this Clause—*that the National Legislature shall have the Authority to appoint Inferior Tribunals.* Carried 7 States against 3—New York divided.

Adjourned till to Morrow.

ROBERT YATES: NOTES ON DEBATES, AS PRINTED BY GENET

Met pursuant to adjournment.

The 9th resolve, *That a national judicial be established to consist of one supreme tribunal, and of inferior tribunals, to hold their offices during good behaviour, and no augmentation or diminution in the stipends during the time of holding their offices.* Agreed to.

Mr. Wilson moved *that the judicial be appointed by the executive,* instead of *the national legislature.*

Mr Madison opposed the motion, and inclined to think that the executive ought by no means to make the appointments, but rather that branch of the legislature called the senatorial; and moves that the words, *of the appointment of the legislature,* be expunged.

Carried by 8 states—against it 2.

The remaining part of the resolve postponed.

The 10th resolve read and agreed to.

The 11th resolve agreed to be postponed.

The 12th resolve agreed to without debate.

The 13th and 14th resolves postponed.

The 15th or last resolve, *That the amendment which shall be offered to the confederation, ought at a proper time or times after the approbation of congress to be submitted to an assembly or assemblies of representatives, recommended by the several legislatures, to be expressly chosen by the people, to consider and decide thereon,* was taken into consideration.

Mr. Madison endeavored to enforce the necessity of this resolve—because the new national constitution ought to have the highest source of authority, at least paramount to the powers of the respective constitutions of the states—points out the mischiefs that have arisen in the old confederation, which depends upon no higher authority than the confirmation of an ordinary act of a legislature—Instances the law operation of treaties, when contravened by any antecedent acts of a particular state.

Mr. King supposes, that as the people have tacitly agreed to a federal government, that therefore the legislature in every state have a right to confirm any alterations or amendments in it—a convention in each state to approve of a new government he supposes however the most eligible.

Mr. Wilson is of opinion, that the people by a convention are the only power that can ratify the proposed system of the new government.

It is possible that not all the states, nay, that not even a majority, will immediately come into the measure; but such as do ratify it will be immediately bound by it, and others as they may from time to time accede to it.

Question put for postponement of this resolve. 7 states for postponement—3 against it.

Question on the 9th resolve to strike out the words, *and of inferior tribunals*.

Carried by 5 states against 4—2 states divided, of which last number New-York was one.

Mr. Wilson then moved, *that the national legislature shall have the authority to appoint inferior tribunals,* be added to the resolve.

Carried by 7 states against 3. New-York divided. (N. B. Mr. Lansing from New-York was prevented by sickness from attending this day.)

Adjourned to to-morrow morning.

GEORGE WASHINGTON: DIARY

Tuesday 5th.   Dined at Mr. Morris's with a large Company, & Spent the Evening there. Attended in Convention the usual hours.

WEDNESDAY, JUNE 6, 1787

JOHN LANSING: NOTES ON DEBATES

Met according to Adjournment.

4th Resolve—C. Pinkney moves—dele *People* and insert *Legislature.*

Messrs. Wilson, Gerry, Sherman spoke in Favor of Amendment. Mr. Mason, Mr. Reed, Mr. Dickinson and Mr. Maddison against it.

Mr. Sherman in the Course of his Remarks observed that the general Government could only have the Regulation of Trade and some other matters of general Concern and not to all the Affairs of the Union.

Wilson moved to reconsider that Part of the System which gives the Executive a Right of objecting to *national Laws* and to *Judicial as a Council of Revision.*

Mr. Maddison seconded it.

Neg. 8 States—Affirm. 3. New York aff.

C. Pinkney gave Notice that on Friday he would move to reconsider the Clause authorizing national Legislature to negative all Laws.

Adjourned till to Morrow.

GEORGE WASHINGTON: DIARY

Wednesday 6th In Convention as usual. Dined at the Presidents (Doctr. Franklins) & drank Tea there—after which returnd. to my lodgings and wrote letters for France.

THURSDAY, JUNE 7, 1787

JOHN LANSING: NOTES ON DEBATES

Met according to Adjourm't.

5th Resolution considered.

C. Pinkney—the Number of which the second Branch was to consist ought previously to be fixed. If each of the smaller States is to have one will amount at least to *86*.

Dickenson—Supposed Legislatures ought to elect—he was for House of Peers or something similar. He moved the following Resolve—

Resolved that the Members of the second Branch of the national Legislature ought to be elected by the Individual Legislatures.

Mr. Williamson moved that after Legislature the words *consisting of* . . . . should be inserted. Supposes *100* Senators would be agreed to—he would be content to reduce them to *25*.

Mr. Wilson—As Convention have already voted a national Government foederal Principles cannot obtain. If so, we ought to try to procure different Views and different Sentiments—Representation cannot be proportioned by Numbers—Propagation by best Calculation so rapid as to double Number of Inhabitants ever *25* Years—Of Consequence if Representation encreased in proportion to Population the older the Government the weaker and more debilitated would it be. He proposed a Division into Districts for Representation—that Division to be permanent.

Mr. Janifer—Representation ought to be proportioned by Contribution.

Mr. Mason—Can Gentlemen suppose that so extended an Empire can be benefited in proportion to the Burthens to which they submit to support it.—Is not for annihilating Individual States—a large Majority of the Legislature on most local Questions cannot be properly informed of those Circumstances which perhaps are indispensibly necessary to enable them to form a Judgment.

Maddison—If each State retained its Sovereignty an Equality of Suffrage would be proper, but not so now.

Dickenson—National Government like the Sun the Centre of the planetary System should rule attract pervade and brighten all the States—but cannot abolish State Governments.

Wilson—Does not wish to extinguish State Governments—but believes they will neither warm or brighten the Sun—Rome in her most powerful

Imperial State could not effectually pervade and protect every Part of its Dominion nor could the U.S.

Moved by Mr. Wilson—*that the second Branch be elected by the People of certain Districts to be formed for that Purpose.* And that the Resolution be postponed.

Mr. Maddison same Opinion.

Question put. *Negatived.*

Question on original Clause as moved by Dickenson.

Carried unanimously.

Adjourned till to Morrow.

PIERCE BUTLER: NOTES ON DEBATES

June the 7th 1787

Mr. Guery. No Matter That the Value of the Landed property depends on the Encouragement given the Trade. Ergo it must not be shackled. The State Government Mr. Willson says will be rivals of the National. Surely they will be more jealous of them if they have no hand in creating them.

PHOTOSTAT (Library of Congress)

JAMES WILSON: DRAFT RESOLUTION[1]

Resolved

That the second Branch of the national Legislature shall be elected in the following Manner—that the States be divided into Districts; the first to comprehend the States of   the second to comprehend the States of   the third to comprehend the States of   the fourth to comprehend the states of   and etc.—that the Members shall be elected by the said Districts in the Proportions following, in the first District

Resolved

That the Members of the second Branch be elected for   Years, and that immediately after the first Election they be divided by Lot into   Classes; that the Seats of the Members of the first Class shall be vacated at the Expiration of the first Year, the second the second Year and so on continually; to the End that the   Part of the second Branch, as nearly as possible may be annually chosen.

Resolved

That it shall be in the Power of the national Legislature, for the Con-

1. This draft appears to have been prepared in connection with Wilson's motion, June 7, "That the second branch of the national legislature be chosen by districts, to be formed for that purpose" (Farrand, 1:157).

venience and Advantage of the good People of the United States, to divide them into such further and other Districts for the Purposes aforesaid as to the said Legislature shall appear necessary.

AD (Historical Society of Pennsylvania)

GEORGE WASHINGTON: DIARY

Thursday 7th. Attended Convention as usual. Dined with a Club of Convention Members at the Indian Queen. Drank Tea & spent the evening at my lodgings.

JONATHAN DAYTON TO DAVID BREARLEY

Contrary to my wish I have been nominated in the Assembly and very contrary to my expectation, appointed in the joint-meeting to a seat in the federal convention. Believe me sir, I feel about me on this occasion all that diffidence with which the consciousness of my youth and inexperience as well as inability to discharge so important a trust, cannot but impress me.

The honor which must naturally attend my being associated with such very respectable characters as colleagues; The improvement to be derived from hearing the sentiments and communications of so learned an Assembly, were, I confess the motives which influenced me, perhaps too powerfully, to accept the appointment. Were I less assured of your friendly aid and advice wherever I might need it, were the gentlemen joined with you, men of less eminent abilities than they are, I should have been utterly discouraged from entering upon the task. I can never, sir, pretend to lay claim to any merit in common with you all but that which my zeal to serve and be useful to my country may give me a title to. I shall return to Elizabeth tomorrow to visit my family where I shall continue until I am informed by a letter from you or one of the other gentlemen that my attendance in Philadelphia is necessary to keep up the representation. When this happens I shall immediately repair thither regretting the necessity which calls either of you from his station and leaves it to be occupied by one so very far his inferior.

Mr. Houston has formally resigned in consequence of his ill state of health—Mr. Clark has also resigned, but in his usual way that is very *informally*, because he thinks there is a kind of incompatibility in the two appointments, I am therefore unfortunately the only one on the list of supernumeraries.

You will oblige *me* much by writing to me by the return of the first post, and at such other times and as often as your leisure will permit.

ALS (Harvard University)

FRIDAY, JUNE 8, 1787

Met according to Adjournm't.

Motion by Mr. C. Pinkney to reconsider *6th* Resolve to substitute instead of the Words *contravening in the Opinion of the national Legislature the Articles of the Union* the Words *which shall appear improper.*

Maddison, C. Pinkney and Dickenson spoke in Favor of it—Williamson, Bedford and Sherman against it.

Question—Massachusetts, Virginia, and Pennsylvania for it, one divided and other 7 States against it.

C. Pinkney—on the above Subject. Indispensibly necessary to vest a great controuling Power in national Legislature, which may like the Centre of the plenetary System retain all the surrounding Planets in their proper Orbits—the Individual States must submit to this Controul for the general Benefit. The Power as expressed in the Resolution must be productive of Contention and if a Difference in Sentiment arises who is to be the Arbiter?

Williamson—The national Legislature ought not to have a Right to negative any Laws but such as may operate to the Prejudice of the Nation.

Madison—wished the precise Line of Power could be ascertained—But totally impracticable—for if a Dispute arises the State Judiciaries are compelled to expound the Laws so as to give those of the individual State an Operation—National Government *centrifugal.*

Gerry—Is doubtful whether it is the Intention of Gentle[men] to give this Power a retrospective Effect—wishes it explained—has no Objection [among others] to extend it to Emission of paper Money.

C. Pinkney—If this acceded to it will operate to abrogate all State Laws and even Constitutions incompatible with national Government.

Wilson—National Government implies the Idea of an Absorbtion of State Sovereignty. Congress in compliance with Wishes of Individual States and from an accomodating Disposition lost those Essential Powers without which a general Government was a mere Sound—The original D[esig]n of Confederation materially different.

Dickenson—repeats some Reasons already urged—for Motion.

Bedford—Objects to these Powers because an undue Weight is intended to be given to some States—Pennsylvania and Virginia are intended to have one third of Representation—The smaller States will be so unconsequential in the general Scale that their Interests will be uniformly sacraficed whenever they are adverse to those of larger States, and the Voice of the solitary Member from Deleware it is not probable will be attended to.

Adjourned till to Morrow.

PIERCE BUTLER: NOTES ON DEBATES

Mr. Pinckney. Antient Republicks fell by their own turbulancy.

Mr. Madison. No Line can be drawn between the State Governments and the General Government.

Willson. Let Us forgett Local and narrow distinctions. Partial Evil must submit to general good.

Maddison. A power in the different States to ratify state Laws. What power is this to be? An individual! a Council! [indecipherable] a Bey or Bashaw. This Assembly must end in Anarchy. We must consider ourselves as One whole that may apply if our resources were common and equal.

Whether the States vote equally or not there can be no danger of the state Governments.

Ans. If the large States get a decisive Majority in the General Government, they may allow the small States the Name and that is all left them. The large States having got a decided Majority in the General Government they will be indifferent about the individual state Governments; besides having a decided Majority they may pass partial Laws.

PHOTOSTAT (Library of Congress)

GUNNING BEDFORD: NOTES FOR A SPEECH[1]

Notes etc.

Embarrassments I labour under. Reliance on experience and wisdom of

1. These notes seem to have been composed at the beginning of the Convention when Rutledge and others complained about the delegates' "shyness" in speaking or, in the words of this document, the "General silence of members." The "two sets of Propositions offered" were the Virginia plan and, apparently, Pinckney's plan of government, although it is possible that the reference is to the Virginia plan and the New Jersey plan, which would date the document after the presentation of the latter, June 15. The notes represent the sentiments of a small state delegate, but they do not conform to any speech in Farrand's *Records*. The sentence, "Independent states to be considered as individuals with regard to superior fortune," is a strong echo of an argument made by William Paterson on June 9 (Farrand, 1:178); otherwise the notes are a digest of small states' sentiment. They may be notes for a speech Bedford intended to deliver and are dated June 8, the date on which he made at least one of the points contained in the notes (Farrand, 1:170). Equally good arguments could be made for other dates.

Convention. General silence of members. But two sets of Propositions offered. Danger of precipitation into question of great importance. The object for which we have convened. Defects in Confederation. Two principal ones. Want of coercive powers and power to regulate trade. Do the propositions reach the express evil we are met to remedy or does it not go much further? The larger states want to improve the present occasion to go farther than we are authorized. They rely on their states approval because to their interest. No such approbation from smaller states. Smaller states rely on Confederation. Breach of faith is greater to ask it of them. Consequences of this breach of faith. Will smaller states be bound to pay their proportions of public engagements. Independent states to be considered as individuals with regard to superior fortune. Smaller states already deceived. The western lands held out as fund for discharge of public Debt. Republican principles prevalent in the states. No aristocracies among us. Shall we make such a division as well as raise an aristocracy? The different mode of representation opens the door to play states off against each other in elections to try which states shall preponderate. This evil increases in proportion as the different objects of men and states. The same disposition in States as in individuals to tyranny. This acknowledged by the gentlemen in opposition. The great unequality of representation in sovereign states. Modern confederated republics will not justify it, as States Genl., Switzerland, nor the states of the Empire. Neither will the ancient republics of Greece, in either each independent state has its vote without regard to size or wealth.

AD (American Antiquarian Society)

GEORGE WASHINGTON: DIARY

Friday 8th. Attended the Convention. Dined, drank Tea, and spent the evening at my lodggs.

SATURDAY, JUNE 9, 1787

Met pursuant to Adjournm't.

Gerry moved to reconsider Appointment of *Executive*—agreed to reconsider it—He then moved that the Executives of the several States should elect national Executive—and that each Executive should have the same Number of Votes in the Election as the State he represents has Members of the first Branch. Reason—Fewer Persons greater Responsibility.

Randolph—Necessary to cloathe national Executive with every possible Confidence—this cannot be obtained in any Mode more effectually than by Election by national Legislature.

Is it probable that all the Executives will be disposed to promote the Growth of the large Oak which is to reduce them to insignificant Shrubs?

Individual Executives not qualified—they have not the Information—their Interests are distinct. It is not their Interest to elect the best Men to fill that Station—It must also cause a *periodical Interregnum.*

On Question—10 Noes—Deleware divided.

The 11*th* Resolve was then read—Upon which Mr. Brearly called for the 2*nd* general Proposition marked C.[1]

Brearly—This Mode of Representation just if all considered as one Nation—but if State Distinctions still obtain—if Measures are pursued to perpetuate their seperate Interests—let the whole be divided into Districts of nearly equal Size and Numbers of Inhabitants—but in our present Situation the Interests of the Smaller States must be sacraficed. He had made a calculation of the relative Representation which had been repeatedly hinted at which need only be read to enable us to determine the probable Consequence—this was on Number of free Inhabitants.

Georgia	1	South Carolina	6
Deleware	1	North Carolina	6
Rhode Island	2	New York	8
New Hampshire	3	Connecticut	8
New Jersey	5	Maryland	6
	Massachusetts	14	

1. I.e., the second resolution of the Virginia plan, which Lansing marked with a "C" when he copied it at the rear of his notes on debates.

Pennsylvania 12
Virginia 16

He was appointed to give foederal Powers—but these too extensive.

Patterson—Powers of Convention inadequate to this System. Confederation is Basis of our proceeding.

Representation exemplified by two Men possessing different Shares of Property—both have a Vote—but the Man of Property has more to protect by Government and he has greater Influence. Equal Division of Territory—Hints had been thrown out by Gentleman from Pennsylvania [Wilson] that a new Confederation between some of States would be formed—If Jersey would not be inattentive to her Interest—that State never would agree to the present System.

Wilson—If Confederation dissolved either *Majority* or *Minority* may Confederate.

Compound Ratio of Property and Numbers would perhaps be best to determine Representation—Pennsylvania has not yet been taught to adapt itself to the Scale of Representation proposed by Jersey—Never will—The States are now as in State of Nature—Each Individual ought to have an equal Weight in Government. He has no Authority to divide States.

He will uniformly vote against every State Establishment.

Postponed.

Adjourned till Monday.

DAVID BREARLEY TO JONATHAN DAYTON

Philadelphia 9th June 1787

Dear Sir:

Your favor of the 7th was delivered to me yesterday by Mr. Elijah Clark: and I do assure you that I was made extremely happy by being informed that the Legislature had joined you to the Delegation. Your abilities and inclination are so well known to me, as to leave no room to doubt of your affording us both able and necessary assistance.

I am distressed that Mr. Houstons health is so bad as to make it necessary for him to decline. He did not hint such a thing to us when he left us; altho it was pretty certain that he could not have attended very closely.

We have been in a Committee of the Whole for some time, and have under consideration a number of very *important* propositions, none of which, however, have yet been reported.

My Colleagues, as well as myself, are very desirous that you should join us immediately. The importance of the business really demands it. Besides one of the Gentlemen, as soon as the state of the business wil admit, is anxious to pay a visit to his family for a few days. We therefore expect the pleasure of seeing you sometime the ensuing week.

I am with every sentiment of respect and esteem

> Dear Sir
> Your obedient humble servant
> David Brearley

ALS (Historical Society of Pennsylvania)

GUNNING BEDFORD: NOTES ON DEBATES

Mr. Brearly. Against. The proposed mode of representation unfair as by calculation made on the last requisitions of Congress. 16 Townships in one County in N. Jersey. One of them as large as any three others. The large one always sends whom she pleases. Agree it is not fair that Georgia should have the same voice as Virginia. The only way to remedy it by equalizing the states.

Mr. Patterson. The powers of Convention not adequate to the present object. If we don't confine ourselves to our powers, our constituents will not assent. Our commissions contain complections of the States. Sovereignty includes equality. Confederation must be made by sovereign states. Equality obtained by equalization. No citizen will be injured by this. A large state should pay more because she has more to protect. By a calculation of the number of Members to be sent to Parliament it appeared they would have one third share. Would this save America from tyranny. The efficacy of Nations depends on the power vested in them and not the source from which the power derived.

AD (American Antiquarian Society)

GEORGE WASHINGTON: DIARY

Saturday 9th.   At Convention. Dined with the Club at the City Tavern. Drank Tea, & set till 10 oclock at Mr. Powells.

SUNDAY, JUNE 10, 1787

GEORGE WASHINGTON: DIARY

Sunday 10th. Breakfasted by agreement at Mr. Powell's, and in Company with him rid to see the Botanical garden of Mr. Bartram; which, tho' Stored with many curious plts. Shrubs & trees, many of which are exotics was not laid off with much taste, nor was it large.

From hence we rid to the Farm of one Jones, to see the effect of the plaister of Paris which appeared obviously great—First, on a piece of Wheat stubble, the ground bearing which, he says, had never recd. any manure; and that the Wheat from whence it was taken was so indifferent as to be scarcely worth cutting—The white clover on this grd. (without any seed being sown & the plaister spread without breaking up the soil) was full high enough to mow, and stood very thick. The line between this and the herbage around it, was most obviously drawn, for there nothing but the naked stubble, some weeds & thin grass appeared with little or no white clover. The same difference was equally obvious on a piece of mowing grd. not far distant from it for where the Plaister had been spread the White and red clover was luxuriant and but little of either beyond it and these thin. The Soil of these appeared loamy—slightly mixed with Isingglass and originally had been good; but according to Jones's account was much exhausted. He informed us of the salutary effect of this plaister on a piece of heavy stiff meadow (not liable however to be wet) where it transcended either of the two pieces just mentioned in the improvement.

This manure he put on the 29th. of October in a wet or moist spot, and whilst the Moon was in its increase, which Jones says he was directed to attend to (but this must be whimsical) and at the rate of about 5 bushls. to the Acre. When it is laid on grass land or Meadow he advises harrowing, previously, to the laying it thereon in order to raise the mould for incorporation.

From hence we visited Mr. Powells own farm after which I went (by appointment) to the Hills & dined with Mr. & Mrs. Morris. Returned to the City abt. dark.

JAMES MADISON TO JAMES MONROE

Philada. June 10. 1787.

Dear Sir

I have been discouraged from answering sooner your favor of
by the bar which opposes such communications as I should incline not less
to make than you must do to receive. One of the earliest rules established
by the Convention restrained the members from any disclosure whatever
of its proceedings, a restraint which will not probably be removed for some
time. I think the rule was a prudent one not only as it will effectually
secure the requisite freedom of discussion, but as it will save both the
Convention and the Community from a thousand erroneous and perhaps
mischievous reports. I feel notwithstanding great mortification in the dis-
appointment it obliges me to throw on the curiosity of my friends. The
Convention is now as full as we expect it to be unless a report should be
true that Rh. Island has it in contemplation to make one of the party. If
her deputies should bring with them the complexion of the State, their
company will not add much to our pleasure, or to the progress of the
business. Eleven States are on the floor. All the deputies from Virga.
remain except Mr. Wythe who was called away some days ago by information from Williamsburg concerning the increase of his lady's ill health.
I had a letter by the last packet from Mr. Short, but not any from Mr.
Jefferson. The latter had sett out on his tour to the South of France. Mr.
Short did not expect his return for a considerable time. The last letter from
him assigned as the principal motive to this ramble, the hope that some of
mineral springs in that quarter might contribute to restore his injured
wrist. Present me most respectfully to Mrs. Monroe. Yrs. Affecy.

Js. Madison Jr.

ALS (Library of Congress)

RUFUS KING TO THEODORE SEDGWICK

Philadelphia, 10 June 1787.

I am happy my Dear Friend that you are a member of the Legislature
for the present year; and cannot but flatter myself that you will have so
respectable a number of your own sentiments that you will be able to check
the madness of Democracy, and hold the political ship at least where she
is, if you shall not be able to manage her agreeably to your own just
opinions. Moderation and firmness will be essential in your measures; I
wish you may have as good a proportion of these excellent qualities as truly
characterise our convention. I know you are anxious, in common with the
virtuous and reflecting characters of every State, to be informed of the
Disposition and projects which have shown themselves in the Convention.

Be a little patient; I think there is some foundation to hope for Good. I am precluded from communicating, even confidentially, any particulars of the proceedings. However I shall ask your opinion by an early post on some points of consequence, which must receive a Discussion in the Convention; the Question must be made to you in confidence, and may serve to give you some Idea of what will be contended for by a respectable number of political characters. Farewel—Remember that the character, nay the most important Interest of Mass. is concerned in their sending men of consequence, and not Dunces to Congress. Probably the most important considerations may be under the deliberation of the next Congress—the public Debt, the claim of the several states, and a number of other Objects equally interesting and consequential:—

Once more, Farewel,
R. King

I am very much pleased with Mr. Strong his mind is what it should be.

ALS (Massachusetts Historical Society)

MONDAY, JUNE 11, 1787

4th Resolve *e* considered.

Mr. Sherman—moved that Right of Suffrage be determined by Number of free Inhabitants in each State.—This Motion not seconded.

Each State ought to have one Vote—Individual States to be considered as representing *House of Lords.*

Governor Rutlege moves *that Representation be apportioned to Contribution.*

King—moves *that Representation be not apportioned by the Rule mentioned in the Confederation—but that some other equitable Mode be adopted.*

Franklin—It does not follow that because States in Union are unequally represented that therefore the greater Representation will oppress the lesser. Instances *Great Britain.*

On Question on Mr. King's Motion—Affirmative 7 States. Negative—New York, New Jersey and D[elaware]—Maryland divided.

Mr. Rutlege's Motion then considered—

Dickenson—Quota of Contribution would throw too great a Share of Power in State that pays most—which Power may be directed to exempt itself from Contribution. Taxes, Contributions and Impost collected in the State ought to be Criterion.

Butler—Individual States ought to retain distinguished Marks of Sovereignty—Let them levy Tax.

Wilson—There are some great national Objects to be attained by Government so constituted as this is supposed—Post Office an important one. Moves that Representation of the first Branch be in Proportion to the free Inhabitants and 3/5 of all others.

Gerry—If Negroes represented why not Horses and Cows—Slaves not to be taken in under any Idea of Representation.

Question on Wilson's. 10 States Affirmative, one Negative.

Sherman moves that in the second Branch of Legislature each State have *one Vote.*

5 Ayes—6 Noes.

Ayes—New York, New Jersey, Connecticut, Deleware, and Maryland. That second Branch be apportioned as the first.

On Question *6 Ayes—5 Noes.*

11*th* Resolve that a Republican Governement and etc.

Mr. Reed moved that *Government* be obliterated and the *Constitution and Laws of each State* be inserted.

Mr. Madison moved that those Words be inserted after *Government*.

Agreed to Mr. Madison's M[otion].

Agreed to strike out Words scored.

13*th* Resolve agreed to.

14*th* Resolve—

Randolph—There is no Constitution that does not contravene Confederation—Judicial Officers sworn to observe Constitution—Wherever National and State Views are opposed those of State will be prefered.

PIERCE BUTLER: NOTES ON DEBATES

Guery. Are we to enter into a Compact with Slaves. No! Are the Men of Massachusetts to put their hands in our purses. No! The Gentleman makes a Calculation of the possibility of four out voting 6. Are not the four bound by the same law. Well if you take the Blacks out of the Question in One way surely they ought in another. This Country will not pay in proportion to its wealth. The Gentleman says 3 10th pray is not that a Compact. The Gentleman says no Acct. of Blacks pray of what Acct. are the Number of White Inhabitants of Massachusetts to the southern states if they cant be brought therein to defend it.

PHOTOSTAT (Library of Congress)

GEORGE WASHINGTON: DIARY

Monday 11th.   Attended in Convention. Dined, drank Tea, and spent the evening in my own room.

WILLIAM BLOUNT TO JOSEPH CLAY

Newyork June 11th 1787

At present there are not States enough represented to form a Congress and I believe will not be untill the Convention rises. The Members of the Convention observe such inviolable Secrecy that it is altogether unknown out doors what they are doing. I shall leave this in a few days to take my Seat among them.

Farrand, 4:64–65.

TUESDAY, JUNE 12, 1787

JOHN LANSING: NOTES ON DEBATES

15*th* Resolve—

Question—5 Ayes, 3 Noes, and two divided.

Connecticut, New York, and New Jersey *No*.

4*th* Resolve was then considered. The Words *for the term of*

Sherman moves that Members of the first Branch be elected every Year.

Rutlege—Triennial Election perhaps best, but moves that the Words *two Years* be inserted in Blank.

Janifer—moves *three Years*.

Madison—Instability of popular Government his Reason for wishing three Years.

Distance of Extremities of Union renders it necessary. The Lessons the Representatives have to learn another Reason.

Gerry—If you fix this at three Years how long must Senate be elected for.

Madison—Public Opinion fluctuating—it has no Standard—is changing Rapidly.

Local Attachments and temporary Opinions ought to be laid aside.

Question on *three Years*.

Aff. 7 Ayes—4 Noes.

Agreed to strike out Clause limiting Age—10 Ayes—1 No.

Motion to insert *fixed* after *liberal*.

Affirmative 8—Negative 3.

Franklin—Moved to strike out *liberal*—carried.

Pierce—moved to add *to be paid out of national Treasury*.

Affirmative 6—Negative 5.

Question on Paragraph to Word Service.

8 Ayes—3 Noes.

Gerry moved after *Service and* to insert *under the national Government*. Carried unanimously.

In Blank after *Space of* agreed to insert *one Year*.

C. Pinkney Moved to strike out *to be incapable* and etc. to the End of Paragraph. Struck out unanimously.

Age of Members of second Branch fixed at *thirty*.

7 *Years* moved by Governor Randolph Duration of Office of second Branch.

Mr. Pierce against it—it will give too much alarm.

Sherman for 5 *Years*.

Question on 7 *Years*.

8 Ayes—1 No and 2 divided.

N.B. New York divided, Judge Yates being in *Negative* and *I* affirmative.

Rutlege moved seconded by Butler that the Clause resp[ectin]g Pay of second Branch be struck out.

3 Ayes—7 Noes—1 divided.

Connecticut, Deleware, and South Carolina Aye, Massachusetts divided.

Question on whole Clause, 10 Ayes—1 No.

9th Resolve resp[ectin]g Judiciary considered.

Piracies and Felonies on the High Seas *struck out*—so *Captures from Enemy*.

C. C. Pinkney moved to insert after *Foreigners* to insert *or Citizens of two distinct States of the Union*.

Postponed.

Adjourned till to Morrow.

GEORGE WASHINGTON: DIARY

Tuesday 12th.   Dined and drank Tea at Mr. Morris's. Went afterwards to a concert at the City Tavern.

WEDNESDAY, JUNE 13, 1787

JOHN LANSING: NOTES ON DEBATES

Met according to Adjournm't.

9*th* Resolve—

Mr. Randolph moved that the 9*th* Article shall extend to Collection of national Revenue Impeachment of any national Officers and Questions which involve the national Peace and Harmony.

Agreed to.

7*th* Resolve—Mr. C. Pinkney moved that the Words to be chosen by the national Legislature be inserted in the Blank left for that Purpose.

Madison moves second Branch to appoint.

Question carried.

6*th* Resolve that each Branch ought to possess Right of originating Acts.

Mr. Gerry moves Exception as to the upper House *excepting* Bills to supply to public Treasury.

8 Noes—3 Ayes.

Committee reported.

Copies of Report ordered—Consideration postponed.

Adjourned till to Morrow.

GEORGE WASHINGTON: DIARY

Wednesday 13th.   In Convention. Dined at Mr. Clymers & drank Tea there. Spent the evening at Mr. Binghams.

THURSDAY, JUNE 14, 1787

JOHN LANSING: NOTES ON DEBATES

Met—on Motion of Mr. Patterson adjourned.

PIERCE BUTLER: NOTES ON DEBATES

To postpone by Mr. Patterson

GEORGE WASHINGTON: DIARY

Thursday 14th.   Dined at Major Moores (after being in Convention) and spent the evening at my own lodgings.

FRIDAY, JUNE 15, 1787

John Lansing: Notes on Debates

Met according to Adjournm't.

Mr. Patterson moved Resolves—which I seconded.

Mr. Madison supposed it would be proper to commit them to a Committee of the whole House. After some desultory Debate agreed to.

Butler—Moved to go into Committee immediately.

I moved for the Morning. I declared that tho I had hitherto given my Vote without joining in the Debates my Sentiments were unaltered—our sole Object ought to be foederal—that these Resolutions afforded an Opportunity of fairly contrasting the Systems, but as the one had been an Object which had engaged the Attention of the Committee a considerable Time—the other recently introduced the House was not prepared to give it that Investigation which its Importance merited.

Randolph spoke in Favor of it. Madison, Wilson, Williamson and Butler against it.

Question unanimously carried.—Copies ordered.

Adjourned till to Morrow.

George Washington: Diary

Friday 15th. In Convention as usual. Dined at Mr. Powells & drank Tea there.

John Dickinson to Polly Dickinson

. . . The Convention is very busy—of an excellent temper—and for Abilities exceeds, I believe any Assembly that ever met upon this Continent, except the first Congress. Give my Compliments to Dr. Wharton and let him know my sentiments concerning this Body. Nothing further said at present. . . .

ALS (Historical Society of Pennsylvania)

WILLIAM BLOUNT TO JOHN GRAY BLOUNT

Newyork June 15th 1787.

Major Pierce returned here last Night from the Convention of which he is a Member and says it is probable and that it is the general Opinion of the Members of that Body that it will not rise before the Middle of October.

I have not learned from him what in particular is done but he says in general Terms very little is done and nothing definitive indeed I suppose he would not like to descend to particulars even to me who am a Member as I have not taken my seat for the Members are under an Injunction not [to] disclose by writing or otherwise any part of their Proceedings to any Persons but siting Members.

Farrand, 4:65

SATURDAY, JUNE 16, 1787

Met according to Adjournment.

I stated the difference between National and foederal Systems—the first subjects all to the Controul of the general Government and draws its Representation from Individuals—the foederal has its Representation from States collectively and subjects great foederal Concerns to general Government.

The one involves a total Subversion of State Sovereignties—the other delegates only Part.—I urged that the Confederation ought to be the Basis of our System. This Power now contended for too great to be given by Implication. Improbable that so many individual States should adopt same Language to describe an Intention which cannot be inferred from the wording of it.

It may be objected *Union* one of the Articles subject to Revision. But the distinct Sovergnties essential to constitute it.

Two Reasons assigned—one that public Mind ripe for System. 2ndly that it must accomodate.

If public Mind to be collected from public Acts instead of being fluctuating—it has been uniform a considerable Time.

Impost an Instance—Most States annexed Clauses expressive of their Distrusts. What Reason to suppose Change?

If public Mind to accomodate it must either happen gradually—then useless—suddenly—then Effect of some great Commotion—it cannot be controul'd or directed.

The national System proposes two Houses.

All Reasoning on Systems unaided by Experience has generally been productive of false Inferences.

Why go into unexplored Ground?

The new Government will be regarded with that Jealousy inseperable from new Establishments.

Congress is a body respected and known.

Patterson—has proposed his Plan.

1. Because it accords with Powers.

2. With Sentiments of the People.

If we wish to meet Approbation walk in Sphere assigned to you.

Practicable Virtue preferable to finest theoretic System.

Larger States have agreed that each should have one Vote. They cannot recal their Assent.

Patterson—Maryland and Jersey came last into Confederation.

Wilson's Principles applied to States totally wrong.

If you will form national Government equalize the States and throw all your public Lands in common.

Two branches of Legislature unnecessary—Congress is competent—the additional Powers ought therefore to be exerted by them.

The Expence of national System another Objection.

Wilson—compares Plans. Observe their relative Merits must be drawn from Experience and Reasoning.

Powers he will first consider.

Supposes himself authorized to propose every Thing—but can conclude Nothing.

State Sovergnties not Idols of People.

A Citizen of national Government will not be degraded.

From every State we hear Complaints that their Governments are inadequate.

Does not mean to collect Sentiments from conversing with People—let the System go to the States—and let them consider it.

Would give *Congress* Power with great Reluctance—

1. Congress is not on Principles of a free Government derived from People.

2. Because only one Body.

Inequality in Representation is a Poison which will contaminate every Branch of Government.

Great Britain Judicial not appointed by a venal Parl't—the Judicial uncorrupt—Not so House of Commons.

United States another Instance—Rhode Island one.

Executive ought to be single.

Triumvirate cemented by Interest—Kings of Sparta and Consuls shew necessity of single Executive.

C. Pinkney—Discovers if Jersey had a single Vote would agree to national System.

Our Powers only recommendatory.

Grecian Confederation—*Lycia League*—23 Towns—Some had 1 others 2 and the largest 3 Votes.

Governor Randolph—The Resolutions from Virginia were drawn under Conviction of reforming Confederation.

If Powers not competent ought not to hesitate.

This a great Occasion—Step boldly beyond prudential Rules.

King of France unpaid, Creditors ruined, and Soldiers languishing.

We would be Traitors to our Country if we did not embrace this parting Angel.

States not Objects of Coercion.

If done by distressing Trade—*some not commercial*—by Inroad—tardy, expensive and dangerous.

Members of Congress particularly dependent on their own States.

This last attempt to confederate—

Adjourned.

PIERCE BUTLER: NOTES ON DEBATES

Mr. Lancey. Without regard to wealth numbers or anything else.

Mr. Patterson. I came not here to sport sentiments of my own, but to speak the mind of my Constituents. Perpetual is a word of Course as in Common Treaties of peace and Alliance. Shall we alter the plans without any tollerable reason. One free man is equal to another but it is not a just deduction that one free State is equal to another. The Quantum of power will depend upon the justice of the Representation. Has Congress been composed of weak or bad Men. This is not a fair Question. Speak of Measures not Men.

Willson. Inequality in representation a poison that must destroy the whole.

Randolph. The Militia are incompetent to the purposes of defence. It would be very difficult to persuade the Militia of One State to march into another. This Argument was brought forward to prove the weakness of Congress.

PHOTOSTAT (Library of Congress)

GEORGE WASHINGTON: DIARY

Saturday 16th. In Convention. Dined with the Club at the City Tavern and drank Tea at Doctr. Shippins with Mrs. Livingstons party.

RUFUS KING TO NATHAN DANE

Philadelphia 16 June 1787

I think that I informed you that by an early order of the Convention the members are restrained from communicating any thing done in convention during the time of their session. The object was the prevention of partial representations, and also the additional consideration of leaving the Report of the convention to stand or fall on its own merits. I am therefore prevented from writing to you with that freedom which otherwise I should do, as well for your information of the proceedings of the convention, as to obtain your sentiments on points of consequence which must here receive their discussion. . . . We hear nothing from N. Hampshire, not even who is president.

Farewell   R. King

ALS (Library of Congress)

GEORGE WYTHE TO EDMUND RANDOLPH

Williamsburgh, 16 of June 1787

Mrs. W.'s state of health is so low and she is so emaciated, that my apprehensions are not a little afflicting, and, if the worst should not befall, she must linger, I fear, a long time. In no other circumstances would I withdraw from the employment, to which I had the honour to be appointed but, as probably I shall not return to Philadelphia, if, sir, to appoint one in my room be judged adviseable, I hereby authorize you to consider this letter as a resignation no less valid than a solemn act for that express purpose. My best wishes attend you and the other respectable personages with whom I was thought worthy to be associated.

ALS (New York Public Library)

SUNDAY, JUNE 17, 1787

GEORGE WASHINGTON: DIARY

Sunday. 17th. Went to Church. Heard Bishop White preach, and see him ordain two Gentlemen Deacons—after wch. rid 8 Miles into the Country and dined with Mr. Jno. Ross in Chester County. Returned in the Afternoon.

MONDAY, JUNE 18, 1787

JOHN LANSING: NOTES ON DEBATES

Met according to Adjournment

Dickenson—wishes the terms *national* and *foederal* to be exploded—Moves to strike out *foederal Constitution* out of Jersey Propositions and alter it so as to read *so as to render the Government of the United States adequate to the Exigencies Preservation and Prosperity of the Union.*

Agreed.

Hamilton—The Situation of the State he represents and the Diffidence he has of his own Judgment induced him to Silence tho his Ideas are dissimilar from both Plans.

No Amendment of Confederation can answer the Exigencies of the States. State Sovereignties ought not to exist—Supposes we have Powers sufficient—Foederal an Association of States differently modified—Diet of Germany has Power to legislate for Individuals—In United States Confederacy legislate for States and in some Instances on Individuals—*Instances Piracies*. The Term *sole* he supposes was to impress an Idea only that we were not to govern ourselves, but to revise Government.

Another Difficulty that the Legislature cannot be supposed to have delegated a Power they did not possess themselves—So far as Respects the State of New York one of the Branches of the Legislature considered it—It was *said they might have Recourse to the People*—this had its Influence and it was carried by one Vote. We ought not to sacrafice the public Good to narrow Scruples. All America, all Europe, the World would condemn us. The only Enquiry ought to be what can we do to save our Country.—Five Essentials indispensible in foederal Government.—

1. A constant and active Interest.
2. Utility and Necessity.
3. A habitual Sense of Obligation.
4. Force.
5. Influence.

Every Set of men who associate acquire an *Esprit de Corps*. This will apply forcibly to States—they will have distinct Views—their own Obligations thwart general Good.

Do not we find a Jealousy subsisting? In the State of New York we had an Instance—The last Requisition was partially paid—the principal Part of their Funds applied to discharge State Obligations—the Individual States hostile to general Interest.

Virginia will in 25 Years contain a Million of Inhabitants—It may then be disposed to give up an Union only burthensome. The Distribution of Justice presents itself to every Eye—this has a powerful Influence and must particular attach Individuals to the State Governments.

Two Modes of Coercion—of Laws—of Military.

Individuals are easily controuled—not so Society—You must carry the Force to Individuals—If only State delinquent it would cause a war—If more they would associate and make a common Cause of it.

We must resort to Influence—Dispensations of Honors and Emoluments of Office necessary—these are all in the Hands of the State Governments— If they exist in State Governments their Influence too great.—Our Situation is peculiar—*It leaves us Room to dream* as we think proper.—Groecian Confederacy lost for Want of adequate Powers—German the same. Swiss Cantons—general Diet has lost its Powers. Cannot combine States but by absorbing the *Ambition and Avarice* of all.

Jersey Propositions—Regulating Trade—Revenue not adequate to meet our Debt—where are we to find it? Requisitions—the several States will deliberate on them.—Requisitions founded on Quotas must always fail. There is no general Standard for Wealth in Communities—Pennsylvania and North Carolina—Connecticut and New York compared. New York derives great Wealth from Commerce—Connecticut none—Indirect Taxation must be multiplied.

Equality of Suffrage ruinous to the Union.

Doubts have been entertained whether the United States have a Right to build a Ship or raise a Reg[imen]t in Time of Peace—this Doubt might involve almost our Ruin.

The Organization of Congress exceptionable—They are annually appointed and subject to recal.—They will of Consequence represent the Prejudices of the States not general Interests—No Power will be executed if the States think proper to obstruct it. If general Government preserves itself it must extinguish State Governments.

If Congress remains Legislature the Sovereignty must ultimately vest in them.

The Expence of national Government is a Consideration with him—it will probably amount to £100,000 per ann.—this however surmountable—It will not do to propose formal Extinction of State Governments— It would shock public Opinion too much.—Some subordinate Jurisdictions—something like limited Corporations. If general Government properly modified it may extinguish State Governments gradually—Representation is another difficulty. British Government the best—Dispairs of ever uniting [?] the great Objects of Government which have been so success-fully attained by the British, public Strength and individual Safety, in any Republican System. He thinks here it would support itself—the Citizens of America may be distinguished into the wealthy well born and well educated—*and the many*. If Government in the hands of the latter they sacrafice the few—are as often in the wrong as right.

You can only protect the few by giving them exclusive Rights—they have Nothing to hope from Change—Monarchy is essential to them. One Branch of Legislature ought to be independent to check popular Frenzy—or Democraties will prevail.—Seven Years is no Check—It is no Object for Men of first Importance—Little Daemagogues will fill Assembly—Undertakers your Senate.

In Republics trifling Characters obtrude—they are easily corrupted—the most Important Individuals ought to be drawn forth for Government—this can only be effected by establishing upper House for good Behaviour. Congress are Objects of foreign Corruption.

Executive ought to be during good Behaviour—He will part with his Power with Reluctance. You ought to interest him in the Government.

This may be objected to as establishing an elective Monarchy—but he will be liable to Impeachment for mal-conduct. The Election it supposed would cause Tumults—To avoid this the People in each District should chuse Electors—those should elect a few in that [?] State who should meet with Electors from the other States and elect *the Governor*.

Roman Emperor—elective—by Army

German Emperor—by great Electors.

Polish King—great Barons who have numerous Dependents.

These were tumultous from their Institutions—We may guard against it.

The principal Citizens of every State are tired of Democracy—he then read his Plan and expatiated on it—See

Adjourned till to Morrow.

JOHN DICKINSON: PLAN OF GOVERNMENT (I)[1]

1. That the Articles of Confederation ought to be revised and amended,

---

1. There are two versions of Dickinson's plan of government, a draft printed here as plan I and a more finished composition printed immediately following as plan II. Dickinson prepared his plan of government after June 15, the date of the New Jersey plan, parts of which it incorporates. It seems likely that he wrote and revised the plan

so as to render the Government of the United States adequate to the Exigencies the Preservation and the prosperity of the Union.

2. That the Government ought to consist of a Legislature Executive and Judiciary.

3. That the Legislative ought to consist of two Branches.

4. That the Members of the first Branch ought to be chosen by the Legislatures of the several States as at present or as in the Report. That immediately after the first Election they be divided by Lot into seven Classes and numbered one two three four five six and seven—that the seats of the Members of the first Class shall be vacated at the End of the first Year, of the second Class at the End of the second Year, and so on continually, to the End that the seventh part of this Branch as nearly as possible may be annually chosen—that if any Member dies the person elected in his place shall only serve for the Residue of the Term for which the deceased was elected.

5. That the Members of the second Branch ought to be elected by the People of the several states for a term of 3 Years or as in the Report— that immediately after the second Election they be divided by Lot into three Classes and numbered one two three—that the seats of the Members of the first Class shall be vacated at the End of the first Year, of the second Class at the End of the second Year, and of the third Class at the End of the third Year, to the End that the third part of this Branch as nearly as possible may be annually chosen—that if any Member dies, the person elected in his place shall only serve for the Residue of the Term for which the deceased was elected—that the people of each state shall chuse the Members of this Branch for the first three Years in the following proportion—New Hampshire Massachusetts Rhode Island Connecticut New York New Jersey Pennsylvania Delaware Maryland Virginia North Carolina South Carolina Georgia—That after the first 3 Years the Right of Suffrage in constituting this Branch ought from time to time to be adjusted in proportion to the sums of Money collected in each state and actually paid into the common Treasury within the preceding 3 Years, except the sums arising from Imposts and provided that the Right of suffrage of the

---

between June 16 and June 18, a period that covered Sunday, when the Convention was in recess. Dickinson was evidently prepared to present the plan on June 18. On June 19 Yates quotes Dickinson as proposing to "contrast" the Virginia and Jersey plans and "consolidate such parts of them as the committee approve" into a new scheme (Farrand, 1:327), but it appears that he had already done so, for on June 18 he moved a resolution that—unknown, apparently, to the other members—was the first article of his plan (Farrand, 1:282). Presumably, the entire plan would have been introduced had the first article been approved.

state contributing most shall never exceed that of the state contributing least more than the proportion of   to one or thus see Margin.[2]

That every new state on admission into the Union shall have the same Right of Suffrage with the state contributing least, until the next adjustment of the Rights of Suffrage and then the Right of such state to be enlarged if entitled thereto, upon the same principle that determines the Rights of the other states,[3] that on the Establishment of part of a state as a new state, the Residue of the Representation previously possessed by the whole, to belong to the State from which the new state shall be separated.

6. That in Addition to the powers vested in Congress by the existing Articles of Confederation, the Legislature of the United States shall be authorized to pass Acts for the Observance of the Laws of Nations for raising a Revenue by levying a Duty or Impost on all Goods or Merchandize of foreign Growth or Manufacture imported into part of the United States by Land or Water—by Stamps on Paper Vellum or parchment—by Postage on all Letters and packages passing through the general Post Office—for the Regulation of Trade and Commerce as well with foreign Nations as with each other and that all punishments Fines Forfeitures and penalties to be incurred for contravening such Acts concerning Revenue and the Regulation of Trade and Commerce shall at present be adjudicated by the Common Law Judiciary of the State in which any Offence contrary to the true Intents and Meaning of such Acts shall be committed or perpetrated with Liberty for the Officers of the United States to commence in the first Instance all suits or prosecutions for that purpose in the superior Common Law Judiciary in such state subject nevertheless to an appeal for the Correction of all Error both in Law and Fact in rendering Judgment to the Judiciary of the United States, for which purpose all the Evidence in such suits and prosecutions shall be put into writing and immediately transmitted upon an Appeal, by the state Judiciary to the Judiciary of the United States, and the Appellee shall give sufficient security to the said state Judiciary, for abiding the final Determination that when hereafter

2. In the margin: "That after the first 3 Years the Right of suffrage in constituting this Branch ought from time to time to be fixed in the following Manner Each state shall for every Dwelling house within its limits be bound annually forever to pay to the United States every 3 years the Rights of Suffrage shall be adjusted for the next ensuing 3 Years in proportion to the said Contribution collected within each state without Coercion and of Quotas of other Contributions on Requisition and at the End of [word undecipherable] so collected and actually paid to the United States within the next preceding 3 years provided that the Right of suffrage of the state contributing most shall never exceed that of the state contributing least, more than in the proportion of   to one."

3. Crossed out: "provided that each state shall always have at least one Representative in this Branch."

Circumstances shall render it necessary for the public good in the Judgment of the Legislature of the United States, they may transfer the Cognizance of such suits and prosecutions to the Inferior Tribunals of the United States.

That the United States shall possess the sole and exclusive Right of emitting Money of any kind, as well as regulating the Alloy and Value of Coin.

That all other Objects of the Legislative Authority of the United States ought to be accurately defined.[4]

That all Laws and Resolves of any states, in any Manner opposing or contravening any Act of the United States made by Virtue and in pursuance of the powers hereby and by the Articles of Confederation vested in them or any Treaties made and ratified under the authority of the United States shall be null and void (then as in the Proposals from N.J.)

Provision to be made for determining Contests likely to disturb the public Peace, within any states as well as between states.

Provision to be made for the punishment of officers in the service of the United States.

Provision to be made for securing the Benefits of the writ of Habeas Corpus and Trial by Juries in proper Cases, and for preventing Contests between the Authority of the United States and the Authority of Individual states.

That the Legislature of the United States be authorized to elect an Executive to consist of 3 persons, one of them a Resident of the Eastern states, another of the Middle States and the third of the southern states to receive a Stipend one of the first 3 to continue in Office 2 Years, another 4 Years and the third 7 Years. Every person appointed upon such Vacancies and so on afterwards to continue in office 7 Years, but if any such officer dies, the person chosen in his place, shall serve only for the Residue of the Term for which the person deceased was elected to be removable by the Legislature of the United States, if they judge it proper, on application by a Majority of the Executives of the several states. The person appointed at the first Election for 7 Years to be President of the Body, and afterwards the person who shall have been the longest Time in the Executive. [One line undecipherable.] Everyone of them to be responsible for every Act of the Body done in his presence, unless he enters his Dissent in writing in the Books of their proceedings—provision to be made in Case of Death or Absence, especially upon Emergencies of Invasion or Insurrection and for convening the Legislature (then as in the proposals from N.J.)

That the Executive shall have a Right to negative any Legislative Act

4. In the margin: "Query: Is Executive to have a Right of Legislation, but without Right of Deliberation or Suffrage in the Legislature. Same Question as to Judiciary."

which shall not afterwards be passed unless by two third parts of each Branch of the Legislature.

The Executive shall never order any Monies to be paid to other purposes than those to which they are expressly appropriated by the Legislature nor out of other Funds than are so appropriated.

That the Judiciary be appointed by the first Branch as [suggested?] in the proposal to consist at present of a supreme Tribunal, the Judges of which to be appointed (as in the proposals from N.J.) except that this Judiciary should have authority to determine in the first Instance in Cases touching the Rights of Ambassadors and other foreign Ministers—That when hereafter in the Judgment of the Legislature of the United States Circumstances shall render it necessary for the public good they may appoint inferior Tribunals.

Then from the 14th Resolution inclusive of the Report to the End.

AD (Historical Society of Pennsylvania)

JOHN DICKINSON: PLAN OF GOVERNMENT (II)

1. That the Articles of Confederation ought to be revised and amended, so as to render the Government of the United States adequate to the Exigencies, the preservation, and the prosperity of the Union.

2. That the Government ought to consist of a Legislative, Executive and Judiciary as in Report.

3. That the Legislative ought to be composed of two Branches as in Report.

4. That the Members of the first Branch ought to be chosen as they now are by the existing Confederation, that is, by the legislatures of the several states, each state having an equal Vote—to be of the Age of thirty Years or as in the 4th Resolution of the Report that immediately after the first Election they be divided into seven Classes, as equal as possible, and numbered 1 2 3 4 5 6 7 that the seats of the Members of the first Class shall be vacated at the End of the first Year, of the second Class at the End of the second Year, and so on continually, to the End that the seventh part of this Branch, as nearly as possible, may be annually chosen that if any Member dies, the person elected in his place shall serve only for the Residue of the Term for which the deceased was elected.

5. That the Members of the second Branch ought to be elected by the People of the several states, for a Term of 3 Years or as in the 3d Resolution of the Report that the People of each state shall choose the Members of this Branch for the first 3 Years in the following proportions: New Hampshire Massachusetts Rhode Island Connecticut New York New Jersey Pennsylvania Delaware Maryland Virginia North Carolina South Carolina

and Georgia that immediately after the second Election they be divided into 3 Classes, as equal as possible, and numbered 1 2 and 3 that the seats of the members of the first Class shall be vacated at the End of the first Year of the second Class at the End of the second Year and of the third Class at the end of the third Year, to the End that the third part of this Branch, as nearly as possible, may be annually chosen that if any Member dies, the person elected in his place shall serve only for the Residue of the Term for which the deceased was elected that after the first three Years, the Right of suffrage in constituting this Branch ought from Time to Time to be adjusted, in proportion to the sum of Money collected in each state and actually paid into the Common Treasury within the preceding 3 Years, except sums arising from Imposts and such other Taxes as might produce too great an Inequality—provided, that each state shall have at least one vote in this Branch and that the Right of suffrage of the state contributing most shall never exceed that of the state contributing least, more than in the proportion of   to one.[5]

That every new state on admission into the Union shall have the same Right of suffrage with the state contributing least, untill the next adjustment of the Rights of Suffrage, and then the Right of such state to be enlarged, if entitled to an Enlargement, upon the same principle that determines the Rights of the other states—that on the Establishment of part of a state as a new state, if such a Case happens, the Residue of the Representation previously possessed by the whole, shall belong to the state from which the new state shall be separated—until adjustment be made in Course, as is before mentioned.

6. That in addition to the powers vested in Congress by the existing Confederation the Legislature of the United States ought to be authorized to pass Acts for enforcing an Observance of the Laws of Nations and an Obedience to their own Laws—for raising a Revenue by levying Duties or Imposts on all Goods and Merchandize of foreign Growth or Manufacture imported into any part of the United States and also a limited Duty on Exports—by stamps on Paper Vellum or parchment by postage on all Letters and packages passing thro the General post office and by such other Modes of Taxation [line undecipherable] for the prosperity of the Union for the Regulation of Trade and Commerce as well with foreign Nations as with each other But before these Acts are passed they ought to be published at least six Months for public Consideration. That all punishments Fines Forfeitures and penalties to be incurred for contravening such Acts concerning Revenue and the Regulations of Trade and Commerce ought

5. Crossed out: "or thus that after the first 3 Years the Right of suffrage in constituting this Branch ought from Time to Time to be fixed in the following Manner Each state shall."

for some Time at least to be adjudged by the Common Law Judiciary of the state in which any Offence contrary to the true Intent and Meaning of such Acts shall be committed or perpetrated, with Liberty for the Officers of the United States to commence in the first Instance all suits or prosecutions for that purpose in the superior Common Law Judiciary of such state, subject nevertheless to an appeal for the Correction of all Error both in Law and Fact in rendering Judgment to the Judiciary of the United States, for which purpose all the Evidence in such suits and prosecutions shall be put into writing and upon an Appeal be fully and immediately transmitted by the said Judiciary of the state to the Judiciary of the United States and the appellee shall give sufficient surety to the said Judiciary, for abiding the final Determination.

That when hereafter, in the Judgment of the Legislature of the United States Circumstances shall render it necessary for the public Good, they may transfer the Cognizance of such suits and prosecutions in the first Instance to the inferior Tribunals of the United States

That all other proper Objects of the legislative Authority of the United States, if any, ought to be accurately defined.

That the Legislature of the United States ought to possess the sole and exclusive Right and power of emitting Money of any kind, as well as regulating the Value and Alloy of Coin that they ought also to possess a Negative on the Acts of the several Legislatures, as in the sixth Resolution of the Report that provision ought to be made for determining Contests within a state, which shall be judged by the United States likely to disturb the public Peace as well as those between two or more states for the punishment of Officers of the United States for securing the Benefits of the Writ of Habeas Corpus and Trial by Jury in proper Cases, and for preventing Contests concerning the Authority of the United States and the Authority of individual states.

7. That all Laws and Resolves of any state in any Manner opposing or contravening the powers now vested or hereby to be vested in the United States or any Act of the United States made by Virtue and in pursuance of such powers or any Treaties made and ratified under the authority of the United States shall be utterly null and void (this nearly as in the proposals from New Jersey).

That the Legislature of the United States be authorized to elect by Ballot, two thirds concurring, an Executive to consist of 3 persons, one of them a Resident of the Eastern States, another of the Middle States and the third of the Southern States to receive a Compensation for Service One of the first 3 to continue in Office 2 Years, another 4 Years, and the third 7 Years—every person appointed upon such Vacancies and so on afterwards to continue in Office 7 years—but if any such Officer dies, the person chosen in his Place, shall serve only for the Residue of the Term for which the person deceased was elected—to be removable by the Legislature of the United States, if they judge it proper on Application by a Majority of the Executives of the several states and to be impeachable for Malconduct or Neglect of Duty. The person appointed at the first Election for 7 Years, to be President and afterwards the person who shall have been the longest Time in the Executive—All their Acts and Appointments to be immediately entered in their Books.—Every one of them to be responsible for every Act and Appointment done or made in his presence, unless he at the Time enters his Dissent in Writing in their Book—Provision to be made in Cases of Death or Absences especially upon Emergencies of Invasion or Insurrection and for convening the Legislature (then as in the proposal from N.J.) that the Executive shall have a Right to negative any Legislative Acts which shall not afterwards be passed, unless by two third parts of each Branch of the Legislature The Executive ought never to order any Monies to be paid to other purposes than those to which they are expressly appropriated by the Legislature, nor out of other Funds than are so appropriated. That the Judiciary be appointed by the Legislature, to consist for some time at least of a supreme Tribunal, the Judges of which to be appointed (as in the proposal from N.J.) except that this Judiciary would have Authority to determine in the first Instance in all Cases touching the Rights of Ambassadors and other foreign Ministers That when hereafter in the Judgment of the Legislature of the United States, Circumstances shall render it necessary for the public Good, they may appoint Inferior Tribunals.

Then from the 14th Resolution of the Report, inclusive to the End

JOHN DICKINSON: NOTES ON DEBATES[6]

1. Espirit de Corps.
2. Love of power.
3. A constant and active Interest in support of a Government.
4. Force.
5. Influence. as to past—will names of Government Monarchy or Republic increase difficulties. No but Force will supply i.e. a standing army. The Espirit de Corps overthrows the whole Plan.

Number 1. No Rule for Quota, yet adopted by the Gentleman for determining Representation.

6. These notes begin with a summary of major points in Hamilton's speech of June 18. The checklist of constitutional provisions, beginning with "Power to regulate Trade," is written in the left margin of the page at right angles to first section of notes. It may relate in some way to Dickinson's Plan of Government or may be the results of continuing reflection on the appropriate components of a constitution. Of course, it is possible that it was written at a different time from the notes preceding it.

Gentleman describes Love of Power and Danger of it in an appointment of the Executive for 7 Years, yet places the Executive in a situation to urge by the most powerful Motives to become a Traytor to his Country.

How the English Constitution grew up. Island No need of standing Armies. Contest between King and Barons. Commons call'd into the Aid of the latter & provided for in every Accommodation. Otherwise in France and all the Rest of Europe where similar Governments were established by barbarous nations. No Instance of a Republic being changed into a limited Monarchy. Always into a despotism and Tyranny.

A Giant simple solitary slow heavy unwieldy.

The States will give Play to Aristocracy. Agreed. better than hereditary Courtiers.

Power to regulate Trade   Imposts Excise Stamp Post
Executive in 3   Office A limited Poll tax
Annual Election of 1st Branch

Right of originating Money Bills—what are such—no Tasks

Representation in House of Commons to be for the first 3 5 or 7 years according to the present Quotas of Contribution. Afterwards in proportion to the sums actually paid into the Common Treasury within every 3 5 or 7 Years. Expence a point of Detail. Not to be taken for granted, that some Taxes besides Imposts and Excises will not be necessary.

$$26 = £13000$$
$$52 - £26000$$

AD (Historical Society of Pennsylvania)

PIERCE BUTLER: NOTES ON DEBATES

Col Hambleton. The Diet of Germany legislated on Individuals of the different Electoral Territories. Not only where they attempt to Contravene the Laws, established Laws of the Diet agreed to in the Diet. The States may be disposed to oppose the general Government and she is adequate to it. the defense the Common Militia of a State is not adequate even to state defence as in Massachusetts foreign powers [indecipherable] disaffected states. A dispensation of honors in every state. No vigorous exertion without a distribution of honors in individual states. Men collectively he says are governed by passions. The states will be rivals of the General. No! Make it their Interest by Laws of General Equity and they will support the general Government. The Amphiction Council, as to those made of raising Money and extending the Quota. Quotas would destroy the whole because there is no standard duty on Exports. Staple states take care. Large states will not agree to the small ones to dispose of their property. We must then resort to Equity. Bad principles will produce their Effects.

Troops cant be brought forward in proportion to the population. Men will try to extend their power. If the General Govt. prevails the Individual must fall. In the British Constitution Individuals are best secured. What are Impressments. The Executive is above all temptation. is it proved so by the Conduct of the Kings of Britain Sweden Prussia. In Poland, he says there are great Barons who overawe. He will leave power in Individual States respecting Finance the power of carrying on War. I am against it. Witness the Stadholder.

PHOTOSTAT (Library of Congress)

GEORGE WASHINGTON: DIARY

Monday 18th.   Attended the Convention. Dined at the Quarterly meeting of the Sons of St. Patrick—held at the City Tavn. Drank Tea at Doctr. Shippins with Mrs. Livingston.

NATHANIEL GORHAM TO THEOPHILUS PARSONS

                                        Philadelphia, June 18, 1787.
My dear Sir:
    It was with singular pleasure I saw your name in the list of Representatives. I hope all the measures of your body will be dictated by the principles of honor and justice. Among the various subjects which will come before you, the requisition of Congress of the last year will undoubtedly be one. I hope you will excuse me for just suggesting to you, that I think it will be burdening the people to no essential purpose to comply with that requisition any further than applies to the cash part of it;—not that I have any doubt of the justice and duty of paying the domestic debt; but it is in vain for Massachusetts alone to expect to support the public credit; for six or seven States have absolutely refused to comply with the one of the year before the last, and, of those who have complied in appearance, very few will make any effectual payments; and I presume there will not be any that will comply with the one that is now to be considered by you, excepting the cash part of it, and with that numbers will comply. In short, the present Federal Government seems near its exit; and whether we shall in the Convention be able to agree upon mending it, or forming and recommending a new one, is not certain. All agree, however, that much greater powers are necessary to be given, under some form or other. But the large States think the representation ought to be more in proportion to the magnitude of the States, and consequently more like a national government, while the smaller ones are for adhering to the present mode. We have hitherto considered the subject with great calmness and temper; and there are num-

bers of very able men in this body who all appear thoroughly alarmed with the present prospect. I do not know that I am at liberty to write anything on this subject. I shall therefore only observe further, that all agree the legislative and executive ought to be separate, and that there should be a national judiciary.

I beg you not to mention having heard anything from me on the subject, except to your brother, to whom I should have written, but I am quite overcome with the heat of the weather. Please to make my compliments to him and to Mrs. Parsons, your brother William, &c. Please to remind your brother Ebenezer about my son John, and believe me to be

Yours, very respectfully,
N. Gorham.

TR (Parsons, *Memoir of Theophilus Parsons*, 461–62)

TUESDAY, JUNE 19, 1787

Met according to Adjournment.

Madison—The Distinction between foederal and national Representation—the one from the State collectively—the other from the People is not well taken—There are two States in the Union in which Delegates are chosen by the People.

Probability of adopting Plan—We must adopt such an one as will ensure Safety—Let us have a Chance. Confederation on same ground as Compact made by a Number of Persons—If one violates it all are discharged—in Treaties it is agreed that a Breach of any is a Dissolution of all—Jersey has refused to comply with Requisitions—He is anxious to perpetuate Union—but will not consent to prolong it on its present Principles.— How is Confederation observed?

Georgia has entered into War and made Treaties in express Violation of Union.

Virginia and Maryland entered into Compact in like Violation.—Massachusetts has a regular Body of Forces without Approbation of Congress.

The conciliatory Resolution of Congress resp[ectin]g Wioming Dicision evinces Weakness of general Government.

The Power retained by the different States Executives of pardoning would alone defeat national Government. The Amphictionic Council had a Right of judging between Members, mulcting Aggressors—drawing out Force of States—and several other important Powers—The Confederacy was however of very short Duration. It will not be denied that the Convention has as much Power as Congress—They have exercised it in recommending a new Rule of Apportionment—11 States agreed to it.

Martin—before the Confederation each State had complete Sovereignty—When confederated they met so and they must remain equal.

Wilson—The Declaration of Independence declares the U.S. collectively to be vested with Power of making War and Peace—this antecedent to framing Constitutions consequently paramount.

Hamilton—agrees with Wilson—this is calculated to destroy many Heresies in Politics—How is general Government to affect Interests of smaller States?—In Agriculture, Commerce and Revenue—large States are remote from each other—Commercial Interests are not the same—on what Principle can they combine to affect agriculteral Interest?

Motion by Wilson to move that the Committee rise and report that it is the Opinion of the Committee that the Plan submitted by New Jersey is inexpedient—This was accordingly done and I was disposed to submit to it because the Sentiments of the Committee on the Question of Representation in the first Instance could not be pointedly taken.

On the first Resolve when Question put—6 States Affirmative—4 against and Maryland divided.

The first Resolution was then considered—(Mr. Elseworth moved) after some Debate on it.

Adjourned till to Morrow.

JOHN DICKINSON: NOTES ON DEBATES[1]

Objection to N.J. Plan

1. One Branch of Legislation which unsafe as Counsils not enough matured and will prevent a Deposit of necessary power.

2. All new states must be admitted on the same principle which is dangerous.

3. Supplies depend on Requisitions and Coercion.

4. Quotas to be settled in an unequal Manner.

The great Defect of antient and modern Confederations was and is that the necessary Legislation of the Nation did not operate with sufficient Energy. Let this be prevented and the Legislation be allowed to operate in all proper Cases.

We should consider the great states have something to part with as well as the smaller. The only question is on what terms we shall agree.

Objection to Report

1. Representation in both Branches founded on Numbers—unreasonable and dangerous.

2. Doubtful Indefinite Expressions which give a power to legislate in *all Cases*.

3. The Executive lodged in a single person. No Instance of its being ever done with safety. The insurmountable Difficulty of effecting a Junction of Government and Territory between two states. What becomes of the Espirit de Corps?

AD (Historical Society of Pennsylvania)

1. Dated by Dickinson's proposal of this date, recorded by Yates, that the New Jersey and the Committee of the Whole House plans be compared and integrated; "Let us therefore contrast the one with the other, and consolidate such parts of them as the committee approve" (Farrand, 1:327).

GEORGE WASHINGTON: DIARY

Tuesday 19th.   Dined (after leaving Convention) in a family way at Mr. Morris's and spent the Evening there in a very large Company.

WILLIAM SHIPPEN TO THOMAS LEE SHIPPEN

. . . The Convention are very busy and very secret. Col. Hamilton spoke 3 hours yesterday and Jackson says well. Madison, Mason, Randolph King etc. are great according to his Idea. . . . They talk of sitting 2 or 3 months longer.

ALS (Library of Congress)

WILLIAM R. DAVIE TO RICHARD CARSWELL

Philadelphia June 19, 1787

Sir:

    We move slowly in our business; it is indeed a work of great delicacy and difficulty, impeded at every step by jealousies and jarring interests.

I have the honor to be with
great respect
Your mo. obt.
William R. Davie

ALS (North Carolina Division of Archives and History)

WEDNESDAY, JUNE 20, 1787

JOHN LANSING: NOTES ON DEBATES

Met according to Adjournment.

Elseworth moved that first Resolve be amended so as to read that the Government of the United States ought to consist of a Supreme Legislative Judiciary and Executive.

Agreed to.

The second Resolve was then considered.

Lansing—moved that it be postponed to take up the following—*"Resolved that the Powers of Legislation be vested in the United States in Congress."* Sherman seconded Motion.

Explained Reasons why the Question on the Propositions from Jersey was not urged—It was brought forward to shew the general Principles on which we would determine. It was however found it could not discover Sentiments of Committee—this will bring it to a Point.

I have urged two Reasons—1. Incompetency of Powers. 2. Public Mind not prep[ared?] The first—general Assertions have only been made that we have Powers—but most Gentlemen seem to have given it up—one Gentleman has offered the Mode of App[ointmen]t in two States as an Argument—Whatever Mode is adopted they are still Representatives of Sovereignties. Another Gentleman admits Incompetency of Powers but will step forward with a generous Confidence. To imitate him we must be convinced of Utility of System—We must be certain that it will secure important and equal Benefits to all.

If destitute of these Convictions we should be Traitors to our Country.

It is said to be unimportant because merely recommendatory.

Let us examine some of Objections to vesting Powers in Congress.

1. Inequality of Representation—Britain has been instanced to prove Evils. So has R. Island. Neither of these applicable.

The Boroughs contain few Inhabitants much impoverished—or the Property of some Man of large Estate. These easily corrupted but it is not from hence to be inferred that several Thousands can be corrupted with equal facility.

Counties in England unequal in *Extent Population* and Wealth. No Complaints from that Source. Rhode Island acted without Confederation—She had a Right to deliberate and to dissent.

But Congress represent *State Interests and Prejudices*. However Representation modified that will be the Case. One Branch appointed in same Mode—the second is intended to be composed of Men avowedly of a less liberal Turn—

It has been said there can be no Inducements for large States to oppress small—If there are no seperate Interests why so solicitous ab[ou]t Represent[atio]n. The Share of Virginia to Deleware as *16* to *1* in Arithmetic Proportion—but in political as *40 to 1* at least. This Legislature to legislate in every Case—they cannot have the necessary Information.

But Congress is more easily corrupted? To obviate this only one Observ[ation]. One appointed annually subject to recall—the other for 7 and 3 Years absolute.

As long as State Sovergnties exist each much an equal Suffrage—this is equitable—it is necessary.

On the new System cannot reason from Experience.

Coercion—in both Systems equal as to their Objects.

Mason—Want of Power strong Objection if we could conclude. We ought to risk it—In Eventual Treaty with G. Britain our Commiss[ioners] did so—Met Approbation of their Country.

No Gentleman can think Citizens of America will trust their Powers to one Set of Men—Will they trust to a *Conclave*, subject to Corruption—certainly not.

In 1778, 79, and 80 Factions in Congress.—States have refused to give Congress Power because one Body, and not elected by the People.

There will be no Coercion in this Government.

He will not consent to Abolition of State Sovereignties.

Martin—The Legislatures have refused to give Congress Powers—no Objection could exist with them that People did not appoint.

10 States must be injured by App[ortionmen]t of Representation. Coercion as compleat in one System as the other. If U.S. only exercise Powers which are not Objects of Odium and leave the Residuum to the individual States they must become completely odious and the Consequence is evident.

Sherman—one Body is sufficient—the great States supposed themselves benefited by Confederacy—Virginia adopted it without a dissenting Vote—Massachusetts had no Objection. Would be content to have two Houses if one represented States.

W[ilso]n—We go contrary to the Principles of App[ortionmen]t if we submit to limit it to one Branch.   On Question

6 Negative	*Affirmative* 4
Massachusetts	
Pennsylvania	Connecticut
Virginia	New York

Maryland divided	North Carolina	New Jersey
	South Carolina	Deleware
	Georgia	

Upon the President's rising to put the Question on original Resolution Bedford moved an Adjournment.

Question 5 for—6 against it—The State of Deleware then put off Question—Adjourned till to Morrow.

[JARED INGERSOLL?]: DRAFT SPEECH[1]

Mr. President

I have preserved a respectfull silence during the debates of the Committee of the whole house; without flattery to others or meaness of spirit

1. Farrand (4:20) ascribed this document to Luther Martin and gave it a probable date of June 19. In a footnote he revealed that he relied on cataloging data in the Library of Congress for his attribution. He also confided that a staff member of the Library's Manuscript Division had challenged his attribution, claiming that Roger Sherman was, in fact, the author of the document.

The draft cannot have been composed by Martin or Sherman. Its author states that he had preserved a "respectful silence" during the debates in the Committee of the Whole House, May 30–June 19. Sherman, however, spoke almost daily during this period and Martin spoke at least twice. The writer, moreover, identifies his home state by its attitude toward slavery: "at the Eastward Slavery is not acknowledged, *with us* it exists in a certain qualified manner, at the Southward in its fullest extent." In 1787 the "Eastward," the eastern states, always meant New England, which excludes Sherman, a resident of Connecticut. Slavery was established in its full vigor in Maryland, the home of Martin, which excludes him as well. Where, in 1787, did slavery exist in a "certain qualified manner"? Having passed a law for the gradual abolition of slavery in 1780, Pennsylvania fits the description. The author of the draft may, then, have been a citizen of Pennsylvania.

On the jacket in which the draft is enclosed in the Library of Congress, Luther Martin's name has been crossed out, Sherman's name has been appended and crossed out, and the name of Pennsylvania delegate Jared Ingersoll has been inserted below Sherman's. On what grounds the attribution of authorship to Ingersoll was made the records of the Manuscript Division do not reveal, but a comparison of the handwriting of the draft with Ingersoll's letter of May 18, above, reveals a striking resemblance between the two that would support an attribution to Ingersoll. The tone of this draft—a skepticism about the feasibility of a strong national government—is not inconsistent with what we know about Ingersoll's political ideas at this time. The reference at the close of the draft to the sentiments of the Connecticut Assembly, which suggested Sherman's authorship, can be explained by Ingersoll's upbringing in New Haven and by continuing family ties and interest in the affairs of his native state.

The draft must have been composed after June 19, for it incorporates Hamilton's observation of that date (Farrand, 1:323, 328) that the states, even if reduced to and considered as corporations, would be formidable entities, threatening the national government. If Ingersoll composed the draft, he never delivered the speech which it outlined. Indeed, he is not recorded as speaking in the Convention.

with respect to myself I can acknowledge my Inferiority, to the Members of this hon[orab]le convention, in an acquaintance with the political history of this Country; a laborious application to the business of my profession has not afforded me much Opportunity for attendance here in order to collect Information, nor time for reflecting on the few Ideas with which my Mind was stored relative to the Object of our present meeting, these considerations operate powerfully in favor of doing no more than [casting] a silent Vote on the several questions to be determined, but other motives still more cogent, impel me, to a full & free communication of my sentiments, the situation of our Country I consider as critical & alarming, I was sent here not to devolve upon others the trouble of thinking for me but to judge & act for myself, I may err but my intentions are the best—

I confess it appears to me that difficulties almost insuperable, attend every possible plan that can be suggested, to introduce a System unexceptionable in itself & relatively so, authorized & yet efficacious, is scarcely within the Sphere of Possibility—

The Attempt however must be made, & the first great Question which presents itself is, shall we delineate a Scheme of Government national or foederal? for I cannot but think that this principle once established, a variety of consequences serious & important are necessarily connected & deducible—

In order to make our Choice between an establishment national or foederal, let us trace the Causes of the present publick Distress, thence we may be able to point out the proper Characteristicks of the new Government, its *Nature* & its *extent.*—

It is a very common error, to mistake a concomitant fact for a cause, perhaps it has happened in the present Instance, & that we have imputed to the want of power in Congress, difficulties inevitable for sometime yet to come, when under the best Government, the most ably administered, the dismemberment of the Empire of Great Britain, by the Independancey of this Country, is an incident peculiarly offensive to that haughty people, those who have conquered may be expected to forgive with equal Magninimity, but a power foiled in its attempts at Dominion, feasts with a malevolent satisfaction at every humiliating circumstance in the Affairs of those whom they could not subdue & therefore wish to disappoint & vex, for this reason the Court of St. James, affects to treat us with comtempt & avoids a treaty, & France[2] our great & good Ally resents the Conduct of our Ministers in the course of the negotiations for a peace, & immediate Interest unites all the powers of Europe, in a combination to exclude from their West-India Islands, if not all our Vessels at least those of considerable burthen & enumerated Articles, comprising nearly every particular, which we can export to those Markets & while enumerating misfortunes that

2. In the margin: "must add 40 for one—alienated Certificates—Commutation."

admit of no immediate relief let us not forget that our domestic Debt is 28,000,000 of Dollars our foreign,

The variety of situations under which the Colonies were situated when they became States, the disproportioned Magnitude of the several independent Sovereignties, & that a very great proportion of the Inhabitants secretly wish destruction to the Polity under which they live, & we must confess, that our Patriotism must in some measure be put to the Test, under any Form of Government that may be introduced—

That the United States, ought to have a Revennue to discharge the Interest of the Debt, incurred by a War undertaken in defence of the inherent rights of human Nature, & eventually the principal, is as far as I know uncontroverted, as a natural attendant & because the States individually are incompetent to the purpose that the United-States should also regulate the Commerce of the United-States foreign & internal, is I believe also a matter of general Consent, & that the United-States should also fix the Currency & determine what should be the circulating Medium, from New-Hampshire, to Georgia would meet but few or no Opponents within these Walls & those who agree to the propositions already stated would certainly as generally concur in the appointment of proper Judiciaries, to carry into execution the laws of the two former descriptions, respecting either Commerce or Impost,—

It is said, this provision is a measure inadequate that our wants require further interference & that should our Deliberations produce no other effect the World will say, that the Fable of the Mountain in labour producing a Mouse is again exemplified—

I will not contend that the additions of power which I have mentioned will answer the expectations of our Constituents, I do not believe that they will, the possibility of reconciling a federal Government with State inferiour Governments I will consider more particularly by & by—I do not hesitate to express my apprehensions that in the present temper of the people in some of the States at least, any power of Congress less than physical will be opposed

But it is contended that the Causes of our troubles are beyond what has been recited, that something more than a federal Union is necessary, a Physical power to carry into effect the measures that the Sovereignty shall determine upon, & to attain the primary objects of Government—

I deny that the situation of any particular state or states is the measure by which we are to regulate our proceedings, we are not to examine whether sufficient powers are properly distributed in the several Governments, to controul the Subjects but whether as between the United-States & the Individual States, the proportion of power is properly distributed—

Still it is contended that this is taking the matter up in a very confined limited view that the Sovereignty of the United States should not act merely on the respective States but immediately on the Individual Delinquent, that in this way, the people lose no Rights altho the Sovereignty acquires Authority & that one Government comprehending the territory now subdivided among thirteen, would secure Liberty & Property & be better able to exercise a Democracy—

This suggestion gives rise to three questions or different views of the subject—First what is best on abstracted principles 2 Secondly what is practicable & Thirdly what are we authorised to do—

Suppose for a moment, that the thirteen united States should be extinguished & annihilated, & that we were about to devise the best & most eligible System of Government unembarrassed by Instructions, & without any reasonable apprehensions of difficulty from the prejudices or prepossessions of the people of this Country and which would be best a national Government or a foederal Union? some Members will be surprised when I add, that I am by no means clear that a national Government would deserve the preference! I shall readily acknowledge & will state particularly by & by, the Inconveniences of a federal Union—we need not refer ourselves to Writers of antient or modern times to know that every political Institution certainly therfore the highest ought to be prepared with a reference to that C[———t] state of property & other local circumstances— these are so different in different parts of the Continent, that no one Form will suit or apply throughout, should this difficulty be got over, still another remains the Laws must be entirely different, the Fisheries & Manufactures of New-England, The Flour Lumber Flaxseed & Ginseng of New York New Jersey Pennsylvania & Delaware The Tobacco of Maryland & Virginia the Pitch Tar, Rice & Indigo & Cotton of North Carolina South Carolina & Georgia, can never be regulated by the same Law nor the same Legislature, nor is this diversity by any means confined to Articles of Commerce, at the Eastward Slavery is not acknowledged, with us it exists in a certain qualified manner, at the Southward in its full extent, time would fail me to enumerate the many particulars, in which such a variety of provisions will be necessary, for descent of Estates, validity of last Wills & Testaments, &c that it would indeed be a political Phenomenon to see the same Legislature enacting at the same time Laws for the abolition of Slavery, for the gradual Abolition of it & for its continuance, & the regulation of the Objects of its Jurisdiction—will it be said that the Laws should be uniform they ought not unless at the same time you can alter the Climate,[3] Produce, Soil, & even Genius of the people—and controul the operation of the common & best established principles of

3. In the margin: "immense extent. thinly settled. doubtfull—too much for a Democracy—too much for a moderate monarchy—expence of the—sit all the time or travel back and forth—what numbers of each branch."

human nature—even in addition from long habits & Education there are principles so interlaced & interwoven that to wrest them would be to burst the common bands of Society—but it is said I am combating imaginary objects that no such one Government is intended, but that the State Governments are to subsist & this general Government only to regulate some few general specified matters, others not particularly needed to remain with the several States—I cannot but think that the present System is more objectionable much than a general Government,—in the first place I conceive & will endeavour to shew, that every person who would object to a general Government would find fault with this they will say as it has been expressed it is the foetus of a Monarchy, in addition to this others will say & I must be of the Number that this Government is consonant to no principle whatever, on the principle of the Union it is too much on the Idea of a general Government it is too little—that it has all the expence of a National Government without its *energy*—will give equal Alarm, equal opportunity to excite prejudice, without affording any dignity to Government or securing Obedience or obtaining any of the primary Objects of Government, that an eternal Contest will be excited between the several Governments & this monstrous sluggard, that the activity of the latter will be able to thwart the overgrown lubber [?], that all that can be expected from it is securing a Revennue, the whole of which will be absorbed in the collection that so much might be obtained nearly in the present system & a great part of the expence saved that it is [?].

If as has been suggested by an hon[orab]le Member from Virginia, we have prejudices to guard against & fears of a Monarchy which will be excited unless circumspection be exercized, this Scheme will most of all excite them, it will be said it is impossible that so much should be done unless more was intended, that it is impossible things should rest here, for all will concur in saying that a Contest between the National Government & the individual States must terminate either in Monarchy or an abolition of the present Systems, concurrent, independent Sovereignties, undefined Imperia in Imperio cannot subsist, none ever did any length of time, that at first the Democratick part will be found too powerfull for the Aristocratick & Executive, the same reasons that began this System must compleat it that it is a mutilated unsistematick Imitation of the british Constitution— If even you denominate the several States Corporations only yet as has been observed they move in such large orbits that they will be able to put themselves in competition with the United-States—if there are these reasons for doubting if the proposed plan be the best even in the minds of the most candid—how far have we reason to believe it practicable—the people of the united-States, excited to Arms by the insidious designs of the then Mother Country have become admirers of liberty warmly & passionately so—they snuff Tyranny in every tainted Gale—they are jealous of their liberty—they are pleased with their present Governments, they think them as energetick as they ought to be framed, they are continually planning subdivisions of the present Governments, they are complaining of the expence of the present Governments—they are jealous of designs to introduce a Monarchy, under specious pretences & different names in the despotick empire of Rome, for some time every thing was transacted under the conciliating Names of the Commonwealth—Consuls—Senate&c—they are apprehensive of designs to abridge the liberties of the common people—to make a greater difference of Ranks than the present Government admits of—even in the Assembly of Connecticutt you see these sentiments—they are prejudiced each against the neighbouring State—of no humour to coalesce.

Farrand, 4:20–28.

GEORGE WASHINGTON: DIARY

Wednesday. 20th.   Attended Convention. Dined at Mr. Meridiths & drank Tea there.

THURSDAY, JUNE 21, 1787

JOHN LANSING: NOTES ON DEBATES

Johnson—Individuality of States ought to be preserved—you deposit Aristocratic and democratic Power in different Bodies—And we can deposit more but then let one Branch represent Sovereignties.

Wilson—As States represented Individually—their Sovereignty to be preserved—Quantum of Power preserved in smaller States as comprehensive as in larger—It will be the Interest of all to represent general Government *if Interest of any*—of Consequence they will co-operate.

Madison—Legislature of States have not shewn Disposition to deprive Corporations of Priviledges—Why should they here.—Question carried d[ivide]d as Yesterday.

C. C. Pinkney moves that *3rd* Resolve be so altered as to read ought to be appointed *in such Manner as the several Legislatures shall direct*—he supposes this will give greater Satisfaction to the People.

Hamilton—If you permit Legislatures to elect you will have *State Interests* represented.

Govr. Rutlege—Legislatures of States ought to appoint—The Representation will be more refined—Whether the People elect themselves or appoint others to elect substantially the same.

Wilson—Official State Influence will defeat the Object of national Government if Election by Legislatures.

King—same Sentiment differently expressed.

Question—Negative—Massachusetts, New York, Pennsylvania, North Carolina, Georgia.

Affirmative—Connecticut, New Jersey, Deleware, South Carolina.

Maryland divided.

N.B. Judge Yates and Colo[nel] Hamilton in Negative—I was for Affirmative.

Randolph moved to obliterate *three Years* and insert *two*.

Sherman—for *one Year*—By suffering them to remain three Years they accomodate their Sentiments to those with whom they associate—they must be oblidged to return Home every Year to remind them of what they owe their Constituents.

Mason—By having annual Elections remote States would generally be unrepresented in Beginning of Sessions.

Hamilton—The Opinion of the People is fluctuating—You must exercise your Judgment, convinced that the Pressure of unavoidable Circumstances will direct the public Mind.

Listlessness prevails in New York on Acc[oun]t of annual Election—Consequence is that Factions are represented in that Government.

Adjourned till to Morrow.

GEORGE WASHINGTON: DIARY

Thursday 21st.   Attended Convention. Dined at Mr. Pragers, and spent the evening in my Chamber.

WILLIAM BLOUNT TO JOHN GRAY BLOUNT

Philadelphia June 21st 1787

Hawkins and myself arrived here on the 19th. He now purposes to leave this on Thursday on board a ship for Petersburg. I am not at Liberty to say what is doing in Convention and if I was the Business is so much in Embryo that I could say nothing that would be in the least satisfactory. All the Members agree that the Convention will sit at least six weekes and it is generally supposed 8 or 10 from this Time, hence the Necessity for more Mony to be remitted to me.

Farrand, 4:65–66; first sentence supplied from ALS in North Carolina Division of Archives and History.

FRIDAY, JUNE 22, 1787

JOHN LANSING: NOTES ON DEBATES

Did not attend Convention being indisposed.

GEORGE WASHINGTON: DIARY

Friday 22d.   Dined at Mr. Morris's & drank Tea with Mr. Frans. Hopkinson.

PHILADELPHIA STREET COMMISSIONERS: MINUTES

PRESENT

Andrew Geyer	Philip Pancake
William Richards	Samuel McLane
Peter Ozeas	Nathan Boys

An order drawn on the Treasurer in favour of Michael Wartman for the Sum of fifteen Pounds on Account for Work done with his Teams at the Common Sewer in Fourth Street £15

Upon Complaint to this Board of the very great difficulty arising from the Carriages passing in front of the State House, so that the Honbl. Convention now setting there, are much interrupted by the Noise of the same—Resolved, that a Quantity of Gravell now haulling out of the Sewer in Fourth Street, be laid on Chestnut Street, in front of the State House.

AD (Records of the Philadelphia Street Commissioners, Independence National Historical Park)

SATURDAY, JUNE 23, 1787

3rd Resolve—*to be paid out of the public Treasury*

Question—five Ayes—five Noes—1 divided.

"to be ineligible to any Office established *by a particular State or* under the Authority of the United States."

C. C. Pinkney moves to strike out *by a particular State or.*

Wilson—If you strike out these Words you confirm Attachments to particular States and give that Attachment a Direction injurious to a general Government.

Sherman—If State and general Governments have separate Interests their Jealousies will be mutual and they already operate very powerfully— hence you must leave the Individual States much Power.

Gorham—It is necessary to give general Government Energy—prevailing Opinions are too democratic.

Question—Ay 8—No 3.

Madison moves after *established* insert *or Emoluments whereof shall have been augmented by the Legislature of the United States during the Time they have been Members or within one Year thereafter*—He wishes Executive to have App[ointmen]t of Officers—He thinks it necessary to hold out Inducements to Men of first Fortune to become Members.

Butler—Executive may be as corrupt as Legislature—It would place too pervading an Influence in him.

Rutlege—We ought not to wish to have place Hunters in Legislature— No Incentives ought to be held out to Men of that Description—Honesty will probably predominate in lower House Ability in the upper.

Mason—He has experienced in Virginia that whenever a Man of the first Character who was not a Member of the Legislature was opposed to a despicable one who was a Member—the latter uniformly succeeded. If the Restriction is continud a Seat in the Legislature will lead the Way to first Offices—this sufficient Inducement—he is against Amendment.

Madison—Men of Ability are not found [?] in Virginia to step forward in Public. Persons of other Descriptions press for Admission.

King—Venality may be as successfully applied in the Appointment of Relations of Members as Members themselves.

Wilson—*Selfish Characters* will endeavor to place *Men of a generous Turn of thinking and Men of Abilities* in a Situation not to be appointed—Executive ought to have app[ointmen]t.

Question 2 Ayes 8 Noes—Maryland divided, *Jersey and Connecticut ay.*

Sherman moves after ineligible to insert *and incapable of holding.* Unanimously agreed.

The Question was then put on the Words *for the Space of one Year after its Expiration.*

4 Ayes—6 Noes—1 divided.

Adjourned till Monday.

GEORGE WASHINGTON: DIARY

Saturday 23rd.   In Convention. Dined at Doctr. Ruston's & drank Tea at Mr. Morris's.

SUNDAY, JUNE 24, 1787

Sunday 24th.   Dined at Mr. Morris's & spent the evening at Mr. Meridiths—at Tea.

RUFUS KING TO ALEXANDER HODGDEN

Philadelphia 24 June 1787

Sir

You must be sensible from the state of my account with the Treasury that I have a much larger demand for arrears of pay than either of my colleagues. I have made it a rule to forbear my importunities on this subject as long as possible. My present situation exposes me to heavy expenses, and I cannot but think that you will unite with me in Opinion that my claims are not behind those of any person who has a Demand on the Treasury.[1] I took an order some months since, on a note of the tax Treasurer's, for 100£. I sold it for 90£. I cannot think of suffering so great a loss of my wages in future. I pray you to inform me when you will authorize me to draw on you for 200£. A much larger sum is due to me but I shall be content to wait some Time for the balance.

With great respect I am, Sir,
your ob. and very Hble. Servant
Rufus King

ALS (Historical Society of Pennsylvania)

1. The straitened financial condition of various delegates is a topic that recurs in this volume and in volume 3 of Farrand. One delegate attempted to alleviate his financial distress by selling information to the British about proceedings in Congress and, presumably, in the Convention. On March 8 Peter Allair, a British agent operating in New York and reporting to secretary of war Sir George Yonge, informed his superior that a member of Congress whose "expenses exceeds his income" was indebted to him and would provide information about Congress for a "liberal" retainer. By April 5 the potential informer had learned that his state had appointed him to represent it at the Philadelphia Convention from which he was, evidently, prepared to send "samples" of information directly to London. The records do not indicate if the proposed agreement between Allair and the Congressman was ever approved in London or if any intelligence was ever sent from the Convention. The identity of the Congressman cannot be conclusively established (Allair to Yonge, March 8, 1787 [two letters], April 5, 1787; P.R.O., F.O. 4/5).

MONDAY, JUNE 25, 1787

4th Resolve. C. Pinkney—We are peculiarly situated—We have no Distinction of Ranks—When Executive hereditary or elective for Life Peers necessary. Not above *100* Men in the United States so rich as to be dangerous—these cannot be considered as a distinct Class on a national Scale—three Classes—professional Commercial and agriculturel—there Interests now generally resolvable into the last. He is therefore for something like the Virginia System, but State Sovereignties must be retained.

The United States too extensive to furnish a general Legislature competent to the Management of domestic Concerns. States ought to be divided into five Classes—to have *from one to five Votes.*

Reed—The Confederacy similar to Articles of Co-partnership—Articles insufficient—before they are revised adjust old Accounts—apply all Lands *acquired and protected by common Arms to discharge public Debt*—this done we may make another Agreement.

Wilson—The System of Hen. IV to unite Europe as a Republic had trifling Objects to those we are now engaged in attaining—The Happiness of *the Globe* involved in it—he has distinct Ideas of State and general Government—has Objection to any Part of Legislature being elected by the State Legislatures—it will *perpetuate local Prejudices*—States are not intended as component Parts of general Government—they need not be represented—The Objects of national Government will be—Commerce—War—Treaties Coins and other great national Concerns. On those Occasions the Proportions of Representation so as to give each State a proper Weight in the Government may be preserved, in the second Branch as well as the first.

If both Branches are elected from same Source they will have same Interests.—Moves that the second Branch be elected *by Electors to be elected by the Citizens of the United States.*

Elseworth—Every Representative will have local Ideas however elected. No existing and distinct Interests to form Ballances—Republican Governments cannot exist throughout U.S. but by support of individual States. Virginia cannot give Law to Kentuckey. Massachusetts cannot extend her Government 100 Miles from Capital. These are strong Instances against an Extension of Republican Government on a general Scale—but the Inhabitants of every State are warmly attached to their several Constitutions—this another Reason.

Johnson—Individuality of States ought to be preserved.

Mason—If Self Defence necessary to general Government it will be as necessary to individual States.—this can only be done by representing the States.

On Question on Wilson's Motion—lost.

Question *on Election by Legislature.*

9 Ayes—2 Noes.

Agreed to expunge *sufficient to ensure their Independence.*

7 Ayes—4 Noes.

Duration of Senate then considered—*seven Years.*

Gorham—wished the upper House to be formed into Classes.

Randolph assents—State Governments will be perpetually tending to the Subversion of general Government—this would give general Government Consistency.

Reed—good Behaviour would be more effectual—If Mr. Hamilton would make the Motion he will second him.

C. C. Pinkney—thinks 4 Years sufficient—otherwise Representatives might be induced to become Inhabitants of State in which Seat of Government established.

Madison—this will weaken it too much.

On Question on striking out *seven Years.*

7 Ayes—3 Noes.

Gorham moved 6 Years—5 Ayes—5 Noes—1 divided. (H[amilton] and myself voted Neg. on Question.)

On Question *five Years.* 5 Ayes—5 Noes—1 divided.

Morris moved that the Senate should be elected for and continue in Office during good Behaviour. Not seconded.

Adjourned till to Morrow.

CHARLES PINCKNEY: DRAFT SPEECH

Our true situation appears to me to be this.—a new, extensive country containing within itself, the materials of forming a government capable of extending to its citizens all the blessings of civil & religious liberty,—capable of making them happy at home.— This is the great end of republican establishments. We mistake the object of our government, if we hope or wish that it is to make us respectable abroad.—Conquest or superiority among other powers is not or ought not ever to be the object of republican systems.—If they are sufficiently active & energetic to rescue us from contempt & preserve our domestic happiness & security, it is all we can expect from them.—It is more than almost any other government ensures to its citizens.

I believe this observation will be found generally true.—that no two people are so exactly alike in their situation or circumstances as to admit the exercise of the same government with equal benefit.—that a system must be suited to the habits & genius of the people it is to govern & must grow out of them.

The people of the U.S. may be divided into three classes. *Professional men* who must from their particular pursuits always have a considerable weight in the government while it remains popular.—*Commercial men,* who may or may not have a weight as a wise or injudicious commercial policy is pursued.—If that commercial policy is pursued which I conceive to be the true one, the merchants of this country will not or ought not for a considerable time to have much weight in the political scale.

The third is the *landed interest,* the owners of & cultivators of the soil who are & ought ever to be the governing principle in the system———.

These three classes however distinct in their pursuits are individually equal in the political scale, & may be clearly proved to have but one interest.—The dependence of each on the other is mutuel?—the merchant depends on the planter—both must in private as well as public affairs be connected with the professional men—who in their turn must in some measure depend upon them.—Hence it is that from this manifest connection & the equality which I before stated exists, & must for the reasons then assigned continue, that after all there is one but one great & equal body of citizens, composing the inhabitants of this country among whom there are no distinctions of rank & very few of fortune.

For a people thus circumstanced, are we then to form a government & the question is, what kind of system is best suited to them.

Will the British government.—no!—why? because Great Britain contains three orders of people distinct in their situation their passions & principles.—These orders combined form the great body of the nation & *as* in national expenses & accounts the wealth & resources of the whole community must contribute so ought each component part to be properly & duly represented.—No other combination of power could form this due representation but the one that exists.—Neither the peers or the people could represent the royalty, nor could the royalty & the people form a proper representation for the peers.—Each therefore must of necessity be represented by itself or the sign of itself & this accidental mixture certainly has formed a government admirably balanced.

But the United States contain but one order that can be assimilated to the British nation———this is the order of commons.—they will not surely then attempt to form a government consisting of three branches two of which shall have nothing to represent . . . they will not have an Executive

& Senate *hostile* because the King & Lords of England are so.—The same reason do not exist & therefore the same provisions are not necessary.

We must as has been observed suit our government to the people it is to direct.—These are I believe as active, intelligent & susceptible of good government as any people in the world.—The confusion which has produced the present relaxed state is not owing to them.—It is owing to the weakness & *impropriety* of a government incapable of combining the various interests it is intended to unite & support & destitute of energy——

The people of the U.S. are perhaps the most singular of any we are acquainted with.—Among them there are fewer distinctions of fortune & less of rank; than among the inhabitants of any other nation.—Every freeman has a right to the same protection & security and a very moderate share of property entitles them to the possession of all the honors & privileges the public can bestow.—Hence arises a greater equality, than is to be found among the people of any other country, and an equality which is more likely to continue. I say this equality is likely to continue; because in a new country, possessing immense tracts of uncultivated lands—where every temptation is offered to emigration & where industry must be rewarded with competency, there will be few poor & few dependent.—Every member of the society almost, will enjoy an equal power of arriving at the supreme offices & consequently of directing the strength & sentiments of the community.—None will be excluded by birth, & few by fortune from a power of voting for proper persons to fill the offices of government—the whole community will enjoy in the fullest sense that kind of political Liberty which consists in the power which the members of the state reserve to themselves of arriving at the public offices, or at least of the having votes in the nomination of those who fill them——

If this state of things is true & the prospect of its continuing, probable, it is perhaps not politic to endeavour too close an imitation of a government calculated for a people whose political situation is, & whose views ought to be extremely different

Much has been said of the constitution of Great Britain.—I will confess That I believe it to be the best constitution in existence, but at the same time I am confident, it is one that will not suit or cannot be introduced into this country for many centuries.—If it were proper to go here into a historical dissertation of the British constitution, it might easily be shewn that The peculiar excellence, the distinguishing feature of that government cannot possibly be introduced into our system.—that it's balance between the crown & the people cannot be made a part of our constitution.—that we neither have, or can have the members to compose it.—nor the rights, privileges & properties of so distinct a class of citizens to guard.—that the materials for forming this balance or check do not exist, nor is there a necessity for having so permanent a part of our legislative until the

Executive power is so constituted as to have something fixed & dangerous in it's principle.—by this I mean a sole, hereditary, tho' limited Executive——

That we cannot have a proper body for forming a legislative balance, between the inordinate power of the Executive or the people is evident from a review of the accidents & circumstances, which gave rise to the peerage of Great Britain.—I believe it is well ascertained that the parts which compose the British constitution arose immediately from the forests of Germany, but the antiquity of the establishment of nobility is by no means clearly defined.—Some authors are of opinion that the dignity denoted by the titles of dux et comes was derived from the old roman to the German Empire, while others are of opinion that they existed among the germans long before the romans were acquainted with them.—the institution however of nobility is immemorial among the nations who may properly be termed the Ancestors of Britain.—At the time they were summoned in England to become a part of the national council & the circumstances which have contributed to make them a constituent part of that constitution, must be well known to all gentlemen who have either had industry or curiosity to investigate the subject.—The nobles with their possessions [?] & dependants composed a body permanent in their nature & formidable in respect of their powers.—They had a distinct interest either from the king or people—an interest which could only be represented by themselves, & the guardianship of which could not be safely intrusted to others.—At the time they were originally called to form a part of the national counsel, necessity perhaps as much as any other cause induced the monarch to look up to them.—It was necessary to demand the aid of his subjects in personal & pecuniary services,—the power & possessions [?] of the nobility would not permit taxation from any assembly of which they were not a part & the blending the deputies of the commons with them, & thus forming, what they called their parler-ment was perhaps as much the Effect of accident as of any thing else.—The commons were at that time compleatly subordinate to the nobility whose consequences & influence seem to have been the only reason for them that superiority.—a superiority so degrading to the commons—that in the first summons, we find, the freemen called upon to consult the commons to consent—from this time the peers have composed a part of the British legislature & notwithstanding their power & influence have deminished & the commons increased yet still they have been found always, an excellent balance against either the incroachments of the crown or the people. . .——

I have said that such a body cannot exist in this country for ages & that until the situation of your people is exceedingly changed no necessity will exist for so permanent a part of the legislature.—To illustrate this I have remarked that the people of the U.S. are more equal in their circumstances than the people of any other country.—that they have few very few rich men among them?—by rich men, I mean those whose riches may have a dangerous influence, or such as are esteemed rich in Europe.—perhaps there are not 100 on the continent.—that it is not probable this number will be greatly increased.—.—that the genius of the people, their mediocre situation & the prospects which are afforded their industry in a country which, must be a new one for centuries are unfavorable to the rapid distinction of ranks.—The distinction of the right of primogeniture & the equal division of the property of intestates will also have an effect to preserve this mediocrity.—for laws invariably affect the manners of a people.—On the other hand that vast extent of unpeopled territory which opens to the frugal [?] & industrious a sure road to competency & independence will effectually prevent for a considerable time that increase of the poor or discontented & be the means of preserving that equality of condition which so eminently distinguishes us.

If Equality is as I contend the leading feature of the U.S. where then are the riches & the wealth whose representation & protection is the peculiar province of this permanent body.—Are they in the hands of the few who may be called rich, in the possession of less than 100 citizens.—*certainly not*——they are in the great body of the people among whom there are no men of wealth & very few of *real property*—is it probable, that a change will, be created, & that a new order of men will arise.—If under the British Government, for a century, no such change was probable, I think it may be fairly concluded it will not take place while even the semblance of republicanism remains.—How Is this change to be effected.—Where are the sources from whence it is to flow.—From the landed interest.—no—they are too unproductive & equally divided in the majority of the States.—From the monied interest if such exists at present, little is to apprehended.—Are they to spring from Commerce——I believe it will be the first Nobility that ever sprung from merchants.—Besides Sir I apprehend upon this point the policy of the U. States has been much mistaken, We have unwisely considered as the inhabitants of an old instead of a new country.—We have adopted the maxims of a state full of people & manufactures & established in credit.—We have deserted our true interests & instead of applying closely to those improvements in domestic policy which would have insured the future importance of our commerce We have rashly & prematuraly engaged in schemes as extensive as they are imprudent.—This however is an error which daily corrects itself & I have no doubt that a few more severe trials will convince us, that very different commercial principles ought to govern the conduct of these states.

The people of this Country are not only very different from the inhabitants of any State we are acquainted with in the modern world, but I assert that their political situation is distinct from either the people of Greece or

Rome or of any state we are acquainted with among the Antients.—Can the orders introduced by the institution of Solon, can they be found in the U.S.—can the military habits & manners of Sparta be assimilated to our habits & manners.—Are the distinctions of patrician & plebian known among us?—Can the helvetic or belgic confederacies, or can the unwieldy, unmeaning body called the Germanic Empire can they be said to possess either the perfection or a situation like ours.—I apprehend not——they are perfectly different, either in their distinctions of rank, their constitutions their manners & their policy. All that we have to do then is to distribute the powers of government in such manner & for such limited periods as while it gives a proper degree of permanency to the magistrate will reserve to the people the right of election they will not or ought not frequently to part with—

I am of opinion that this may be easily done & that with some amendments the propositions before the committee will fully answer this end

No position appears to me more true than this that the general government cannot effectually exist without retaining the states in the possession of their local rights.—They are the instruments upon which the Union must frequently depend for the support & execution of their powers however immediately operating upon the people & not upon the states.

Much has been said about the propriety of *removing* the distinction of state governments, & having but one general system, suffer me for a moment to examine this Question.

Farrand, 4:28–37

PIERCE BUTLER: NOTES ON DEBATES

Mr. Willson. Because a State Government ought to elect a general Government the general Government ought as well to appoint the State Governments. He objects to the state Governments having anything to do in electing the general Governments. The general Government is not to be considered as composed from different States. Commerce, he says must be common.

PHOTOSTAT (Library of Congress)

GEORGE WASHINGTON: DIARY

Monday 25th.   Attended Convention. Dined at Mr. Morris's—drank Tea there—& spent the evening in my chamber.

TUESDAY, JUNE 26, 1787

JOHN LANSING: NOTES ON DEBATES

Reed moved to insert *nine Years* in the Blank.

Madison—The Advantages of Government cannot be extended equally to all—Those remote from Seat of Government cannot be placed in a Situation equally advantageous with such as near it—Distinctions will always exist—that of Debtor and Creditor—Property had made Distinctions in Europe before a Nobility was created—Inequality of Property will produce the same Distinctions here—The Man in affluent Circumstances has different Feelings from the man who daily toils for a Subsistence. The landed Interest has now the Supreme Power—a Century hence the commercial may prevail—The Government ought to be so organized as to give a Balance to it and protect one Order of Men from the predominating Influence of the other.—The Senate ought to represent the opulent Minority—If this is not done the System cannot be durable.

Sherman—Permanency and Security appear the great Objects of pursuit—In Connecticut have had annual Elections for 135 years—It has protected Property effectually and no Imputations of Instability on it.

Hamilton—We are now considering the Cause of Democracy—he is attached to a free Government and would chearfully *become a Martyr to it*—The occasional Violence of Democracy and the uniform Tyranny of a Despot are productive of the same Consequences—to prevent them he is for tuning the Government high—In the ordinary Progress of Things we must look to a Period as not very remote when Distinctions arising from Property will be greater—You must devise a Repository of the Rights of the wealthy—At Rome after the Institution of the tribunitian Power greater Distinctions arose from the unequal Distribution of Riches and *Rich* and *Poor* were more oppressive Distinctions than *patrician* and *plebeian*. Under the Colonial Government of Connecticut its Objects were contracted—but we have taken a new Station—Its Powers ought to be enlarged in Proportion to the Magnitude of the Objects it is intended to embrace. He will therefore go beyond any of the Ideas advocated by either Party.—Is for nine Years.

Wilson—Foreigners in making Treaties will naturally be inclined to wish a permanent Body to treat with—This will give their Measures Respect and Permanency—Great Britain will not make Treaty with us because Congress instable.—*2nd* Branch have that [?] Power.

On Question Delaware Georgia and Pennsylvania Aye—8 Noes.

Gorham moves *six Years one third to go out biennially*.

7 Ayes—4 Noes—New York New Jersey South Carolina and Georgia No.

C. C. Pinkney—moves that *to receive fixed Stipends* be struck out—It is the prevailing Idea that *2nd* Branch ought to represent the Wealth of the Nation—If so they ought to serve without Compensation.

Franklin—Is of the same Opinion—We will always be able to command the Attendance of a sufficient Number of Men, whose Wealth will enable them to serve Gratis—On Question 5 Ayes—6 Noes.

Elseworth moves *To be paid out of the State Treasurys*.

Madison—by making Elections six Years distant from each other we evince a Disposition to make them independent.—This can only be done by a Payment from national Treasury.

Strong—If you fix the Provision it will not comport with oeconimical Ideas of the Day—It will alarm the Public—Let Legislature provide for themselves.

On Question 5 Ayes—6 Noes.

To be paid out of the Treasury of the United States.

Mason—The second Branch is intended as a Check to the democratic Spirit—Would it not be best to insert *a Qualification of Estate?*

On Question 5 Ayes—6 Noes.

To be ineligible *to any Office by any particular State.*

On Question 3 Ayes—8 Noes.

Or United States during the Time for which they were elected and for one Year thereafter.

On Question—Unanimously affirmative.

5th Resolve—carried unanimously without Debate.

Adjourned till to Morrow.

PIERCE BUTLER: NOTES ON DEBATES

Maddison. Each Interest ought to be represented. Property ought to be defended against the will of even the Majority. If we do not give it a just ballance or proportion of power, the Government can not last.

PHOTOSTAT (Library of Congress)

GEORGE WASHINGTON: DIARY

Tuesday 26th.   Attended Convention. Partook of a family dinner with Govr. Randolph and made one of a party to drink Tea at Grays ferry.

OLIVER ELLSWORTH TO ABIGAIL ELLSWORTH

Philadelphia, June 26, 1787

Mrs. Ellsworth

Our business is yet unfinished and it yet remains uncertain when I shall return home. I am sure I wish for the time for this city has no charms for me. I mix with company without enjoying it and am perfectly tired with flattery and forms. To be very fashionable we must be very trifling and make and receive a thousand professions which everybody knows there is no truth in. Give me a little domestick circle where affection is natural and friendship sincere and I do not care who takes the rest.

I seldom write long letters to anybody and I am sure I need not to you to convince you that I am with the truest and tenderest affection.

Yours   Oliver Ellsworth

Love to the little ones.

Chauncey is well through the smallpox

ALS (Connecticut Historical Society)

JOHN LANSING TO PHILIP SCHUYLER

Philadelphia, June 26th, 1787

. . . The business of the Convention is going on very slowly and it is still in such a Stage as to render the Result very dubious.

ALS (New York Public Library)

EDMUND RANDOLPH TO BEVERLEY RANDOLPH

Philadelphia, June 26th, 1787

Sir:

I beg leave to enclose to your honorable board a letter from Mr. Wythe, resigning his seat in the federal convention. As it rests wholly with them to decide on the propriety of appointing a successor, I shall only assure you, that, if the vacancy should be supplied, the delegation will receive with pleasure any gentleman, whom you may think proper to associate with them. . . .

ALS (Virginia State Library)   .

WEDNESDAY, JUNE 27, 1787

Rutlege moves that *6th* Resolve be postponed to take up *7th* and *8th*.—
Agreed to.

7th Article—the Words *ought not to be according to the Rule established by the Confederation* first to be considered.

Martin—general Government only intended to protect State Governments.

National Objects for Legislative and Executive Exertion ought to be defined and much contracted. If after the greatest Caution defective, it may be revised by a future Convention.

While national Government acts for general Good in the Sphere prescribed for it—no hostility to be apprehended from individual States—it will receive their Patronage and Protection.

The Respect shewn *to a general Government* weak to Excess evinces the amicable Disposition of the Individual States to it.

Virginia and Maryland made Convention for settling Navigation in *Chesepeak and Potowmack*—this is no Breach of Confederation.

The Troops of Massachusetts were drawn out to quell Rebellion—Neither of those Instances prove a Disrespect to Articles of Union.

In every Confederation Equality of Suffrage indispensable.

The larger States have more to protect and their superior Wealth and Strength give them a proportionate Influence.

The three larger States can carry the most injurious Points to the other States—unless the others miraculously combine.

The Executive and Judicial will be from them. The Executive has a Right to subject Laws to a Revision—this will protect them effectually. But what is to prevent them from making decided Arrangements to assume all the Power of general Government?

Athens—Sparta and Thebes pursued same Line of Conduct. From the Journals of Congress it appears that Virginia was sole for apportioning Representation by Numbers or Contribution—She has gained many Proselytes since.

The smaller States gave up their Share to the common Territory acquired by their joint Exertions—this was an important Sacrafice.

Jersey Maryland and several other States have contributed as essentially to repel the Enemy as the large States who now suppose themselves entitled to Preeminence—he would not trust a Legislature so constituted to legislate for Carolinian Slaves or Massachusetts oxen.—the one was to form Part of Rule for Representation—He cannot give his Assent to subject the Rights of Freemen to them.

It has been observed that great States have great Objects, which they will not permit the small States to thwart—If those Objects are directed to general Good they will be pursued by all—if not, it would be right to defeat them.

Adjourned till to Morrow.

GEORGE WASHINGTON: DIARY

Wednesday 27th.   In Convention. Dined at Mr. Morris's. Drank Tea there also and spent the evening in my chamber.

WILLIAM SAMUEL JOHNSON TO ANNE JOHNSON

. . . My time has been so much taken up with company from which I could not excuse myself, that I have but a very few Moments left to acknowledge the rect. of your dear favor of the 22d instant. . . .

ALS (Connecticut Historical Society)

WILLIAM PIERCE TO ST. GEORGE TUCKER

Philadelphia, June 27, 1787

My dear Sir:

. . . I wish it was in my power to give you some information respecting the proceedings of the Convention, but we are enjoined to secrecy. I dare not say any thing.

You may suppose that where there are a variety of interests, there will be a variety of projects. Nothing can conquer the force of local habit. Some are for one thing, and some for another, but I believe we shall ultimately agree on some sort of Government.

Burlemaqui relates a circumstance which he has borrowed from Herodotus that is a good deal in the style of our various sentiments. On the death of Cambyses of Persia there was an attempt made to re-establish the Government and to effect the punishment of the Magus who had usurped the Throne as a descendant from Cyrus. A question was proposed in the Council of the seven Chiefs, of this sort—what is the best kind of Government for the present state of Persia? One was of opinion that Persia ought to be a Republic; another was of opinion that it ought to be a strong

Aristocracy, and a third (who I think was Darius) was convinced that no other Government would suit it but a Monarchy.

I pray you not from this story to conclude that we are to have a Monarchy. I related it merely to give you some idea of the various opinions which we have sometimes started. . . .

ALS (College of William and Mary)

Convention Delegates to Benjamin Franklin

The Gentm. of the Convention at the Indian Queen present their compliments to his Excellency the President of the State of Pennsylvania and request the honor of his company to dinner at their Quarters on Monday next at half after three o'clock.

Wednesday June 27th

The favour of an answer is requested.

Farrand, 4: 66.

THURSDAY, JUNE 28, 1787

JOHN LANSING: NOTES ON DEBATES

Martin—It is in State Capacities we are taxed—The Majority of States ought to tax.

In arguing it has been said that Protection ought to be extended to *rich* and *poor*—they ought only to protect States. Daily Experience shews the Genius of People is in Favor of small Governments—they are for seperating whenever they are remote from its Seat.

In Amphictionic Council each State had two Votes. Sparta attempted to exclude three Cities.

Destruction of Confederacy owing to large States.

In the Dutch and Swiss Confederacies each has one. Berne and Zurich are equal to all the Rest—each has one Vote.

Happiness is preferable to the Splendors of a national Government.

Admission of large States into the Confederation dangerous to the others if they are admitted on Principles of perfect Equality—but more so if they have a constitutional Predominance.

There is no Danger of not having another Convention unless the Conduct of the present prevents it.

The greater States as now circumstanced are not Objects of Terror.

Massachusetts convulsed—Pennsylvania Commerce in the Power of Jersey and Deleware—Virginia weak and divided. It is as much their Interest to confederate as any of the smaller States—If they will not do it on the Footing of Equality let them take their own Course.

Madison—Fallacy of Argument owing to a Connection of Legislative Ideas with Right of making Treaties.

Are the larger States congenial to each other by Proximity common Interests or Similarity of Pursuits?—They are not—they are so situated as to perpetuate Diversity of Interests.

The Staple of Massachusetts is *Fish* and she has carrying Trade—that of Pennsylvania *Wheat* and Virginia Tobacco.

Equality will uniformly excite Jealousy—Did Rome and Carthage combine to destroy their Neighbours?

This Question will determine whether we shall confederate at all or partial Confederations shall be formed.

Williamson—Mathematically Demonstrable that Representation ought to be proportioned to Individuals.

If the Taxes are laid by smaller States what would prevent them from surcharging the greater?

Wilson—Is it not unjust that old Sarum should send two Members and London only four? If this admitted it applies forcibly to the present Case.

Lansing—moved that Word *not* be struck out.

Madison—Efficient Government can only be formed by apportioning Representation.

The States may be equalized by general Government.

The State of New Jersey being unrepresented by the Indisposition of Governor Livingston the Question was put off by New York.

Previous to which L . . . .

Adjourned till to Morrow.

PIERCE BUTLER: NOTES ON DEBATES

Williamson. States Cannot be taxed according to Numbers.
Sherman. It will not be reasonable that the Interior States should pay as much as the Commercial States.

PHOTOSTAT (Library of Congress)

GEORGE WASHINGTON: DIARY

Thursday 28th. Attended Convention. Dined at Mr. Morris's in a large Company—(the news of his Bills being protested, arriving last night a little mal-apropos). Drank Tea there, & spent the evening in my chamber.

WILLIAM BLOUNT TO JOHN GRAY BLOUNT

Philadelphia June 28th 1787

. . . I am not at Liberty to say what is done or doing in Convention but I can say things are so much in Embryo that I could give you no satisfactory account if I were so much at Liberty. It is generally supposed that the Convention will continue to sit for 2 Months at least.

Yours
William Blount

ALS (North Carolina Division of Archives and History)

FRIDAY, JUNE 29, 1787

JOHN LANSING: NOTES ON DEBATES

Johnson—Must unite Ideas of *States* with Districts of Country containing a certain Number of Inhabitants.

Gorham—three Members of Massachusetts are Descendants of Persons who resided in three different Provinces now united in Massachusetts—this Circumstance does not influence their Measures. If all the States go off excepting one—Massachusetts will stay with that one and recommend System.

Reed—Has no Doubt resp[ectin]g it—will agree to Report so far as respects this Point.

Hamilton—In the Course of his Experience he has found it difficult to convince Persons who have been in certain Habits of thinking. Some desultory Remarks may not be improper. We can modify Representation as we think proper.

The Question simply is, what is general Interest. Larger States may submit to an Inequality of Representation to their Prejudice for a short Time—but it cannot be durable. This is a Contest for Power—the People of all the States have an Inequality of Representation.

So long as State Governments prevail State Influence will be perpetuated.

There may be a Distinction of Interests but it arises merely from the carrying and noncarrying States.

Those Persons who have had frequent Opportunities of conversing with the Representatives of European Sovereignties know they are very anxious to perpetuate our Democracies. This is easily accounted for—Our weakness will make us more manageable. Unless your Government is respectable abroad your Tranquility cannot be preserved.

This is a critical Moment of American Liberty—We are still too weak to exist without Union. It is a Miracle that we have met—they seldom occur.

We must devise a System on the Spot—It ought to be strong and nervous, *hoping* that the good Sense and principally *the Necessity of our Affairs* will reconcile the People to it.

Pierce—The Difficulty of carrying on Business in Congress is owing to local Prejudices and Interests. Must sacrafice States Distinctions.

Madison—Examine Journals of Congress—see whether States have been influenced by Magnitude. Small States have embarrassed us—Embargo agreed to by twelve States during the War—Deleware declined it.

On Question whether *not* should be struck out. Massachusetts Pennsylvania Virginia North Carolina South Carolina and Georgia—Noes.

New York—New Jersey. Connecticut and Deleware—Ayes. Maryland divided.

Question put on Resolve carried—6 Ayes—4 Noes—1 divided.

Elseworth—moves to postpone Remainder of 7*th* Resolve to take up the 8*th*. Question 9 Ayes—2 Noes.

Elseworth—In first Branch you draw Representation from Numbers—the Individuals will have their Rights protected here.

He will move that *each State have an equal Vote in second Branch.*

This will preserve State Sovereignties—

In any Community select a fifth, a tenth, or any other Proportion from all the different Classes of Citizens—give them an exclusive Right of governing—they will become a distinct Order and oppress the Rest. So it will be with the States.

It will be much easier for the three States to confederate than the others to join to defend themselves.

Baldwin—wishes Powers to be modified—but Property ought to be represented in one Branch—

Madison—If there was any Difference of Interests would agree to equal Representation.

Let Gentleman recollect the Experiments that have been made to amend Confederation—they always miscarried. The Dutch Republics made four several Experiments all ineffectual.

Adjourned till to Morrow.

PIERCE BUTLER: NOTES ON DEBATES

Ellsworth. The second Branch to be a Check on the first. To Establish a National Legislature that shall reach property. If We do not go upon a system that shall establish bad habits.

PHOTOSTAT (Library of Congress)

JOHN DICKINSON: NOTES FOR A SPEECH[1]

But the Majority of the larger states in Congress and the local situation of the smaller are not the only two sureties for the Interest of the former

1. So dated because the remark about the "Candor by an Honorable Gentleman from Virginia yesterday" in acknowledging the primacy of large states in a confederacy is apparently a reference to James Madison's speech of June 28 (Farrand 1:448–49).

against the latter. There are two more. 1st The national Influence of the larger states from a Variety of Causes of the larger, in the National Councils. This acknowledged with Candor by an Honorable Gentleman from Virginia Yesterday.

2d The Representation in the first Branch of Legislature which will most probably take place with the future consent of the smaller states in Proportion to numbers or actual Contribution to the national Uses. Our situation from Delaware. Let the Property of the larger states be secured. Let the Property and Liberty of the lesser be also secured. Let Neither dictate to the other. What will be the Condition of the larger in this Case? Their Property cannot be disposed of without their Consent.[2]

What will be the situation of the smaller, if in *both* branches, the Representation is *in the* Proportion mentioned? They will [be] delivered up into the absolute power of the larger.[3] They may injure them in a Variety of Ways. I will mention but two. They may destroy their Trade and draw it wholly to themselves.[4] They may tax them to relieve themselves. Is this too monstrous a supposition? Athens did it. Britain attempted it. What did Athens. She with rash Hands tore Taxes from the Allies that were confederated with her in the most solemn Manner. For Prosperity of the Confederation. No. To exhibit with Asiatic Magnificence the Tragedies of Sophocles and Euripides.

Signal Vengeance at length overtook the luxurious Tyrant. What has been may be. There is not a great State in the Union but is as eminent in every public and private Virtue as the Smaller, but power Grandeur and Prosperity mingle an intoxicating Draught. too generally too strong for the limited Understanding and fallible Virtue of Mortality.

We are not forming plans for a Day Month Year or Age, but for Eternity.[5] Let us endeavour with united Councils to establish a Government that not only may render our Nation great respectable free and happy but also VIRTUOUS. Let us try to combine political Establishments with moral Virtue that if possible the first may be equal with the Duration of this World and an aid or at least not a Hindrance to the Enjoyment of another.

AD (Historical Society of Pennsylvania)

2. In the margin: "Jersey proposal impracticable inadmissible. What others. Mine. of the different Representation. The smaller states will be swallowed up if every *new* State is established an equal Vote, which they must have. Proportion of Taxes will secure Us. Nothing else can."

3. In the margin: "if perhaps legislation is in proportion to Numbers or Quotas of Contribution—only in one Branch. If *Numbers* or *Quotas* are assumed—The new States to be created may rule the present states as Vassals, under the form of Laws. They will do it. The Fate."

4. A phrase, undecipherable, was added by Dickinson with a caret here.

5. Here Dickinson wrote an undecipherable Latin phrase, ending with "*Eternitati.*"

GEORGE WASHINGTON: DIARY

Friday 29th.   In Convention. Dined at Mr. Morris and spent the evening there.

JOHN F. MERCER TO WILLIAM SMALLWOOD

Annapolis. June 29. 87.

Having been apprized by yr. Excellency, that difficulty had or would occur, to prevent the advance of money to those Gentlemen who have been appointed by the Legislature to attend the Convention now sitting in Philadelphia, no money having been appropriated to this purpose—I woud beg leave on this to remark to yr. Excellency, that such advances are, I am authorized to say usual in other States on this occasion & as far as it respects myself woud be now convenient—but as I fear that a cause of this nature may still have its future operation, I am led to be explicit with your Excellency on my part, that private circumstances do not permit my sparing any part of my own resources for any length of time, & that unless I coud receive assurance of a speedy restitution of my expences to the amount of the allowance the State has affixed, it will be wholly out of my power to attend—In making this communication, I hope your Excellency will remain persuaded, that I strongly regret the necessity, which obliges me on an occasion of this moment to suggest any difficulty of this nature.

Farrand, 4:66–67

SATURDAY, JUNE 30, 1787

JOHN LANSING: NOTES ON DEBATES

Mr. Hamilton left Town this Morning.

Brearly—moves that President write to Executive of New Hampshire to send Delegation.

Question. New York and New Jersey Ayes—5 Noes 1 divided.

Each State shall have equal Vote.—Wilson—Gentlemen have declared the Reluctance of Eastern States to acceed to national Government.—If a Minority are inclined to separate it never can be on stronger or better Principles. State of Votes now as 22 to 90—Shall the one fourth controul the Remainder.

Can we forget for whom we form Governments—for Men not imaginary Beings called States.

Elseworth—On this Occasion each State has only a preventive Vote—the Minority is not to govern but to prevent its own Destruction—this is not novel—it is useful.

It is said the Equality of Suffrage has embarrassed us—Can Gentleman Instance salutary Measure being lost by not having a Majority of States in its Favor.

Rhode Island did not defeat Impost under Confederation. If Security be the principal Object of the great States they have it here.

All the Reason in favor of national Government founded on Ideas of State Interests having too powerful Operation—as they are permitted to exist they must still influence.

Madison—Equality of Representation was dictated by the Necessity of the Times. The larger States cannot be safe unless they have a greater Share in Government. Connecticut has shewn a Disregard to her foederal Compact—She has declined complying with Requisition.

Elseworth—That Connecticut has not complied with Requisition is owing to her superior Exertions during the War—to keep her Regiments compleat she incurred an enormous Expence—She was exhausted—that was Reason of Delinquency.

Sherman—That Legislature of Connecticut did not comply with Requisition is no Impeachment of Congress. If the Argument is to have any Weight shew that the State frustrated it in Congress.

Davie—90 Members are proposed for Senate—As States accede the

Numbers will be much increased—this will embarrass—they ought to be less.

The Preservation of the State Governments is the only Object of Confederation. but if each State has a single Vote it will defeat the whole System.

Wilson—he subscribes to Justice of Davies Remark—the Senate ought to consist of a few. In apportioning Representation he will agree that every 100,000 Persons shall be represented by one Member and that every State having less should have one.

Franklin—We must do like a Joiner in making a Table—take off the Protuberances—pare the different Opinions to a common Standard. He has prepared a Proposition with that Intention—Each State ought to have a certain Number of Votes in Senate.

On some Occasions an Equality of Suffrage to be admitted in States, in others to be apportioned. but thinks Equality is inequitable.

In the last War the U. States and King of France had not an equal Vote in the Disposition of the Money expended for common Defence!

King—Every Vice of the present System will be perpetuated by adopting Amendment—We subject our minds to imaginary Evils—Is much affected—has heard no Arguments in Favor of it.

Dayton—If Gentlemen will substitute Declamation for Argument it is not surprising that they are unattended to—A Number of Reasons forcible in their Nature have been assigned in Favor of Amendment—they have not been answered. He is convinced this can never receive Approbation of the People.

Bedford—Will rather agree to consolidate Government than apportion Representation unequally.

Ambition and Avarice influences us—We represent the different Interests of our States—the larger States wish to aggrandize themselves at the Expence of the others. The Language of the greater States is *give us Power we will exert it for your Benefit*.

If a Combination does not destroy us a Rivalship of the large States will.

The smaller States are entrapped—you get a Representation under one *View* you give into another.

Is a Breach of the Union so trifling as to be told with *a Smile*—that a few States will confederate—they dare not—It is only calculated to intimidate.

The People expect an Amendment of the Confederation—they will be surprised at our System—they are not ripe for it.

King—When Scotland and England united the same Arguments were adduced—Their Rights however still exist. If there is a Power which from its Prevalence may absorb all others, it will have that Effect whether you confederate or not.

Adjourned till Monday next.

JOHN DICKINSON: NOTES ON DEBATES[1]

The Line drawn for Alteration General Powers cannot be particularized. Map of America.

Mr. Wilson—Waters of Bitterness have flowed from unequal Representation Men or States cant confederate wont participate with same Rights True—but they may—what they will part with—a party in [one word undecipherable] under Sanction of Compact.

Mr. Wilson—Smaller states cant be injured, but protected by Executive—doubtful—Is there no other Mode of Injury. On this Proposal, every Man may give his Vote, and therefore may be equally represented—answer—Here is a substantiation of every Reason on which our objection is founded, i.e., the Representatives chosen in Virginia will carry into the public councils that Momentum of Attention to Virginia which animated their Electors. This can only be counteracted by a supposition that the Citizens of Virginia are as ardently attached to the Interests of New Hampshire or Delaware as to those of Virginia a supposition which the Honorable Gentleman will not make especially as two Interests may sometimes be opposite.

Resolved, that a national Executive be chosen in the Manner following, that is to say—the Freeholders of each state respectively shall every two Years at the Election of the Members of the first Branch nominate person Resident within the same out of whom the national Legislature shall chuse the said Executive.

1. So dated because a list of states, their quotas of taxes, and their delegate strength proportioned thereupon—identical to that printed by Farrand at June 9 (1:190)—appears at the head of the document with the addition of the assignment of one to four senators to each state, the basis of apportionment being one senator per 100,000 inhabitants, as James Wilson proposed on June 30 (1:488). Also, Dickinson's brief notes on Wilson's speech appear to fit Wilson's remarks of June 30, especially those in which he argued that an executive chosen from one of the large states could provoke the opposition of the other large states and that the ensuing tension would protect the small states (1:483).

A case can be made for dating this document June 9, the date of the appearance in the Convention of the list of states and their quotas. On that day Brearley of New Jersey argued that the only way to solve the problem of representation was "that a map of the U.S. be spread out, that all the existing boundaries be erased, and that a new partition of the whole be made" (1:177). Wilson followed Brearley with a defense of proportional representation. This sequence may be indicated in this document, with its reference to "Map of America" followed by Wilson's statements on representation.

Militating against a June 9 dating, however, is the requirement, in the first of Dickinson's resolves, of biennial election of members of the first branch. Dickinson favored triennial elections, but on June 21 the Convention established biennial elections (1:360–62). Dickinson's specifying the latter would, therefore, indicate a post–June 21 date and corroborate the June 30 dating.

Rates of Representation in the first Branch to be founded on Taxes actually collected and paid every Year.

A Negative by the national Legislature on the Legislative Acts of Individual States to be retained.

Equal Laws as to persons and places.

Rotation in 2d Branch.

Exclusive Right of emitting Money of every kind.

Also of terminating Contests within a State.

So of punishing their officers—Habeas Corpus and Trial by Jury.

AD (Historical Society of Pennsylvania)

JOHN DICKINSON: NOTES FOR A SPEECH (I)[2]

The sense of all Confederations
1. Policy in allowing an equal Vote
2. Justice

In a Confederation no Danger from small states

Their Interest is peace prosperity Ballance

Their Condition teaches them political Virtues and suppresses political Vices.

This Reason teaches

Experience confirms

Instances in several Republics

The amphyctionic League

Athens and Sparta

Archaia

2. The following Dickinson documents form a unit. Document I is an outline of a speech; the other three contain phrases and ideas sketched in it. The speech for which these documents were the raw material was never delivered. Dickinson seems to have been moved to attempt a major speech by Madison's speech of June 28, for it is to that effort that he alludes in Document II by mentioning the "Distinctiaon made by Virginia," that is, the distinction made by Madison between the force of a compact and a treaty (Farrand, 1:446–47). In his June 28 speech Madison also surveyed ancient and modern confederacies from the Amphictyonic League to Austria; Dickinson treats the same topics. A more precise date for the preparation of Dickinson's notes can be derived from his use of the word "Lamb" in Document I, which he amplified in Document III to "Lessons in the Language of Fable," concerning a "Lamb." The only reference to a lamb in Farrand's *Records* is in William Paterson's notes of June 30, which indicate that he intended to examine the claim that "The Lesser States will destroy the larger—Lamb and Lyon" (1:506). June 30, then, would appear to be an approximate date for Dickinson's notes, a surmise strengthened by their subject matter—a plea for equal representation of the smaller states, the issue that was monopolizing the Convention's attention at that time.

Germany

Call for opposite Instances

What Experience in Congress

What are the Causes of our Distress

Not the Voice of smaller states but the Want of greater powers

What Instances of Injury by the Interests of the smaller states being different from the rest

None

A Majority of States are large

Others of competent size to be formed by them—as they a real Majority

Little Being Enemy passed [two words undecipherable] neither great states to dictate to smaller ones nor smaller ones to great ones

Large states may [undecipherable phrase]

A large Commercial State ought to patronize the smaller ones in her Neighborhood that depend on her no harm

I was of same opinion at the Beginning when representing Pennsylvania

We are settling general Principles. The Eyes of Europe of the World upon Us.

Great sentiments have settled often general principles that obtained the universal pleasing Homage of Mankind because approved by the understanding and dear to the uncorrupted Heart.

Liberty Benevolence Justice

Lamb

The equal Vote allowed in allmost every Confederation Compact. Distrust between State and Individuals unfounded.

An Experiment more cruel than curious like opening a living Animal to examine the palpitations of its dying Heart.

The World will know the Force.

The Reasons urged against it.

What will they say?

The Highest Authority declaring that Justice and Compact must give way to *Convenience*—to *Necessity*.

The Plea of Tyrant. A Necessity in words not in facts.

Is this a foundation for Empire? What an Example

Talk no more of Tender Laws and violations of Treaties. They were *convenient*.

Let not the large states dictate to the smaller nor the smaller to the larger.

AD (Historical Society of Pennsylvania)

JOHN DICKINSON: NOTES FOR A SPEECH (II)

I pass to the second point. The Justice Compact

Distinction made by Virginia inadmissible between states and Individuals. What are Treaties? Compacts between states to be violated. No. Answer Reservation dreadfull that this Compact was temporary tho declared perpetual. A Despot may hereafter use the same Language. What Degradation of Character have we suffered on that Account? What Treaties what Compacts more solemn more sacred than those made by States Neighbours Brethren of the same Blood Family? In a [one word undecipherable] are imminent a dreadful Danger? Did not our Hearts dictate our Words. Our Hands confirm the stipulation by subscription for perpetual Remembrance. Did we not call the Nations of the Earth and Heaven itself to witness our agreement with each other?

All to be dissolved in the short period of 11 Years. Is American fidelity only to be retained in Clouds and Storms, like the Travelers Cloak, and to be thrown away, as soon as the bright and warm sun breaks thro them. Did our fellow Citizens shed their Blood, lose their Limbs, and encounter every difficulty Distress and Danger upon this Compact that an opportunity might be purchased by their suffering for violating it?

Is this the Return as above. Under the auspices of Heaven we are where we are and what we are. Let us recollect the Pythagorean maxim and "revere ourselves." What is the pretence for this Violation? No Injury in the public Councils no perfidy in the public Cause.

Not so well acquainted with Particulars as to the other smaller states. What has N.J. done or neglected to do to merit this treatment. Overwhelmed with hostile Armies. her people plundered her towns burnt her Matrons and Virgins butchered. Did New Jersey falter. No. A mournful Monument of human Virtues assailed yet faithful.

Thro the little State of Delaware, the Army of the Enemy passed, while her whole seaboard was exposed to the continual Hostilities of her naval forces darting upon her whereever they pleased and not to be protected because the points of attack were unknown, till the Injuries were committed. Weak as her arm was yet did her Mind ever waver? No. All succor cut off. Held by the Throat. swords incontinantly pointed. She was ready and willing to be sacrificed rather than renounce the Fate of her Country.

What pretence then for this Conduct to the smaller states. Is it necessary. I hope what has been said on the first Head demonstrates that it is not. Is Necessity a proper plea in the Mouths of those who are to gain by that Plea. What did the Patriots of England think and say of such a Plea in the Days of Charles the II. I will not repeat what they said. What did the patriots of America say of this Plea in the Days of George the 3d. I need not repeat what they said.

But it is perhaps convenient. Convenient for whom. for those who are to profit by it? So are Tender Laws to Debtors and the Violation of Treaties to some Individuals. But does this Convenience outweigh the Considerations for an adherence to sacred Obligations?

AD (Historical Society of Pennsylvania)

JOHN DICKINSON: NOTES FOR A SPEECH (III)

Is the most august Assembly upon Earth to declare to Mankind that Justice and Compact must give Way to partial Convenience, a pretended Necessity. To my poor judgment it appears, that this blending too much of Metaphysics with Politics. The inspired Apostle "All Things to thee are lawful but not convenient." He meant lawful things for the sake of others, but he must be a bold Metaphysician who reverse his rule and say that all things are lawful that are convenient. I think myself at least at liberty to conclude that they who reverse it cannot be inspired by the same spirit that he was. The lesser states will never resign their Dignity. It must be wrested from them by violence. Nor will they then be silent. They will appeal to the awful Tribunal of Mankind plead their Cause urge their Reasons.

Impartial Mankind will decide upon the Question. Is this a Foundation for Empire. It is a copy of Caesar's favorite adage "si violandre" and worse than Caesar's for then every Thing tended to a Monarchy at Rome. worse than Romulus' fractricide for he was in a passion. What an Example to other Nations to our own Posterity. Punica fide. This will be an indelible stigma to our national Character. No individual in this Room no Example within these walls will be able to justify it. What a precedent. What a Doctrine for future Ambition to follow. We shall only be pioneers for succeeding Tyrants. If they follow our steps, they must obtain the summit of their Wishes. This Convenience or Necessity or whatever other Name is in fact but a Plan for the Aggrandizement of some states at the Expence of others. There is no other Convenience no other Necessity.

Test of this. Throw all Governments and Territories into Common Stock and divide de novo. Then we shall have the Equity and Equality talked of not otherwise.

Let not gentlemen think so meanly of the smaller states as to believe they will be contented while a beautiful sign of Equality is held out with one Hand but the substance taken away with the other.

This is a mere Novelty an Experiment in Government. Humbly submit if not too costly too curious too useless too cruel. And how far it resembles those I have read of, where living Creatures have been cut up overnicely to examine the palpitation of their dying Hearts.

Great Theatre Eyes of Europe and the World upon us Caution.

We are settling General Principles. Let them be well founded. Great sentiments sagacious sages have in different Countries and Ages been employed also in forming other sets of General Principles. Have succeeded because they have established general Principles to which Mankind has paid an universal pleasing Homage because approved by the Understanding and dear to the Heart. Inculcating Liberty Benevolence Justice. These wise admired Instructors of the World have modestly cloathed their

Lessons in the Language of Fable. I beg leave to recite one of them.
A Lamb

AD (Historical Society of Pennsylvania)

JOHN DICKINSON: NOTES FOR A SPEECH (IV)

1. Policy What Guilt?
2. Justice Benefit of Union Passed & signed Policy

Throw all into common stock & divide de novo. If old Things are to be done away let all Things be new. My Opinion allways the same and advocated the Cause of the small states when I had the Honor of representing Pennsylvania in the first Congress. I speak in a public Character. The general Sense of Mankind in forming Confederations between independent and sovereign states of the Justice of allowing equal Votes to each. In a Confederation no Danger from smaller states. Their interest is peace Protection Ballance. Their Condition teaches them the political Virtues of a Confederation suppresses the political Vices of a Confederation. It is situation in Individuals and Societies that prompts and inflames Passions pernicious to Mankind. A Sulla and a Cromwell had virtue enough to serve their Country till Ambition convinced and urged them to enslave it. Athens was regarded as a tutelary Angel by her Allies, till she found she could plunder them with Impunity. And even Britain was the Idol of these states till in the Dream of Insolence she flattered herself she could make them Drawers of Wood.

These Truths therefore Reason teaches History confirms. States of Greece ruined by Contests between the powerful states of Sparta and Athens. The same Dissensions ruined the Achaian League. Germany and Danger from the House of Austria. Prussia raised up as a Ballance.

Call for opposite

Doctrine of Mr. M. I recollect not any Confederation destroyed by smaller states unless irritated by greater. Macedon called in to oppose Sparta. Denmark.

What are the Causes of our Distress. Not the Votes of the smaller states. Mention Cases if any. No. The Want of greater powers in Congress and a better organized Government. What single Instance of the Interests of the greater States being injured by the interests or votes of the smaller states? None. A Majority of states are large. They therefore may erect others of competent size to protect them from the dangerous Desires or daring Enterprises of their weaker Associates. The smaller states must of Necessity decrease in their Importance. They are content to dye a natural Death, for states as well as Men must dye. All they ask—and when I survey this Assembly I may say they ask with Confidence with utmost affection—that they may not be put to death by their Brethren. One Empire was founded in [word undecipherable] by Romulus, but his Brother had provoked him by Insults. This a changeful World. This Consideration reminds me of some words I have read in a little Book: "And they said one to another, we are verily guilty concerning your Brother, in that we saw the Anguish of his soul, when he besought Us; and we would not hear: therefore is this Distress come upon Us. And Reuben answered them saying, spake I not unto You, saying, Do not sin against that Child; and you would not hear? therefore, behold also, his Blood is required."

I look for better Things. Yesterday's Vote proves that instead of a Giant unwieldy slow heavy. A Father surrounded by a Family of hearty, affectionate strong sons [undecipherable phrase] attached to him and each other not by fear or servile dependance but by a generous tender participation of Blessings and a Reciprocity of Kindnesses and Advantages.

If in every small state should arise a Caesar as brave as Alexander as artful as Hannibal and as infamous as Borgia he could not injure the greater.

What is their Situation one at each Extremity Two others separated by a very powerful a very commercial State closely connected with her by Blood by Marriage by Friendship by every kind of Interest and almost wholly dependent upon her in Commerce. The supplyers of her Exports The Consumers of her Imports. From the first Moment of their Existence they have been thus connected to, I had almost said, devoted to her, constantly and cheerfully contributing to extend her fleets and to spread her sails upon the ocean. Unsuspecting and affectionate they rejoice in the Connections. The deare Ties not to be dissolved but by an imprudent and unneighbourly Attempt on her side to stab them to the Heart. She will then be esteemed by them as selfish in her politics, as she is just liberal and magnanimous in every other point of View.

AD (Historical Society of Pennsylvania)

George Washington: Diary

Saturday 30th   Attended Convention. Dined with a Club at Springsbury—consisting of several associated families of the City—the Gentlemen of which meet every Saturday accompanied by the females of the families every other Saturday. This was the ladies day.

[JUNE?]

GEORGE MASON: MEMORANDUM[1]

At a time when our Government is approaching to Dissolution, when some of its Principals have been found utterly inadequate to the Purposes for which it was establish'd, & it is evident that without some material Alterations it can not much longer subsist, it must give real concern to every man who has his Country's Interest at Heart to find such a Difference of Sentiment & Opinion in an Assembly of the most respectable and confidential characters in America, appointed for the special purposes of revising and amending the federal Constitution, so as to obtain and preserve the important objects for which it was instituted—the protection Safety & Happiness of the people. The Treatys & Leagues & Confederacies between different sovereign independent powers have been urged as proofs in support of the propriety and Justice of the single & equal representation of each individual State in the American Union; & thence conclusions have been drawn that the People of these United States would refuse to adopt a Government founded more on an equal representation of the People themselves, than on the distinct representation of each separate individual State. . . . If the different States in our Union always had been as now run substantially & in reallity distinct sovereign & independent nations, this kind of reasoning would have great Force; but if the premises on which it is founded on mere Assumptions not ground on Facts or at best upon Facts to be found only upon a paper of yesterday, & even then contradictory to each other; no satisfactory conclusions can be drawn from them.

DRAFT MOTION[2]

The 1st to be chosen by Numbers as per the reported resolution 2d by the Legislatures of the respective states not exceeding 3 persons from each State each attending member to have one voice 3d viz. Executive by the Members of both branches by way of Ballot

AD (Dickinson Papers, Historical Society of Pennsylvania)

1. Not dated by Farrand but placed chronologically at the end of August (Farrand, 4:75–76). The memorandum must have been composed in June or early July, however, when representation in the legislature—the topic it addresses—was being actively debated.

2. In an unidentified hand.

SUNDAY, JULY 1, 1787

GEORGE WASHINGTON: DIARY

July. 1st.   Dined and spent the evening at home.

LUTHER MARTIN TO NICHOLAS LOW

Philadelphia July 1st 1787

Sir:

I procured a Judgment to be ordered up in your Suit on the Terms proposed at our last Court.

The Gentleman who on your behalf employed me in the Suit informed me on a Judgment being obtained I should receive twenty Guineas as a fee for my Services. I have as yet received nothing, on the contrary have in the first Instance to answer to the Different Officers the Costs of prosecuting the Suit as you live out of the State of Maryland.

I am at present attending the Convention in this City and shall be for a considerable Time. A Remittance to me in this City or a Draught on some your Correspondent here for the above Sum would be particularly acceptable as I never wanted it more.

Your very humble Servant
Luther Martin

PHOTOSTAT (Maryland Historical Society)

MONDAY, JULY 2, 1787

On Question for Equality of Suffrage—Massachusetts Pennsylvania Virginia North Carolina—South Carolina for Affirmative and Connecticut New York New Jersey Deleware and Maryland Negative. Georgia divided.

C. Pinkney—He is one of those who believes that if Proportion is adjusted in both Branches as in first it will operate in the Mode stated by Minority.

North Carolina South Carolina and Georgia have Interests different from great States—their Staples are Indigo and Rice.—Must make a Compromise so as to preserve all.

Proposes 4 Classes—States to have from one to four Votes.

G. Morris—2nd Branch is Check on the first—to correct Precipitancy, Changeableness and Excess—all these have marked Acts of Congress—2nd Branch must be Men of great Property—composed of those Men who are disposed to lord it over the Rest.—We ought to contrive that Men of established Property should fill it—they must be chosen for Life—Aristocracy should keep down Democracy.—It is objected they will immediately do wrong—he believes so—he hopes so—that will form Ballance.—they ought not to be paid they will pay themselves.

The Executive should fill second Branch.

If our Establishments are good they must be supported and will take a proper Direction—If the State Governments have Distribution of Loaves and Fishes the general Government cannot prevail—You must give them Disposition of Offices and *Baubles*—The Senatorship will operate as a Lure.

Governor Randolph—Warmth has formed a Barrier to Conviction—A Security may be offered to smaller States—Executive may correct it by giving him additional Powers—Give second Branch an Equality of Vote in his Election—in Distribution of Offices and in determining on Impeachments—the Executive will be oblidged to interpose in Favor of 2d Branch.

If however every Attempt to make a general Confederation is inefficient it would influence him to seek elsewhere.

Some desultory Conversation then took Place the Result of which was the Appointment of a Committee of a Member from each State to try to settle Representation—the Committee balloted for consisted of Gerry, Elseworth, Yates, Patterson, Franklin, Martin, Bedford, Mason, Davie, Rutlege and Baldwin. Adjourned till Thursday 5th July.

GEORGE WASHINGTON: DIARY

Monday. 2d.   Attended Convention. Dined with some of the Members of Convention at the Indian Queen. Drank Tea at Mr. Binghams, and walked afterwards in the state house yard.

Set this Morning for Mr. Pine who wanted to correct his portrt. of me.

WILLIAM PATERSON TO EUPHEMIA PATERSON

Philada., 2d July, 1787

The Burlington court did not continue as long as I expected. I arrived here on Friday last, about 10 o'clock at night.

This letter will be handed to you by the Gov'r [Livingston], who will set out tomorrow. It is impossible to say when the Convention will rise; much remains to be done, and the work is full of labour and difficulty. . . .

ALS (Rutgers University)

TUESDAY, JULY 3, 1787

Tuesday. 3d.   Sat before the meeting of the Convention for Mr. Peale who wanted my picture to make a print or Metzotinto by.

Dined at Mr. Morris's and drank Tea at Mr. Powells—after which, in Company with him, I attended the Agricultural Society at Carpenters Hall.

RICHARD DOBBS SPAIGHT TO JOHN GRAY BLOUNT

Philadelphia 3 July 1787

Dear Sir,

I have twice wrote to you on the subject of receiving for me and re-mitting to me two months salary which the deputies have wrote to the Governor to advance to them, but have not had the pleasure of receiving any answer to them: I shall however rely upon your friendship in this instance, and depend upon the remittance being made by you. Indeed if you do not undertake it I know not to Whom to apply.

The time which I expected to stay here is already elapsed and as I did not provide for a longer stay, my cash is already expended. Judge then my situation should I receive no further supplies.

Your Brother left this yesterday morning for New-York, from whence he will return in eight or nine days. It is still uncertain when the Con-vention will rise. You will much oblige me by forwarding the inclosed to Jacob Johnston.

I am with Regard

Yours Sincerely

Richd. Dobbs Spaight.

ALS (North Carolina Division of Archives and History)

WEDNESDAY, JULY 4, 1787

GEORGE WASHINGTON: DIARY

Wednesday 4th.   Visited Doctr. Shovats Anatomical figures and (the Convention having adjourned for the purpose) went to hear an Oration on the anniversary of Independance delivered by a Mr. Mitchell, a student of Law[1]—After which I dined with the State Society of the Cincinnati at Epplees Tavern and drank Tea at Mr. Powells.

MARY NORRIS TO ———

Philada. July 4th. 1787
I am very Sorry to hear Cousin Dickinson continues so very poorly, such constant daily attendance at the Convention was too fatueging for his Constitution at this Season of the Year, but Rest & quiet I hope will soon restore his health.

Farrand, 4:67

MARY BUTLER TO THOMAS BUTLER

New York July 4th 1787
. . . Your Papa I left ten days since at Philadelphia. My health was so bad that I could not support the excessive heat of that Climate, and was obliged to come to a more temperate one. . . . Your Papa being a Member of the Federal Convention, that have met at Philadelphia, obliges him to remain there; although He has suffer'd in his health extremely. . . .

PHOTOCOPY (British Library, Additional Manuscripts, 16603)

---

1. "Wednesday next being the Anniversary of Independence, Race Street Church has been procur'd for the Delivery of an annual Oration. I am desired to open the Performance by Prayer, the whole will be rendered agreeable by frequent *Flights* of Music, vocal and Instrumental. We go in Procession from the State House, honor'd by the Company of the Convention and Executive Council" (William Rogers to Enos Hitchcock, June 27, 1787, Rhode Island Historical Society).

THURSDAY, JULY 5, 1787

ROBERT YATES: NOTES ON DEBATES, AS PRINTED BY GENET[1]

Met pursuant to adjournment.

The report of the committee was read.

Mr. Gorham. I call for an explanation of the principles on which it is grounded.

Mr. Gerry, the chairman, explained the principles.

Mr. Martin. The one representation is proposed as an expedient for the adoption of the other.

Mr. Wilson. The committee has exceeded their powers.

Mr. Martin proposed to take the question on the whole of the report.

Mr. Wilson. I do not chuse to take a leap in the dark. I have a right to call for a division of the question on each distinct proposition.

Mr. Madison. I restrain myself from animadverting on the report, from the respect I bear to the members of the committee. But I must confess I see nothing of concession in it.

The originating money bills is no concession on the part of the smaller states, for if seven states in the second branch should want such a bill, their interest in the first branch will prevail to bring it forward—it is nothing more than a nominal privilege.

The second branch, small in number, and well connected, will ever prevail. The power of regulating trade, imposts, treaties, &c. are more essential to the community than raising money, and no provision is made for those in the report—We are driven to an unhappy dilemma. Two thirds of the inhabitants of the union are to please the remaining one third by sacrificing their essential rights.

When we satisfy the majority of the people in securing their rights, we have *nothing* to fear; in any other way, *every thing*. The smaller states, I hope will at last see their true and real interest.—And I hope that the warmth of the gentleman from Delaware will never induce him to yield to his own suggestion of seeking for foreign aid.

1. For the significance of this and the following document, see the introduction to this volume.

ROBERT YATES: NOTES ON DEBATES, AS COPIED BY LANSING

Thursday July 5.	Met pursuant to adjournment.
	Report of the Committee Read.
Mr. Gorham.	Calls for an Explanation.
Mr. Gerry.	Explains the principle of it. But they want their powers, in determining the original money bills.
Mr. Martin.	The one Expedient is on Condition of an adoption of the 2d.
Mr. Wilson.	The Committee gone beyond their powers.
Mr. Martin	proposes to take the question on the whole.
Mr. Wilson.	A Leap in the dark. Right to call for a division of the question, hopes we shall take the Senti[ment]s on each dist[inct] prop[osal].
Madison.	Restrained from animadverting on them from the Respect of the Committee. Made from a view to an accommodation. He sees nothing of concession in it, the orig[inating] Bills. If seven States in the second, want a bill—cant they prevail on the other of originating such a Bill. Exp[erience] in Vi[rginia] and S[outh] C[arolina]. it has no effect. no more than a nominal priviledge. 2 Branch small in number connected with each other, and will prevail. power of regulating Trade impost Treaties etc. no provisions made, and greater powers, than raising money. Drove to the dilemma to please ⅓ to the detriment of the ⅔ of the people—with the Majority we have nothing to fear, the other way everything. The small states may at last see the true interest. The warmth of Delaware will ever yield to his suggestion of foreign Connections. And Jersey will upon reflection will also yield. Rather a report or plan of 3 or 4 States or even an anonymous[?] production than the present[?]. The op[inion] of the Com[mittee] will be regulated by the wisdom of the plan.
Mr. Butler.	To take up the whole *in toto*. It will be hard task—lose time. Moves whether we shall agree to it as wrote.
G. Morris.	Respect for the Committee. Extraordinary that propositions without amendment. We come here as Rep[resentatives] of America, nay even human

Race. ought to extend our Views beyond the Moment of the day. Appears as Ambas[sador] to make a sort of bargain or truck. Opinion of the people rather a figure of Rethoric than a serious assertion. The small and greater states rather imaginary. suppose the smaller states do not accede. make all the Int[erest] in their states as much as they could. Example of N. Jersey would be disposed to follow Penn and N. York. [one word indecipherable] they persist.

It must be united. If persuasion wont—the sword must. Look on it with horror. What is here a difference of opinion may end in Contrav[ersy] and even blood. Foreign interference he thinks probable. What the horrors of it in[?] a patriotic bosom.

Returns to the report. 2d. Branch cannot answer the End proposed. Will in Event[?] in war and an annihilation of the G[eneral] G[overnment]. Congress can recommend but cant enforce obedience. The Senate thus organized would take part with the state. Germany. Aulic Council. Suppose R[hode] I[island] and Vir[ginia] cast one vote—Source of dispute. vote different. The great State will say you have the Con [rest of word indecipherable] for Children Childrens to form our nation? to overturn the inequality of the states is impractical but we may allay the sting. Why persist in the distinct[ion] of states.

May add to a [one word indecipherable] everything the 1st branch to controul everything. Nothing can be made right to the conviction being right.

Mr. Bedford. To explain himself—Did not mean a wish to call foreign assistance. But if the larger states dissolved the Contract. Breach of faith. Those powers would take us by the hand. not wished by the smaller. professional habits and his own feelings. Plan are Accomodation[?]. The small states like the preservation of the G[eneral] G[overnment] was to be preserved.

Judge Elsworth.
Rutlegde.
Mr. Paterson. Warmth tends not to recom[mend] conviction—nor

| | will the sword or Bayonet do it. The manner of the Gentlemen[?] of Pennsylvania and Virginia have given cause of the Alarm. |

Mr. Mason.   The report recommending[?] no more, in order to see whether it could not be the basis of our accomodation. shews how the question of Representation was agitated in Convention. Some Gent[lemen] will appeal to the world at larger rather agree. If an agreement could be made, he would stay till he was burryed here.

Mr. Butler.   Against both propositions as they stand—property not represented Taxation and representation ought to go together—if otherwise suppose they tax away my property and wander like a Tartar, with Liberty indeed, but a baggor. Rather would not have a second Branch.

G. Morris   Thinks property ought to have weight—Liberty most enjoyed by the savages—Numbers will amuse the Logycian and Matephysician but not reducable to practice.

Mr. Butler.   Holland grumbling, because she has only one vote and pays one half of the Expence.

G. Morris.   Is for defining the number of votes for each state in perpetuity. It is better for small States. R.I. now one of 75. would she not agree to this rather than have 757 votes against it.

Mr. Gorham   Has no obj[ection] to the Motion of SC provided the property could be ascertained. It cannot be done by any way. In past. partial.

JOHN LANSING: NOTES ON DEBATES

Mr. Gerry reports from Committee that each State shall have a Vote in 2d Branch, provided it is generally agreed that every 40,000 shall send one Member in the first. Money Bills to originate exclusively in lower House.

Sherman—as we are pretty equally divided, it is best to put Question on the whole.

Wilson—We are not to be misled by Sounds—there is no equal Division—More than 2/3ds of one Sentiment.

Madison—Altho' the House was equally divided on the 2nd Branch—on the first there was a considerable Majority for departing from Equality—All the Concessions are on one Side—We are reduced to the Alternative of displeasing *Minority* or *Majority*—by deciding for the latter we have Nothing to fear—the former every Thing.—He would rather have a System received by three or four States than none.

G. Morris—If the smaller States persist, if Argument is unavailing, the Sword will determine it.—To overturn the States is impracticable—but you may extract the Teeth of the *Serpents.*—We have been too warm.

Bedford—He has been warm—that not owing to a Want of Respect—but while he acknowledges that he was apparently warm, he cannot help remarking that he has Reason to be so—The Language of Intemperance is by no Means peculiar to himself.—Gentlemen have threatened in Terms very indelicate, tho' they have generally moderated their Voices when they did so. One Gentleman has declared the smaller States must agree another that *two-thirds* ought to give the Law and a third has pointedly declared that Force must be used—Do those Gentlemen suppose that Sentiments of that Kind can produce any other Effect than a Smile—they are mistaken if they do; we know their Language is calculated to make Impressions in favor of their System—but it cannot have that Effect—We know the States who have Recourse to it are impotent.

Patterson—same Sentiments differently expressed.

Rutlege moves that Representation in the first Branch be in proportion to Contribution.

Butler seconds it—You may either take this Rule or whole *Number of Whites and Slaves.*

Adjourned till to Morrow.

JOHN RUTLEDGE: MOTION

Proposition by Mr. Rutledge

That the Sufrages of the several States be regulated and proportioned according to the sums to be payd towards Revenue, by the Inhabitants of each state respectively. That an apportionment of suffrages according to the ratio aforesaid shall be made and regulated at the End of —— Years from the first meeting of the Legislature of the U.S. and so from time to time at the end of every —— Years thereafter but that for the present and untill the end 1st above mentioned Delaware shall have one suffrage.

PHOTOSTAT[2] (Library of Congress)

PIERCE BUTLER: NOTES ON DEBATES

Maddison. By giving Negative to the 2d Branch they will finally govern the Republick.

2. In the Pierce Butler papers in Pierce Butler's hand.

GEORGE WASHINGTON: DIARY

Thursday 5th.   Attended Convention. Dined at Mr. Morris's and drank Tea there. Spent the evening also.

NATHAN DANE TO RUFUS KING

New York July 5 1787

. . . It seems to be agreed here that the Virginia plan was admitted to come upon the floor of investigation, by way of experiment, and with a few yieldings on this point and that keeps its ground at present. The contents of this plan was known to some, I believe, before the convention met. . . .

ALS (New-York Historical Society)

FRIDAY, JULY 6, 1787

After a Repetition of Sentiments frequently urged before by several Gentlemen it was agreed on Motion of Mr. G. Morris to refer the first Proposition in Report of Committee to a Committee of five—The Motion was carried 9 States against 2. Committee appointed consisting of Mr. Gorham, Mr. Randolph, G. Morris, Rutlege and King.

Adjourned till to Morrow.

N.B. Before the Appointment of the Committee Question was put on Part of Report which had in Object confering the exclusive Right of originating Money Bills in first Branch.

On which Question there were *five Ayes,* three Noes—and 3 States divided—New York Massachusetts and Georgia divided. A Dispute arose whether it was carried in Affirmative—Some Debate on Subject—postponed.

George Washington: Diary

Friday 6th.   Sat for Mr. Peale in the Morning. Attended Convention. Dined at the City Tavern with some members of Convention and spent the evening at my lodgings.

Abraham Baldwin to Joel Barlow

July 6, 1787

Dear Sir

. . . The conjectures of people on the great political subjects now before the convention are very various and not a little amusing. So many forms of government I believe never were contrived before. They are floating about here in all directions like Spectators worlds some half-finished some a quarter the great part but just begun—meer political tadpoles.

I am now sitting in the big room. Your old acquaintance Governeur Morris is now speaking. They call off my attention so often I know not what I have written. Anything to the purpose I am not permitted to tell you, and therefore it is I have been talking so long to no purpose. The connection is of not so much importance when one is talking nonsense, as you probably know by experience.

I send you enclosed the newspaper of the day to let you see that every body has as barren a paper today as yourself. Lean fare we have had for some time. Some of our cooks are for making rich sauces and I think if they had their way we should have a plenty of red goose. . . .

ALS (Yale University)

SATURDAY, JULY 7, 1787

John Lansing: Notes on Debates

Question whether the last Question was carried in Affirmative. 9 Ayes—2 Noes.

Equality of Suffrage.—After some Debate in which Nothing new was offered the Question was put and carried—6 Ayes—3 Noes—2 divided.

Ayes—Connecticut—New York—New Jersey—Delaware—Maryland and North Carolina.

Noes—Pennsylvania—Virginia and South Carolina—

Divided—Massachusetts and Georgia.

Adjourned till Monday next.

George Washington: Diary

Saturday 7th.   Attended Convention. Dined with the Club at Springsbury and drank Tea at Mr. Meridiths.

William Jackson to William Rawle

Sir   Philadelphia July 7 1787

In obedience to a vote of the Convention, I do myself the honour to request that you will be pleased to communicate the thanks of that honourable Body to the Directors of the Library Company of Philadelphia for their polite attention, expressed in the resolve, which your letter enclosed to His Excellency the President.[1]

1. Rawle wrote Washington, July 6, 1787, enclosing a resolve of the directors of the Library Company of Philadelphia, July 5, 1787, offering members of the Convention borrowing privileges (Farrand, 1:548). Some members abused the privileges. On October 2, 1788, the directors noted that Luther Martin had not returned "Jones' Asiatic Poems"; as late as March 5, 1789, Rufus King had not returned "Grosse's Voyages, 2 vols. and Andrews' letters on France." Both delegates blamed their servants for neglecting to return the books and offered restitution (Library Company, minutes, October 2, 1788; March 5, 1789).

> I have the honor to be, very respectfully,
> Sir, your obedient humble Servant
>   W. Jackson Secretary

ALS (Library Company of Philadelphia)

SUNDAY, JULY 8, 1787

GEORGE WASHINGTON: DIARY

Sunday 8th. About 12 Oclock rid to Doctr. Logans near German town where I dined.[1] Returned in the evening and drank Tea at Mr. Morris's.

1. "He came with his friend Daniel Jennifer Esq. of Maryland and passed a day at Stenton in the most social and friendly manner imaginable, delighted with the fine Grassland and beautiful experiments with Gypsum and other subjects of rural economy which Dr. Logan had then to shew" (biographical memoir of Dr. George Logan, Historical Society of Pennsylvania).

MONDAY, JULY 9, 1787

John Lansing: Notes on Debates

The Committee of five reported the following Apportionment of Representation in first Branch of Legislature for first Meeting consisting of 56 Viz.

New Hampshire 2	Deleware 1
Massachusetts 7	Maryland 4
Rhode Island 1	Pennsylvania 8
Connecticut 4	Virginia 9
New York 5	North Carolina 5
New Jersey 3	South Carolina 5
	Georgia 2

The Rule of Adjustment was required to be explained—It was answered it was a combined Ratio of Numbers and Property. This was postponed to take up the subsequent Part of Report in these Words—

"But as the present Situation of the States may probably alter as well in point of Wealth as in the Number of Inhabitants that the Legislature be authorized from Time to Time to augment the Number of Representatives and in Case any of the States shall hereafter be divided or any two or more States united or any new States created within the Limits of the United States the Legislature shall possess authority to regulate the Number of Representatives in any of the foregoing Cases upon the Principles of their Wealth and Number of Inhabitants."

Question—9 Ayes—2 Noes—New York No.

It was then moved to refer the Apportionment of Representation to a Committee of 11.—a Member from each State.

Agreed to and Committee appointed accordingly.

Adjourned till to Morrow.

John Dickinson: Notes for a Speech (I)[1]

Contemplate the Increase of the Empire

Proportion from Numbers is allmost universally the best Rule but our peculiar Circumstances render it imperfect if not unsafe.

---

1. This and the following document were apparently portions of a speech (or speeches) Dickinson intended to deliver during the period July 9–14, when the representation of the west and of slaves in the House of Representatives was under consideration.

16 or 17 new States will arise if We have not introduced all the southern states. Pennsylvania New York Massachusetts will most probably be subdivided.

The old parts of these states will contribute greatly more to public uses. Is each new state instantly to start into an Equality of power by its Numbers only? The Inhabitants will undoubtedly be very numerous but poor in Comparison with the others. They will contribute little or Nothing. The Laws will be slighted. They will be broken and yet they will have and exercise a Right of legislating for the older states.

The best Philosophy is drawn from Experiments The best Policy from Experience. I know of late where the utmost Frugality was practiced while the Members of Assembly were chosen in some proportion to the Taxes of each County. When Numbers were admitted as the principle the very Reverse took Place. The Members from Counties that paid little or Nothing disposed of the whole Property of the State. No State ever to exceed the proportion of 20 to 1 to the smallest. The present proportion to be established. Every new state to be put on the same footing with the smallest then Contributions to determine provided.

JOHN DICKINSON: NOTES FOR A SPEECH (II)

Acting before the World

What will be said of this new principle of founding a Right to govern Freemen on a power derived from Slaves in preference to other property themselves incapable of governing yet giving to others what they have not. The omitting the *Word* will be regarded as an Endeavour to conceal a principle of which we are ashamed. Every Importation of Slaves will increase the power of the state over others. This principle I wish to avoid. A Calculation of the Value of Property I acknowledge to be impractical. Why not admit *actual Contribution* as the Rule. Objection from Massachusetts.

Is it to be taken for granted that no other Imposition is to be laid by the national Legislature. It is next to impossible. England and Holland with their vast Commerce and their Imposts and Excises have land taxes. Tis true their Laws extend to the Affairs and Expenses of the whole Nation. Here divided with the particular Legislatures but this national Legislature will certainly comprehend especially in Time allmost the whole Expenses of the Nation. The rest will be but a Drop in the Bucket. National Debt and arrears of Expenses committees Proposition Objection from Massachusetts holds not in that Case if even Imposts and Excises were to be computed, yet the Inconvenience apprehended might be totally removed by a provision that the Representation of no state should rise beyond a certain proportion to its Neighbors.

Emotion shall submit Half a Slave if adopted Ruinous to the whole
system. Former jointments the same. 3 arguments only used. 1. Equality
of Representation 2. England and Holland. 3. Resolution of Sept. 1774.
As to the first. It subtracts the only Reason on which our Objection is
founded. Attention to Interests of particular states. Dependencies not parts.
Government of Republics over their Dependencies. As to second they are
selected by the same King equal to all his subjects. Despotism will be
thought better than such a Dominion of fellow Citizens. As to the 3 absolutely perpetually confirmed afterwards by the Confederation. Having
endeavoured to remove these Objections I now pass to the Consideration
of the System on Policy and Justice.

GEORGE WASHINGTON: DIARY

Monday 9th.   Sat in the Morning for Mr. Peale. Attended Convention.
Dined at Mr. Morris's & accompanied Mrs. Morris to Doctr. Redmans
3 Miles in the Country where we drank Tea and returned.

CHARLES COTESWORTH PINCKNEY: NOTES[1]

The Numbers in the United States being supposed to be 2,500,000, the proportions or numbers from the States are supposed to be as follows—

The Numbers in the United States. Those marked with an Asterisk are from actual Numeration, the others from Calculation, including three fifths of the Negroes

New Hampshire	97,847		
Massachusetts	374,045		
Rhode Island	53,863		
Connecticutt	220,152		
New York	213,739		
New Jersey	138,930		
Pennsylvania	341,983		
Delaware	37,405		
Maryland	235,864		
Virginia	427,474		
North Carolina	181,655		
South Carolina	93,643		
Georgia	27,060		

Number of Representatives alotted to the states

New Hampshire*	102,000	3	
Massachusetts*	360,000	8	
Rhode Island*	58,000	1	
Connecticutt*	202,000	5	
New York*	238,000	6	
New Jersey*	138,000	4	
Pennsylvania*	360,000	8	
Delaware*	37,000	1	*Negroes*
Maryland*	218,000	6	80,000
Virginia	420,000	10	280,000
North Carolina	200,000	5	60,000
South Carolina	150,000	5	80,000
Georgia	90,000	3	20,000
	2,573,000	65	*Three fifths of these are included in the first Numbers*

Endorsed: An Account of the Numbers in the United States

AD (Library of Congress)

1. This and the following document were generated by the debates of early July on the apportionment of representation in the "first branch" of the legislature. Farrand prints similar documents at July 10, 1:572–74.

PIERCE BUTLER: NOTES

New Hampshire	2	3
Massachusetts	7	8
R. Island	1	1
Connecticut	4	5
New York	5	6
New Jersey	3	4
Pensylvania	8	8
Delaware	1	1
Maryland	4	6
Virginia	9	10.
North Carolina	5	5
So. Carolina	5	5
Georgia	2	3*

*This principle is grounded, I am told on the following—
    The number of white Inhabitants in the U.S. supposed to be 2,500,000—the proportions alloted to Each State will be as follows

		Returnd from Actual Numeration Vidzt.	
New Hampshire	97,847	N. Hampshire	102 000
Massachusets	374,045	Massachusets	353,000
Rhode Island	53,863	Connecticut	202,000
Connecticut	220,152	New York	238,000
New York	213,739	New Jersey	140,000
New Jersey	138,930	Pensylvania	—
Pensylvania	341,983	Delaware	40,000
Maryland	235 864	Maryland	218,000
Virginia	427 474	Virginia Supposd	400,000
N. Carolina	181 655	No. Carolina	250,000
Georgia	27,060	So. Carolina	170,000
		I suppose Negroes are included in the last 3 states	

Representation as fixd by the Convention
in the proportion of one Member in the House of Representatives to 35,000—the Blacks reckend at the rate of 3/5ths.

New Hampshire 102 000	3	Delaware	1	
Massachusetts ... 352 000	8	Maryland	6	
R. Island	1	Virginia	10	
Connecticut	5	No. Carolina ..	5	
N. York	6	So. Carolina ...	5	
Jersey	4	Georgia	3	
Pennsylvania	8		30 total 65.	
	35.			

PHOTOSTAT (Library of Congress)

GEORGE WASHINGTON: DIARY

Tuesday. 10th.   Attended Convention. Dined at Mr. Morris's. Drank Tea at Mr. Binghams & went to the Play.

WEDNESDAY, JULY 11, 1787

GEORGE WASHINGTON: DIARY

Wednesday 11th   Attended Convention. Dined at Mr. Morris's and spent the evening there.

RUFUS KING TO HENRY KNOX

Philadelphia 11 July 1787

I wish it was in my power to inform you that we had progressed a single step since you left us—I say progressed; this expression must be defined by my own political Creed, which you are very well acquainted with—I can form no conjecture of the Report, or separation, of the convention—If I had returned to N-Yk with you or with our very able and segacious Friend Hamilton, I should have escaped much Vexation, enjoyed much pleasure and have gratified the earnest wishes & desires of Mrs. King—

Farrand, 4:68.

RUFUS KING TO NATHAN DANE

Philadelphia 11 July 1787

Dear Sir

I Thank you for your letter by Monday's post. The period of the Convention is as uncertain as when they first assembled. I hope they will agree in some just and reasonable reform of the Articles of Union. But you are too well acquainted with the situation of our Country not to be sensible that there are a variety of considerations which will operate against an unanimity in the Opinions of the Delegates of the several states. Perhaps however they may unite in their Judgments. . . .

ALS (New England Historic Genealogical Society)

WILLIAM PATERSON TO EUPHEMIA PATERSON

Philada. 11 July, 1787

My dear Affa.

The Heat here is and has been intense. Philada. is, I think, the warmest Place I have been in. . . .

ALS (Rutgers University)

THURSDAY, JULY 12, 1787

ELBRIDGE GERRY: DRAFT MOTION[1]

That in the original Formation of the Legislature of the U.S. the first
branch thereof shall consist of 65 Members—of which Number

NH *shall have*	3
M	8
R	1
Con	5
N York	6
NJ	4
Penn	8
D	1
M	6
V	10
NC	5
SC	5
G	3

But as the present Situation of the States may probably alter as well in
point of Wealth as in the Number of their Inhabitants that the Legislature
be authorized from Time to Time to augment the Number of Representatives and in Case any of the States shall hereafter be divided or any two
or more States united, or any new State created within the Limits of the
U.S. the Legislature shall possess authority to regulate the Number of
Representatives in any of the foregoing Cases upon the principle of Wealth
and Number of Inhabitants. Provided always that Representation ought to
be proportioned according to direct Taxation and in order to ascertain the
alteration in the direct Taxation which may be required from Time to
Time by the Changes in the relative Circumstances of the States Resolved
that a Census be taken with [indecipherable word] six years from the first

1. This document must have been prepared by Gerry in his capacity as chairman of
the "grand committee," appointed on July 2, to consider the problem of representation
in the legislature. It is a combination of portions of committee reports of July 9 and 10
and of James Wilson's motion of July 12, as amended on that date. The document cannot
have been written after July 13, because it contains phrases—apportionment based on
"wealth"—which the Convention deleted on that day (Farrand, 1:557, 563, 590, 599,
603, 606).

Meeting of the Legislature of the U. States, and once within the term of every 10 years afterward of all the Inhabitants of the U. States in the Manner and according to the ratio recommended by Congress in their Resolution of Ap. 18 1783 and that the Legislature of the U.S. proportion the direct Taxation accordingly.

AD (Sang Collection, Southern Illinois University)

EDMUND RANDOLPH TO BEVERLEY RANDOLPH

July 12 1787

Sir

The deputation here have desired me to obtain a further sum of money. I have accordingly drawn for an hundred pounds; which the executive will oblige us by paying.

I beg leave to enclose my own account. It contains an article charge without authority, but arising from circumstances, which I could not avoid. A Cherokee chief came hither under the conduct of an interpreter, who urged me to send a talk and a present. I could not refuse the one the other and conceived that a silver pipe with some symbols of Virginia and Cherokee friendship, would be an ornament to the townhouse of the Indians, and a small medal would conciliate the chief, who visited me. I do not, however, wish that the entertainment should be paid for by the public, unless the fullest propriety should dictate the measure. If it should not appear to be perfectly allowable, I hope that there will not be the least hesitation in rejecting it; as I consider myself wholly unauthorized to make such a present. Mr. Wythe left fifty pounds with us, of which an account will be rendered by us.

I have the honor sir to be with
great respect yr. mo. ob. serv.
Edm. Randolph

Dr. Edm. Randolph	To the commonwealth of Virginia
1787	£100
May to cash	50
June to cash to Mrs. R	
	£150

Cr. By attendance on the convention, together with travelling expenses from the 6th of May inclusive to 19th July inclusive, being 74 days at 6 dollars per day, which are equal to 144 dollars which are equal to £133. 4

By cash paid for a silver medal and a silver pipe for the Cherokees
£11. 6. 6. Penna. Cy.

$$\begin{array}{r} £9.\ 9.\ 3 \\ \hline £142.\ 13.\ 3 \end{array}$$

ALS (Virginia State Library)

GEORGE WASHINGTON: DIARY

Thursday 12th.   In Convention. Dined at Mr. Morris's & drank Tea
with Mrs. Livingston.

FRIDAY, JULY 13, 1787

GEORGE WASHINGTON: DIARY

Friday 13th.   In Convention, drank Tea, & Spent the Evening at Mr. Morris's.

JONATHAN DAYTON TO WILLIAM LIVINGSTON

Philadelphia July 13th 1787

Sir

I have the mortification to inform your Excellency that, altho' we have been daily in Convention, we have not made the least progress in the business since you left us. It is unnecessary and would perhaps be improper, to relate here the causes of this delay. They will very readily occur to your Excellency from your knowledge of them heretofore.

I must request that your excellency will be pleased agreably to the arrangement made at parting, to return to this place on Tuesday or Wednesday next at the farthest.

Mr. Paterson must leave this town the first day of August, and I must consequently be here to relieve him the last day of this month, let my stay at home be ever so short. I shall therefore at best have ten days.

I have the honor to be Your Excellency's
most obedient very humble servant
Jonathan Dayton

ALS (Massachusetts Historical Society)

FARRAND: NOTE ON CONVENTION SITE

Robert P. Reeder, in a footnote to a paper "The First Homes of the Supreme Court of the United States" published in the *Proceedings of the American Philosophical Society*, LXXVI, 567–68 (n. 136), commented upon this quotation from Watson's *Annals*.[1] "The passage was

---

1. The passage, quoted by Farrand (3:59 n.), reads: "The Convention which met to form the Constitution of the United States, met *up stairs*, and at the same time the street pavement along Chestnut Street was coverd with earth to silence the rattling of wheels."

in the 1843 edition of Watson, I, 402, but not in the 1830 edition. The statement of an unnamed person so long after the event carries but limited weight."

Mr. Reeder then adds the following important information: "On the other hand, the *Columbian Magazine* for July, 1787, said that the sessions were held 'in the same hall which enclosed the patriots who framed the Declaration of Independence.' The *Diary of Jacob Hiltzheimer,* a member of the General Assembly, for September 5, said the Convention had been meeting downstairs and that the Assembly, which had been in recess, would meet upstairs.[2] The Minutes of the Assembly for that date appear to make the same statement. Madison's Debates for September 17 quotes a remark by Franklin about looking often at a carving on the President's chair which appears to show that from time to time through the Convention he had been looking at the chair in which Washington sat on September 17. Mease, *A Picture of Philadelphia* (1811), 319, says that the Convention sat in the east room on the first floor. It thus seems probable that the Convention met downstairs usually if not always, although it is possible that when the Assembly was not in session the choice of the Convention as to its meeting-place depended upon whether it gave more weight to the accessibility of the lower room and the associations connected with it or to the desire for the utmost secrecy at some stages of its proceedings. Secrecy may have been more desirable in June and July than it was later on. Yet we must remember that during the war, when there was some need for secrecy, the Congress sat downstairs and the Assembly upstairs. It is also possible that the use of the courtroom in July, 1787, when Cutler was in Philadelphia, made it desirable for the Convention to sit upstairs while the court was in session."

Farrand, 4:68–69

---

2. "Met the Assembly at the State House in the Lower room, and adjourned to meet tomorrow half past 9 oClock in the upper room, Leaving the Lower room as before to the Gentlemen of the Convention" (Jacob Hiltzheimer, diary, American Philosophical Society; September 5, 1787).

SATURDAY, JULY 14, 1787

GEORGE WASHINGTON: DIARY

Saturday. 14th.   In Convention. Dined at Springsbury with the Club and went to the play in the Afternoon.

RICHARD HENRY LEE TO FRANCIS LIGHTFOOT LEE

New York July 14th, 1787.

I found the Convention at Phila. very busy and very secret. it would seem however, from variety of circumstances that we shall hear of a Government not unlike the B. Constitution, that is, an Executive with 2 branches composing a federal Legislature and possessing adequate Tone.

Farrand, 4:70

SUNDAY, JULY 15, 1787

GEORGE WASHINGTON: DIARY

Sunday 15th.   Dined at Mr. Morris's & remaind. at home all day.

MONDAY, JULY 16, 1787

GEORGE WASHINGTON: DIARY

Monday 16th.   In Convention. Dined at Mr. Morris's and drank Tea with Mrs. Powell.

TUESDAY, JULY 17, 1787

GEORGE WASHINGTON: DIARY

Tuesday 17th. In Convention. Dined at Mrs. Houses, and made an excursion with a party for Tea to Grays Ferry.[1]

WILLIAM PATERSON TO EUPHEMIA PATERSON

Phila. July 17th 1787

I expect to be with you on or about the first of next month and hope that I shall not be under the necessity of returning.

The business is difficult and unavoidably takes up much time, but I think we shall eventually agree upon and adopt a system that will give strength and harmony to the Union and render us a great and happy people. This is the wish of every good, and the interest of every wise man.

Farrand, 4:70

---

1. Jacob Hiltzheimer reported that on this day he went "in the afternoon . . . to Mr. Gray's ferry, where we saw the great improvements made in the garden, summer houses, and walks in the woods. General Washington and a number of other gentlemen of the present Convention came down to spend the afternoon" (Jackson and Twohig, eds., *Diaries of Washington*, 5:176).

WEDNESDAY, JULY 18, 1787

GEORGE WASHINGTON: DIARY

Wednesday 18th. In Convention. Dined at Mr. Milligans and drank Tea at Mr. Meridiths.

THURSDAY, JULY 19, 1787

GEORGE WASHINGTON: DIARY

Thursday 19th. Dined (after coming out of Convention) at Mr. John Penn the youngers. Drank Tea & spent the evening at my lodgings.

WILLIAM LIVINGSTON TO JOHN JAY

July 19, 1787

. . . By notification I received yesterday from Philadelphia that one of my colleagues is obliged to return home I am obliged to set out for that cool city and excellent fish market tomorrow. . . .

ALS (Columbia University)

HUGH WILLIAMSON TO JOHN GRAY BLOUNT

Philadelphia 19th July 1787

Dear Sir

The several members of Convention from our State, some Weeks ago wrote to the Governor that their Continuance here would certainly be longer than had at first been expected. For this reason they submitted to his Excellencies Consideration the granting them a farther allowance of 2 Months in Draughts on the Treasury. By a separate Letter to the Governor, I requested him, if he should issue a Certificate in my favour, to forward it to your care. If you have received any such Draught I wish you to try to get mony on the same & to vest it in some thing for my Account. Though I wish that some thing may be bought I do not at this Instant know any thing that can be purchased at a moderate loss. I know that Tobacco is not to be had nor are Corn or Pork. Naval Stores are too subject to waste, else Tar might do some thing. The Value of Pitch and Tar must ever go Hand in Hand; If Pitch is to be had I think it would be preferable to any other Article of Produce. It is now worth—in this Place. You doubtless know the Inclination of some People to make Mony by selling soft or tarey Pitch or by scooping up a good deal of Sand or Clay along with the Pitch, but if Pitch is to be had from People of reputation for a moderate Share of Honesty I would greatly prefer it to any other Article that is like to be had.

If the Governor has not sent you the Certificates I wish you would be so good as to write him a Line. If the Mony is not to be had at Washington or Tarborough perhaps it may be had at Edenton.

Col. Davie alledges that it will be necessary for him to return Home on or about the Beginning of next Month—He must attend the Circuits of the Superiour Courts. Col. Martin proposes returning with him, for he says that he will be out of Cash. Perhaps you may wonder at my saying that I would rather lose the assistance of the last than the first of those Gentlemen, but things of this sort will often happen. When your brother came here some Time ago from N. York he suspected that where there were 4 there might be a 5th Person required to prevent a divided Vote but was soon convinced that he might return to N. York & serve the State there, whose Service had been deserted by all its Delegates in Congress except Hawkins. There has not in a single important Question been a Division in our Representation nor so much as one dissenting Voice.

I am

Your obed^t. Servt.
Hugh Williamson

ALS (North Carolina Division of Archives and History)

WILLIAM BLOUNT TO JOHN GRAY BLOUNT

Newyork July 19th 1787.

I had yesterday a letter from Davie in which he says "since you left us We have progressed obliquely and retrogaded directly so that we stand on the same Spot you left us" and when I left them much Progress was not made. My Colleagues were very unanimous. H. W. are there Head and were in Sentiment with Virginia who seemed to take the lead Madison at their Head tho Randolph and Mason are also great. The general outlines were to have a National Assembly composed of three Branches the first to be elected by the People at large and to consist of about 70 Members, the second Branch of a less Number to be chosen by the respective Legislatures for a longer Duration and the third an Executive of a single Man for a still longer Time. I must confess not withstanding all I heard in favour of this System I am not in sentiment with my Colleagues for as I have before said I still think we shall ultimately end not many Years just be seperate and distinct Governments perfectly independent of each other. The little States were much opposed to the Politicks of the larger they insisted that each State ought to have an equal vote as in the present Confederation.

Farrand, 4:71

FRIDAY, JULY 20, 1787

GEORGE WASHINGTON: DIARY

Friday 20th.   In Convention. Dined at home and drank Tea at Mr. Clymers.

SATURDAY, JULY 21, 1787

GEORGE WASHINGTON: DIARY

Saturday 21st.   In Convention. Dined at Springsbury with the Club of Gentn. & Ladies. Went to the Play afterwards.

OLIVER ELLSWORTH TO ABIGAIL ELLSWORTH

Philadelphia July 21st 1787

Dear Mrs. Ellsworth

I believe the older men grow the more uneasy they are from their wives. Mr. Sherman and Doctor Johnson are both run home for a short family visit. As I am a third younger than they are I calculate to hold out a third longer, which will carry me to about the last of August.

My health holds better than I feared. To preserve I walk a good deal in the cool of the afternoons and frequently stop in and take a little chat and tea sipping with good Connecticut women who are dispersed about in different parts of the city. They are all very agreeable, but as Mrs. Lockwood I think is the most like yourself you will allow me to like her a little the best. I can add however, if it will be any satisfaction to you that my friend Mr. Lockwood is a home man and generally makes one of the party.

I yesterday dined with Mrs. Gibbs and Nancy Ferry whose company was the more acceptable because they inquired so particularly about you, and your little ones. I go to Mr. Gibbs's the oftener for the sake of conversing with Billy, who since his return from Europe where he's spent five years travelling through different nations and examining everything curious, is to me a pleasing and profitable companion. Curiosity and the love of information you know has no bounds. My curiosity was highly gratified the other day by clasping the hand of a woman who died many hundred years ago. The ancient Egyptians had an art, which is now lost out of the world, of embalming their dead so as to preserve the bodies from putrification many of which remain to this day. From one of those an arm has lately been cut off and brought to this city. The hand is intire. The nails remain upon the fingers and the wrapping cloth upon the arm. The flesh which I tried with my knife, cuts and looks much like smoked beef kept till it grows hard. This will be a good story to tell Dr. Stiles, which is all the use I shall probably make of it. His avidity for food of this kind you know is strong enough to swallow the arm and body whole. This letter is so much lighter than what I commonly send you that I will not pursue it any further lest you should imagine I am growing light headed and which may for ought I know be the case before we get through the business of the Convention. Love to Nabby and the little boys and a smack to Fanny.

Oliver Ellsworth

TR (Connecticut Historical Society)

SUNDAY, JULY 22, 1787

GEORGE WASHINGTON: DIARY

Sunday 22d.   Left Town by 5 oclock A.M. Breakfasted at Genl. Mifflins. Rode up with him & others to the Spring Mills and returned to Genl. Mifflins by Dinner after which proceeded to the City.[1]

1. "This day Gen. Washington, Gen. Mifflin and four others of the Convention did us the honor of paying us a visit in order to see our vineyard and bee houses. In this they found great delight, asked a number of questions, and testified their highest approbation with my manner of managing bees" (Peter Legaux, diary, American Philosophical Society).

MONDAY, JULY 23, 1787

GEORGE WASHINGTON: DIARY

Monday 23d.   In Convention as usual. Dined at Mr. Morris's and drank Tea at Lansdown (the Seat of Mr. Penn).

TUESDAY, JULY 24, 1787

GEORGE WASHINGTON: DIARY

Tuesday 24th. In Convention. Dined at Mr. Morris's and drank Tea, by appointment & partr. Invitation at Doctr. Rush's.

WEDNESDAY, JULY 25, 1787

GEORGE WASHINGTON: DIARY

Wednesday 25th. In Convention. Dined at Mr. Morris's, drank Tea, & spent the evening there.

WILLIAM PIERCE TO WILLIAM SHORT

New York, July 25th 1787

Dear Sir

. . . In January last I took my seat in Congress and continued untill May, when I met the Delegates from the different States, in Convention, at Philadelphia. After continuing in that Council untill all the first principles of the new Government were established, I came on again to New York, and am now in Congress. The business of the Convention is now going on with some degree of harmony. I dare not communicate any of its proceedings. . . .

ALS (Library of Congress)

EDMUND RANDOLPH TO DAVID SHEPHERD

. . . I presume that your part of the world, like this city [is] anxious to be informed of the proceedings of the Convention. It would give me pleasure to contribute to the gratification of the friends of the united states. But we are not yet discharged from the obligation of secrecy. This much I can only tell you that we have been employed in settling general principles of government and yesterday a committee was appointed to prepare a constitution conformable to those principles. Our western friends, beyond the Allegheny, may be assured that we shall not be unmindful of their interests in our regulations.

TR (Independence National Historical Park)

THURSDAY, JULY 26, 1787

EDMUND RANDOLPH: DRAFT SKETCH OF CONSTITUTION[1]

In the draught of a fundamental constitution, two things deserve attention:

1. To insert essential principles only; lest the operations of government should be clogged by rendering those provisions permanent and unalterable, which ought to be accommodated to times and events: and

2. To use simple and precise language, and general propositions, according to the example of the (several) constitutions of the several states. (For the construction of a constitution necessarily differs from that of law)

1. A preamble seems proper. Not for the purpose of designating the ends of government and human polities—This (business, if not fitter for the schools, is at least sufficiently executed) display of theory, howsoever proper in the first formation of state governments, (seems) *is* unfit here; since we are not working on the natural rights of men not yet gathered into society, but upon those rights, modified by society, and (supporting) *interwoven with* what we call (states) the rights of states—Nor yet is it proper for the purpose of mutually pledging the faith of the parties for the observance of the articles—This may be done more solemnly at the close of the draught, as in the confederation—But the object of our preamble ought to be briefly to (represent) declare, that the present foederal government is insufficient to the general happiness; that the conviction of this fact gave birth to this convention; and that the only effectual (means) ⟨mode⟩ which they (could) ⟨can⟩ devise, for curing this insufficiency, is the establishment of a supreme legislative executive and judiciary—(In this manner we may discharge the first resolution. We may then proceed to establish)[2] Let it be next declared, that the following are the constitution

1. This sketch with emendations in the hand of John Rutledge was a working document used by the Committee of Detail. Farrand printed it from the original in the Mason Papers, Library of Congress. His rendering of the document is used here. Parts of the text in parentheses were "crossed out in the original, italics represent changes made in Randolph's handwriting, and the emendations in Rutledge's handwriting are enclosed in angle brackets" (Farrand, 4:37).

2. Marginal note crossed out: "1st resolution."

and fundamentals of government for the United States[3]—After this introduction, let us proceed to the

   2. First resolution—This resolution involves three particulars:
- 1. the style of the United States; which may continue as it now is.
- 2. a declaration that (an) ⟨a⟩ supreme (execu) legislative executive and judiciary shall be established; and
- 3. a declaration that these departments shall be distinct, (except) and independent of each other, except in specified cases.

In the next place, treat of the legislative, judiciary and executive in their order, and afterwards, of the miscellaneous subjects, as they occur; bringing together all the resolutions, belonging to the same point, howsoever they may be scattered about *and leaving to the last the steps necessary to introduce the government.*—(Tak) The following plan is therefore submitted

    I   The Legislative

1. shall consist of two branches: viz:
   - a) a house of delegates; and
   - b) a senate;
2. which together shall be called "the legislature of the United States of America."
3. a) The house of delegates
   1. (shall never be greater in number than
      To effect this, pursue a rule, similar to that prescribed in the 16th. article of the New-York constitution.)
   2. Each state shall send delegates, according to the ratio, recommended by congress.
   3. to ascertain this point, let a census be taken *in due time* as the national legislature shall direct; within six years from the first meeting of the legislature; and once in every term of ten years thereafter.
   4. the census being taken and returned, the legislature shall apportion the representation:
   5. The qualifications of (a) delegates shall be the age of twenty five years at least: and citizenship:[4] (and any person possessing these qualifications may be elected except)
   6. Their duration in office shall be for two years.
   7. The elections shall be *biennially* held on the same day through the *same* state(s): except in case of accidents, and where an adjournment to the succeeding day may be necessary.

3. Marginal note crossed out: "2d resolution."
4. Marginal note crossed out: "qu: if a certain term of residence and a certain quantity of landed property ought not to be made by the convention further qualifications."

8. The place shall be fixed by the (national) legislatures from time to time; or on their default by the national legislature.

9. So shall the presiding officer.

10. (Votes shall be given by ballot, unless ⅔ of the national legislature shall choose to vary the mode.)

11. The qualification of electors shall be the same (throughout the states; viz.) *with that in the particular states, unless the legislature shall hereafter direct some uniform qualification to prevail through the states.*

> (citizenship:
> manhood
> sanity of mind
>
> previous residence for one year, or possession of real property within the state for the whole of one year, or inrolment in the militia for the whole of a years.)[5]

(12. All persons who are may be elected;)

12. A majority shall be a quorum for business; but a smaller number may be authorized by the house to call for and punish non-attending members, and to adjourn for any time not exceeding one week.

13. (quaere. how far the right of expulsion may be proper.) The house of delegates shall have power over its own members.

14. The delegates shall be privileged from arrest[6] (or assault) *personal restraint* during their attendance, for so long a time before and after, as may be necessary, for travelling to and from the legislature (and they shall have no other privilege whatsoever.)

(15. Their wages shall be)

16. They shall be ineligible to *and incapable of holding* offices under the authority of the united states, during the term of service of the house of delegates.

17. Vacancies *by death disability or resignation* shall be supplied by a writ from the (speaker or any other person, appointed by the house.)[7] *governor of the state, wherein they shall happen.*

18. The house shall have power to make rules for its own government.

19 The house shall not adjourn without the concurrence of the senate for more than one week, nor without such concur-

---

5. Marginal note crossed out: "These qualifications are not justified by the resolutions."

6. "Arrest" underscored in the original.

7. Underscored in the original before being crossed out.

rence to any other place, than the one at which they are sitting.

4 b) The Senate—

(1. shall consist of   members; each possessing a vote)

2. *the legislature of* Each state shall (send) *appoint* two (members) senators using their discretion as to the time and manner of choosing them.

3. the qualification of (a) senator*s* shall be
the age of 25 years at least:
citizenship in the united states:
and property in the amount of

4. (Their duration in office shall)
They shall be elected for six years and immediately after the first election they shall be divided by lot *as near as may be* into (four) *three* classes, (six in each class,) and numbered 1, 2, 3: and the seats of the members of the first class shall be vacated at the expiration of the (first) second year, of the second class at the expiration of the fourth and of the third class at the end of the sixth year, and so on continually, that a third part of the senate may be biennially chosen.

5. A majority shall be a quorum for business: but a smaller number may be authorized to call for and punish non attending members and to adjourn (for any time not exceeding one week) ⟨from day to day⟩.

6. *Each senator shall have one vote*

(6) 7. The senate shall have power over its own members.

(7) 8. The senators shall be privileged from arrest[8] *personal restraint* during their attendance,
and for so long a time before and so long after, as may be necessary for travelling to and from the legislature (and they shall have no other privileges whatsoever.)

(8) 9. The senators shall be ineligible to and incapable of holding any office under the authority of the united states, during the term for which they are elected, and for one year thereafter, (except in the instance of those offices, which may be instituted for the better conducting of the business of the senate, while in session.)

(10. Vacancies)

(10. The wages of the senators shall be paid out of the (nat) treasury of the united states.:
those wages for the first six years shall be   dollars per diem—

8. "Arrest" underscored in the original.

at the beginning of (the) every sixth year after the first, the supreme judiciary shall cause a special jury of the most respectable merchants and farmers to be summoned to declare what shall have been the averaged value of wheat during the last six years, in the state, where the legislature may be sitting: And for the six subsequent years, the senators shall receive per diem the averaged value of   bushels of wheat.)

11. The (house) *Senate* shall have power to make rules for its own government

12. The Senate shall not adjourn without the concurrence of the house of delegates for more than (one week) ⟨3 days⟩, nor without such concurrence to any place other than that at which they are sitting.

The following are

       (1) the legislative powers; *with certain exceptions; and under certain restrictions*

       (2 with certain exceptions and)

       (3 under certain restrictions.)

agrd. 1. To raise money by taxation, unlimited as to sum, *for the (future) past (or)* ⟨&⟩ *future debts and necessities of the union* and to establish rules for collection.

       Exception(s)

agrd. No Taxes on exports.—Restrictons 1. direct taxation proportioned to representation 2. No (headpost) capitation-tax which does not apply to all inhabitants under the above limitation—3. no (other) *indirect* tax which is not common to all. (4. Delinquency shall be by distress and sale, and officers of state bound to conform)

  2. To regulate commerce ⟨both foreign & domestic & no State to lay a duty on imports—⟩

     Exceptions

     1. no Duty on exports.

     2. no prohibition on (such) ⟨the⟩ importations of ⟨such⟩ inhabitants ⟨or People as the sevl. States think proper to admit⟩

     3. no duties by way of such prohibition.

  Restrictions.

  1. A navigation act shall not be passed, but with the consent of (eleven states in) ⟨⅔ds. of the Members present of⟩ the senate and (10 in) ⟨the like No. of⟩ the house of representatives.

(2. Nor shall any other regulation—and this rule shall prevail, whensoever the subject shall occur in any act.)

(3. The lawful territory To make treaties of commerce

(qu: as to senate)   Under the foregoing restrictions)

4. (To make treaties of peace or alliance)

(qu: as to senate) under the foregoing restrictions, and without the surrender of territory for an equivalent, and in no case, unless a superior title.)

5. To make war⟨:(and)⟩ raise armies. ⟨& equip Fleets.⟩

6. To provide tribunals and punishment for mere offences against the law of nations.

⟨Indian Affairs⟩[9]

7. To declare the law of piracy, felonies and captures on the high seas, and captures on land.

⟨to regulate Weights & Measures⟩[10]

8. To appoint tribunals, inferior to the supreme judiciary.

9. To adjust upon the plan heretofore used *all* disputes between the States ⟨respecting Territory & Jurisdn⟩

10. To (regulate) ⟨The exclusive right of⟩ coining ⟨money (Paper prohibit) no State to be perd. in future to emit Paper Bills of Credit witht. the App: of the Natl. Legisle. nor to make any (Article) Thing but Specie a Tender in paymt. of debts⟩[11]

11. To regulate naturalization

12. (To draw forth the) ⟨make Laws for calling forth the Aid of the⟩ militia, (or any part, or to authorize the Executive to embody them) ⟨to execute the Laws of the Union to inforce Treaties to repel Invasion and suppress internal Comns.⟩

13. To establish post-offices

14. To subdue a rebellion in any particular state, on the application of the legislature thereof.

⟨of declaring the Crime & Punishmt. of Counterfeitg it.⟩[12]

15. To enact articles of war.

16. To regulate the force permitted to be kept in each state.

(17. To send embassadors)

⟨Power to borrow Money—

To appoint a Treasurer by (joint) ballot.⟩[13]

---

9. Marginal note.
10. Marginal note.
11. Marginal note.
12. Marginal note.
13. Marginal note.

18. To declare it to be treason to levy war against or adhere to the enemies of the U.S.

19. (To organize the government in those things, which)
⟨Insert the 11 Article⟩

(All laws of a particular state, repugnant hereto, shall be void: and in the decision thereon, which shall be vested in the supreme judiciary, all incidents without which the general principles cannot be satisfied, shall be considered, as involved in the general principle.)

⟨That Trials for Criml. Offences be in the State where the Offe was comd—by Jury—and a right to make all Laws necessary to carry the foregoing Powers into Execu—⟩

2. The powers belonging peculiarly to the representatives are those concerning money-bills

3. The powers destined for the senate peculiarly, are
   1. To make treaties of commerce
   2. to make ⟨Treaties of⟩ peace. ⟨& Alliance.⟩
   3. to appoint the judiciary
   4. ⟨to send Embassadors⟩

4. The executive ⟨Governor of the united People & States of America.⟩[14]
   1. shall consist of a single person;
   2. who shall (hold) be elected by the Legislature ⟨by (joint) Ballot (& in) each Ho. havg a Negative on the other⟩
   3. and *shall* hold his office for the term of (six) *seven* years
   4. and shall be ineligible thereafter.
   5. His powers shall be
      1. to carry into execution the national laws.
      2. to (command and superintend the militia,) ⟨to be Commander in Chief of the Land & Naval Forces of the Union & of the Militia of the sevl. states.⟩[15]
      (3. to direct their discipline)
      (4. to direct the executives of the states to call them or any part for the support of the national government.)
      5. to appoint to offices, not otherwise provided for. ⟨by the constitution⟩
      ⟨shall propose to the Legisle. from Time to Time by Speech or Messg such Meas as concern this Union⟩[16]
      6. to be removeable on impeachment, made by the house of representatives and (on) conviction (of malpractice or neglect of duty,) before the supreme judiciary

14. Marginal note.
15. Marginal note.
16. Marginal note.

⟨of Treason Bribery or Corruption.⟩

7. to receive a fixed compensation for the devotion of his time to public service the quantum of which shall be settled by the national legislature: to be paid out of the national treasury. ⟨no Increase or decrease during the Term of Service of the Executive⟩[17]

8. (and) to have a qualified negative on legislative acts so as to require repassing by ⅔.

9. and shall swear fidelity to the union, (as the legislature shall direct.) ⟨by taking an oath of office⟩

10. receiving embassadors 11. commissioning officers. 12. convene legislature ⟨The Presidt. of the Senate to succeed to the Executive in Case of (death) Vacancy untill the Meeting of the Legisle The power of pardoning vested in the Executive (which) his pardon shall not however, be pleadable to an Impeachmt.⟩[18]

5. The Judiciary

1. shall consist of one supreme tribunal:

2: the judges whereof shall be appointed by the senate:

3. and of such inferior tribunals, as the legislature may (appoint:) ⟨establish⟩

(4. the judges of which shall be also appointed by the senate—)

5. all the judges shall hold their offices during good behaviour;

6. and shall receive punctually, at stated times a (fixed) compensation for their services, to be settled by the legislature; in which no diminution shall be made, so as to affect the persons actually in office at the time of such diminution. and shall swear fidelity to the union.

7. The jurisdiction of the supreme tribunal shall extend

1. to all cases, arising under laws passed by the general; ⟨Legislature:⟩

2. to impeachments of officers: and

3. to *such* other cases, as the national legislature may assign, as involving the national peace and harmony; in the collection of the revenue in disputes between citizens of different states

⟨in disputes between a State & a Citizen or Citizens of another State⟩[19]

in disputes between different states; and in disputes, in which subjects or citizens of other countries are concerned ⟨& in Cases of Admiralty Jurisdn.⟩

17. Marginal note.
18. Marginal note.
19. Marginal note.

But this supreme jurisdiction shall be appellate only, except in ⟨Cases of Impeachmt. & (in)⟩ those instances, in which the legislature shall make it original: and the legislature shall organize it

        8. The whole or a part of the jurisdiction aforesaid, according to the discretion of the legislature, may be assigned to the inferior tribunals, as original tribunals.

Miscellaneous provisions

1 New states soliciting admission into the Union
    (1. must be within the present limits of the united states:)
    2. must lawfully arise; that is
      (a—in the territory of the united states, with the assent of the legislature.)
      (b—within the limits of a particular state, by the consent of a major part of the people of that state:)

⟨States lawfully arising & if within the Limits of any of the prest. States by Consent of the Legisle. of those States.⟩[20]

    3. shall be admitted only on the suffrage of ⟨⅔ds.⟩ in the house of representatives and ⟨the like No. in the⟩ Senate
    4. & shall be admitted on the same terms with the original states (but the number of states or votes required on particular measures shall be readjusted—)
    5. provided always, that the legislature may use their discretion in (refusing) *admitting* or rejecting, and may make any condition concerning the (old) debt of the union ⟨at that Time.⟩
    (6. provided also, that the western states are entitled to admission on the terms specified in the act of congress of)

2. The guarantee is
    1. to prevent the establishment of any government, not republican:
    (2) ⟨3.⟩ to protect each state against internal commotion; and
    (3) ⟨2.⟩ against external invasion.
    4. But this guarantee shall not operate ⟨in the last Case⟩ without an application from the legislature of a state.
    5.
3. The legislative executive and judiciaries of the states shall swear fidelity to the union, as the national legislature shall direct.
4. The ratification of the reform is—After the approbation of congress—to be made by a special convention ⟨in each State⟩ recommended by the assembly to be chosen for the express purpose of considering and approving or rejecting it in toto: and this recommendation may be used from time to time
5. (An alteration may be effected in the articles of union, on the appli-

20. Marginal note.

cation of two thirds *nine* ⟨⅔d⟩ of the state legislatures ⟨by a
Convn.⟩⟩ ⟨on appln. of ⅔ds of the State Legislatures to the Natl.
Leg. they call a Convn. to revise or alter the Articles of Union.⟩
(6. The plighting of faith ought to be in solemn terms.)

Addenda

1. The assent of the (major part of the people) ⟨Conventions⟩ of
   states shall give (birth) operation to this constitution
2. Each assenting state shall notify its assent to congress: who shall
   publish a day for its commencement, not exceeding *After such
   publication, or* (on) *with* the (failure thereof) *assent of the major
   part of the assenting states,* after the expiration of   days *from the
   giving of the assent of the ninth state,*
   1. each legislature shall direct the choice of representatives, *according
      to the seventh article* and provide for their support:
   2. each legislature shall also choose senators; and provide for their
      support.
   3. they shall meet at ⟨the Place &⟩ on the day assigned by congress,
      (or as the major part of the assenting states shall agree, on any
      other day.)
   4 They shall as soon as may be after meeting elect the executive: and
      proceed to execute this constitution.

The object of an address is to satisfy the people of the propriety of the
proposed reform.

To this end the following plan seems worthy of adoption

1. To state the general objects of a confederation.
2 To shew by general, but pointed observations, in what (particulars)
   respects, our confederation has fallen short of those objects.
3. The powers, necessary to be given, will then follow as a consequence
   of the defects
4. A question next arises, whether these powers can *with propriety* be
   vested in congress. The answer is, that they cannot.
5. *But* As some states may possibly meditate partial confederations, it
   would be fit now to refute this opinion briefly.
6. It follows then, that a government of the whole on national principles, with respect to taxation &c is most eligible.
7. This would lead to a short exposition of the leading particulars in
   the constitution.
8. This done, conclude in a suitable manner.

This is the shortest scheme, which can be adopted. For it would be
strange to ask (for) new powers, without assigning some reason—it matters
not how general so ever—which may apply to all of them. Besides we
ought to furnish the advocates of the plan in the country with some general

topics. Now I conceive, that these heads do not more, than comprehend the necessary points.

Farrand, 4:37–51.

GEORGE WASHINGTON: DIARY

Thursday 26th.   In Convention. Dined at Mr. Morris's, drank Tea there, and stayed within all the Afternoon.

ABRAHAM BALDWIN TO JOEL BARLOW

Philadelphia, July 26, 1787

We are still at work at this great building so much talked of. I fear we are not of the true craft, by the slowness of our progress, and I shall not hesitate to call you a lazy fellow for not furnishing even one stone in the building.

I am in hopes we shall have a resting spell of a few days before long, but I fear not long enough to avail myself of the pleasure of visiting old friends. Messers. Johnson and Sherman have left us for a few weeks. I had determined to get with them but dared not leave the state unrepresented. I believe that they expected we should adjourn immediately. I trust we have got the greater part of the materials together. And shall soon appoint the workmen to put it together, but there is so much to be said about *foundations, cornerstones* and all the rest of the stones, that I expect we shall not have the raising for several days. If we should have a leisure of two or three weeks I will come and see you.

I hear our poor Georgians are again using the old play of Indian war and am sure it will be attended with very bad consequences. That is one great source from which I expect the troubles of my life.

The New Hampshire Deputies Langdon and Gilman are here. It gives me pleasure to see that all the states have sent their Representatives except Rhode Island that she may be left alone and unsupported in her disgrace. I fear my colleagues will leave here in a few days. I shall stay as long as my money or credit lasts till the business is finished. Tell the girl I am getting some miniatures for her here, but as I prefer young workmen it will be some time before they will be done.

Adieu.

ALS (Yale University)

OLIVER ELLSWORTH TO SAMUEL HUNTINGTON

Philadelphia, July 26 1787

Sir

I received your Excellency's letter of the 9th instant, in the absence of Doctor Johnson and Mr. Sherman, who are on a short visit to their families; and am happy to be informed that the troubles in Massachusetts, which wore so threatening an aspect, not only in the government of that but of the adjoining states, have so far subsided.

The business of the Convention, Sir, is yet progressing, and will, I hope, in a few weeks more, come to a close. A report from a committee of the whole, containing principles of a reform of the federal government, has after a very long discussion and a variety of amendments been agreed to. And is referred to a smaller committee to throw into form and detail after which it will undergo one revision more. The convention may perhaps incur censure for being too long about its work, but I apprehend it will not for not having done or attempted enough.

Your Excellency's letter of the 22d of June was duly received and would have been immediately answered by my colleagues and myself but we had just done ourselves the honor of addressing a letter to you with all the little information in our power.

> I have the honor to be, Sir,
> with very great respect
> Your Excellency's humble Servant
> Oliver Ellsworth

ALS (Connecticut Historical Society)

FRIDAY, JULY 27, 1787

Friday 27th.   In Convention, which adjourned this day,[1] to meet again on Monday the 6th. of August that a Comee. which had been appointed (consisting of 5 Members) might have time to arrange, and draw into method & form the several matters which had been agreed to by the Convention as a Constitution for the United States.

Dined at Mr. Morris's, and drank Tea at Mr. Powells.

WILLIAM PATERSON TO JOHN LANSING

Philadelphia 27 July 1787

Dear Sir:

The Convention adjourned yesterday to meet on Monday the 6th of next Month, by which Time, it is expected, the Business will be detailed. It is of Moment, that the Representation should be complete, and I hope, that Mr. Yates and yourself will not fail to attend on the very Day. The Commissioners from New Hampshire arrived a few Days ago: so that with a Representative from your State, all the States, except Rhode Island, will be on the Floor.

I hope to see you and Mr. Yates at New Brunswick on your Way to Philadelphia.

My best respects await the Judge.

Yr. Ob. hb. Serv.
William Paterson

Honorable Mr. Lansing

ALS (New-York Historical Society)

DAVID BREARLEY TO JONATHAN DAYTON

Philadelphia 27 July 1787

Yesterday we completed the great Principles, which we have been so long considering, and Committed them to five Gentlemen to put into proper form and detail.—The Committee are, Mr. Gorham, Mr. Ells-

---

1. An obvious slip of the pen; the Convention adjourned the preceding day.

195

worth, Mr. Wilson, Mr. Randolph and Mr. Rutledge. We have adjourned to monday the sixth day of August, at which time it is expected that the Committee will be ready to report. The most exact punctuality has been enjoined the members in meeting at the day and hour to which they are adjourned; and every one appeared so sensible of the propriety of this measure, that there is not a doubt of its being strictly complied with. Mr. Paterson expects that you will attend at the time, as he is under the necessity of being absent. We (the members of Jersey) purpose returning to this place on the Saturday previous to the day of meeting, in order to prevent any delay on our part. If you come on in the Stage on Saturday, I shall join you at Witts and take a seat with you to Philadelphia.

Farrand, 4:72

WILLIAM SAMUEL JOHNSON TO SAMUEL PETERS

Stratford, 27th July 1787.

I have been all Summer at Philadelphia attending the Convention of the States, assembled by Recommendation of Congress, for the purpose of strengthening and consolidating our Union, and vesting more ample powers in our General Government than they at present possess. Whether we shall be able to agree upon any Plan which will be acceptable to the People I cannot determine, but there appear at present many circumstances in our favor. . . .

Farrand, 4:72–73

SATURDAY, JULY 28, 1787

GEORGE WASHINGTON: DIARY

Saturday 28th.   Dined with the Club at Springsbury. Drank Tea there
and spent the Evening at my lodgings.

SUNDAY, JULY 29, 1787

GEORGE WASHINGTON: DIARY

Sunday 29th.   Dined and spent the whole day at Mr. Morris's principally in writing letters.

MONDAY, JULY 30, 1787

GEORGE WASHINGTON: DIARY

Monday. 30th.   In company with Mr. Govr. Morris, and in his Phaeton with my horses; went up to one Jane Moores in the vicinity of Valley-forge to get Trout.

CALEB STRONG TO ALEXANDER HODGDEN

Philadelphia July 30 1787

Sir

When I came forward to this Place as one of the Deputys in the Convention I had no Expectation of staying more than five or six Weeks. I have already been here nearly double that Time and it is now very uncertain when I shall be able to return. The Situation of Affairs renderd it extremely difficult to obtain Money in the Part of the Country where I live and a Variety of Disappointments prevented my procuring so much as I wished. Indeed untill within a few days before I left Northampton I expected Judge Dana would have been able to come forward in which Case I should have been excused from the Service. I wrote to Mr. Lyman while in Boston inclosing an Order for the Sum for which a Warrant might be drawn in my Favour. He informs me that a Warrant was drawn and that you gave him Encouragement that part at least of the Money might be procured. You will easily conceive that it will be very convenient and even necessary for me that the Order should be answered at least a considerable part of it and I have the fullest Reliance on your Endeavors for that Purpose and that they will not be unsuccessful.

I am Sir with Esteem and Respect your
most obedt. and hble. Servt.
Caleb Strong

ALS (New York Public Library)

TUESDAY, JULY 31, 1787

George Washington: Diary

Tuesday 31st. Whilst Mr. Morris was fishing I rid over the old Cantonment of the American [army] of the Winter 1777, & 8. Visited all the Works, wch. were in Ruins; and the Incampments in woods where the ground had not been cultivated.

On my return back to Mrs. Moores, observing some Farmers at Work, and entering into Conversation with them, I received the following information with respect to the mode of cultivating Buck Wheat, and the application of the grain. Viz.—The usual time of sowing, is from the 10th. to the 20th. of July—on two plowings and as many harrowings at least—The grain to be harrowed in. That it is considered as an uncertain Crop being subject to injury by a hot sun whilst it is in blossom and quickly destroyed by frost, in Autumn—and that 25 bushls. is estimated as an average Crop to the Acre. That it is considered as an excellent food for horses, to puff and give them their *first* fat—Milch cattle, Sheep, and Hogs and also for fatting Beeves. To do which, 2 quarts of Buck Wheat Meal, & half a peck of Irish Potatoes at the commencemt. (to be reduced as the appetite of the beasts decrease or in other words as they encrease in flesh) mixed and givn. 3 times a day is fully competent. That Buck wheat meal made into a wash is most excellent to lay on fat upon hogs but it must be hardened by feeding them sometime afterwards with Corn. And that this meal & Potatoes mixed is very good for Colts that are weaning. About 3 pecks of Seed is the usuall allowance for an Acre.

On my return to Mrs. Moores I found Mr. Robt. Morris & his lady there.

WEDNESDAY, AUGUST 1, 1787

GEORGE WASHINGTON: DIARY

Wednesday 1st.   About 11 oclock, after it had ceased raining, we all set out for the City and dined at Mr. Morris's.

JOHN LANGDON TO JOSHUA BRACKET

Philadelphia, August 1, 1787

My Dear Sir:

Shall I forget my old Friend Bracket. No surely my whole Soul forbids it; I arrived at this place, twelve days after I left home having made some tarry at New Haven and New York. If it was not for the Importance of the Errand which I came upon, should most heartily wish myself at home; notwithstanding the Riches and Splendor of this City the fatiguing sameness makes me sick.

The Convention, well now see the Convention; Figure to yourself the Great Washington, with a Dignity peculiar to himself, taking the Chair. The Notables are seated, in a Moment and after a short Silence the Business of the day is open'd with great Solemnity and good Order. The Importance of the Business, the Dignified Character of Many, who Compose the Convention, the Eloquence of Some and the Regularity of the whole gives a Ton to the proceedings which is extreamly pleasing. Your old Friend takes his Seat. Conscious of his upright Intentions, and as far as his poor Abilities will go keep his eye single to what is righteous and of good Report.

The Convention has adjourned for a few days, to give time to a Committee to detail the Business. Give my kind Respects to Sister Bracket, Mr. and Mrs. Lowell, and all Friends. Please deliver Mrs. Langdon the inclosed.

I am your Friend
John Langdon

ALS (Harvard University)

THURSDAY, AUGUST 2, 1787

GEORGE WASHINGTON: DIARY

Thursday 2d.   Dined, Drank Tea, & Spent the Evening at Mr. Morris's.

FRIDAY, AUGUST 3, 1787

GEORGE WASHINGTON: DIARY

Friday 3d. In company with Mr. Robt. Morris and his Lady and Mr. Gouvr. Morris I went up to Trenton on another Fishing party. Lodged at Colo. Sam Ogdens at the Trenton Works. In the Evening fished, not very successfully.

SATURDAY, AUGUST 4, 1787

GEORGE WASHINGTON: DIARY

Saturday 4th.   In the morning, and between breakfast & dinner, fished again with more success (for perch) than yesterday.

Dined at Genl. Dickenson's on the East side of the River a little above Trenton & returned in the evening to Colo. Ogden's.

SUNDAY, AUGUST 5, 1787

GEORGE WASHINGTON: DIARY

Sunday 5th.   Dined at Colo. Ogdens, early; after which in the company with which I came, I returned to Philadelphia at which we arrived abt. 9 Oclk.

JAMES MCCLURG TO JAMES MADISON

Richmond Augt. 5. 87.

Dear Sir,

I am much obliged to you for your communication of the proceedings of the Convention, since I left them; for I feel that anxiety about the result, which it's Importance must give to every honest citizen. If I thought that my return could contribute in the smallest degree to it's Improvement, nothing should keep me away. But as I know that the talents, knowledge, & well-establish'd character, of our present delegates, have justly inspired this country with the most entire confidence in their determinations; & that my vote could only *operate* to produce a division, & so destroy the vote of the State, I think that my attendance now would certainly be useless, perhaps injurious.[1]

I am credibly inform'd that Mr. Henry has openly express'd his disapprobation of the circular letter of Congress, respecting the payment of British debts; & that he has declared his opinion that the Interests of this state cannot safely be trusted with that body. The doctrine of three Confederacies, or great Republics, has it's advocates here. I have heard Hervie support it, along with the extinction of State Legislatures within each great department. The necessity of some independent power to controul the Assembly by a negative, seems now to be admitted by the most Zealous Republicans—they only differ about the mode of constituting such a power. B. Randolph seems to think that a Magistrate annually elected by the people might exercise such a controul as independently as the King of G.B. I hope that our representative, Marshall, will be a powerful aid to Mason in the

1. Farrand omitted the remainder of this letter, although it contains suggestive comments about two issues which were important in the Convention: the national legislature's negative of state laws and the possibility of partial confederacies.

next Assembly. He has observ'd the continual depravation of Mens manners, under the corrupting Influence of our Legislature; & is convinc'd that nothing but the adoption of some efficient plan from the Convention can prevent Anarchy first, & civil Convulsions afterwards. Mr. H——y has certainly converted a Majority of Prince Edward, formerly the most averse to paper-money, to the patronage of it. The opposers of this Scheme are generally favourers of Installments, together with a total prohibition of foreign Luxuries; that people having no temptation to spend their money, may devote it to Justice. The Importance of the next Assembly, with respect to so many objects of great public Interest, makes me wish most sincerely that Congress was deprived of you, at least for this Session.

Mr. Jones has left town, on a pilgrimage to the Temple of health, somewhere about the Mountains. He had been very sick, but seem'd well enough recover'd before he left us.

You will please to present my Compts. to your Colleagues, & my Acquaintance in your house, & believe me, with perfect esteem & regard, Dear Sir, Your friend, & humble Servt.

James McClurg

ALS (Library of Congress)

On July 24 the Convention appointed a committee—John Rutledge, Edmund Randolph, Nathaniel Gorham, Oliver Ellsworth, and James Wilson—"to report a Constitution conformable to the Resolutions" that it had passed. On July 26 the Convention adjourned until August 6 to give the committee (soon called the Committee of Detail) an opportunity to work in peace. The Committee finished its assignment in time to present a printed copy of its report to the Convention when it reconvened on August 6. Of the approximately sixty copies printed, eighteen are known to have survived: the proof sheets, corrected by Edmund Randolph, at the Historical Society of Pennsylvania; five copies at the Library of Congress—William Samuel Johnson's, William Jackson's, James Madison's, Charles Cotesworth Pinckney's, and Hugh Williamson's; two copies at the National Archives—George Washington's and David Brearley's; two copies at the Huntington Library—George Mason's and an unidentified owner's; two copies at the Massachusetts Historical Society—Elbridge Gerry's and Nathaniel Gorham's; a copy at the Pierpont Morgan Library—Abraham Baldwin's; a copy at the University of Indiana—owner unidentified; a copy at the Library Company of Philadelphia—John Dickinson's; a copy at the New Hampshire Society of the Cincinnati—Rufus King's; and two copies in private hands—Pierce Butler's and James Wilson's.

The Committee reports were printed with unusually wide left hand margins, to permit the delegates to record substitute motions, revisions, and other alterations in constitutional language. In addition, all copies contain cancellations and interlineations, some in profusion. In most cases the additions, revisions, and marginalia contain the changes in the Committee report made as the Convention inched forward clause by clause. The annotated reports served, then, as legislative diaries, permitting individual delegates to record the evolution of the Constitution. A few delegates, however, used the Committee report to enter independent observations on proceedings in the Convention. The more substantial of these marginal reflections, suggestions, and queries are printed below.

In identifying marginalia as original material, caution must be used on several counts. Many delegates, either capriciously or from a desire to rearrange the report, made marginal entries which transposed actions taken late in the Convention to an earlier period and thus gave a false impression of prescience and inventiveness. For example, next to article VII, section 1, first clause, approved August 16, George Mason made the following marginal entry: "Sec. 1st. The Legislature shall fulfill the Engagements and discharge the Debts of the united States." Mason was here merely copying the motion adopted by the Convention on August 23 (Farrand, 2:392), not anticipating his colleagues by a week. Care has been taken to print only those marginal entries which are both substantive and original, although different selections would be possible in some cases.

ARTICLE III

In a marginal note, keyed to the phrase "the Legislature shall meet on the first Monday in December every year," Williamson wrote: "It was proposed to strike out this Provision, on the allegation that frequent Meetings of the Legislature may occasion changes of Measures etc. I no."

ARTICLE IV, SECTION I

Across from this section Williamson wrote: "It was proposed to confine the Election to freeholders. I no."

ARTICLE IV, SECTION III

In the margin Williamson wrote: "Sept. 8th motion made by HW to reconsider sect. 3rd so as to increase the number of representatives to 100. Question lost. pro. 7. 8. 9. 11.[1] con. the other six states."

ARTICLE IV, SECTION IV

Last phrase revised by Dickinson to read: "according to the Rule hereinafter for direct Taxation not exceeding the rate of one for every forty thousand, provided that every state have at least one Representative and that the Representation of the most populous state shall not

1. In entering his marginalia Williamson numbered the states 1 to 13, descending the coast from New Hampshire (number 1) to Georgia (number 13).

exceed that of the least populous more than on the proportion of twenty to one."

ARTICLE VII, SECTION I

Opposite to "regulate commerce with foreign nations" Dickinson wrote: "no Preference or Advantage to be given to any persons or place—Laws to be equal." Mason wrote: "See the provision in Section 6, & the Note upon the 8th Article."

Opposite to "regulate the value of foreign coin" Dickinson wrote: "no money to be drawn out of the National Treasury, unless by an appropriation thereof by Law."

Opposite to "appoint a Treasurer" Dickinson wrote: Q[uery] Board." Mason wrote: "Amend by inserting—or Treasurers by joint ballot."

Opposite to "declare the law and punishment of piracies" Dickinson wrote: "and offenses by persons in the service of the United States." Mason wrote: "Why not also foreign Current Coin, the Bills of Credit, and the Public Securitys of the United States?"

Opposite to "raise armies" Dickinson wrote: "to erect forts."

Opposite to "call forth the aid of the militia" Dickinson wrote: "to create Offices to fix the Salaries."

ARTICLE VII, SECTION III

Opposite this section Dickinson wrote: "Q[uery] Meaning of Direct Taxation."

ARTICLE VII, SECTION IV

Opposite Section IV Dickinson wrote: "on the Exportation of Livestock Wheat or other Grains, Flour, Rice, Fish, Lumber, Iron, Tobacco, Indigo or the Manufactures of any state."[2] Mason wrote: "Report of the Committee upon Entrys and Duties to be inserted here."

ARTICLE IX, SECTION I

Opposite Section I Mason wrote: "As Treaties are to be the Laws of the Land and commercial Treaties may be so framed as to be partially injurious, there seems to be some necessity for the same Security upon the Subject as in the 6th Section of the 6th Article."

2. Directly above this entry Dickinson copied the full faith and credit clause from Article IV of the Articles of Confederation.

ARTICLE IX, SECTION II

Opposite Section II Dickinson wrote: "A Power to terminate all Discensions with a state, likely to disturb the public peace."

ARTICLE X, SECTION I

After "elected by" Mason added: "by the joint Ballot of"

ARTICLE X, SECTION II

Dickinson entered the following series of observations in the margin: "To lay Embargos. The offices should be established by the Legislature. Proroguing. Convening at some other place than that adjourned to. Independance of Salary. and shall appoint to all offices established by this Constitution, except in Cases herein otherwise provided for and to all offices that shall be created by Law."

Mason noted at "Ambassadors": "this was not the Idea of the Convention"; before "Commander in Chief": "Q[uery]. Whether the President ought to command the Army personally"; before "execute the Office": "He ought also to swear, to the best of his Power and Knowledge to preserve the Constitution."

ARTICLE XI, SECTION II

Opposite Section II Dickinson queried: "Should they not be removable on Application by the two Branches of the Legislature."

ARTICLE XI, SECTION III

Opposite "such as shall regard Territory or Jurisdiction" Dickinson wrote: "Q[uery] Appeals in Cases relating to Territory Jurisdiction or Disputes with foreign Powers."

After "such regulations as the Legislature shall make" Mason commented: "a more explicit Definition seems necessary here."

ARTICLE XI, SECTION IV

Opposite Section IV Dickinson wrote: "Q[uery] Offences committed out of the United States."

ARTICLE XI, SECTION V

Opposite Section V Mason wrote: "No Mode of impeaching the Judges is established; and the Mode of Indictment and Punishment for all the great Officers of the Government should be designated."

ARTICLE XII

Opposite this article Dickinson wrote: "nor to lay Duties or Imposts on the postage of Letters or the Carriages employed therein nor on Exports unless they be the produce or Manufacture of the state exporting the same nor to lay embargos."

ARTICLE XIII

Dickinson keyed the following marginal note to "specie": "coined or regulated by the Legislature of the United and at the Rate or Value by them established." At the end of the article he added: "and then to continue no longer than Congress shall otherwise determine."

ARTICLE XIV

At the end of the article Dickinson added: "except the priveledge of electing and being elected to office."

ARTICLE XXII

Opposite the article Dickinson wrote: "the Union to be perpetual." Williamson wrote on the back of page six of his copy of the report: "Art:22. Question first put for filling up the Blank with 10, the number 7 had been proposed. Question lost. The question was then put for 9 and carry'd. 10. 11. 12. 13. HW ay."[3]

ARTICLE XXIII

At the end of the article Dickinson added: "If within   Months after the Government ordained declared and established by this Constitution shall be agreed to in Congress, the same shall not be confirmed by the Legislature of every State, then, to introduce this Constitution, it is the Opinion of this Convention, that Delegates should be appointed by Conventions to be called by the Legislatures of such states as shall assent to this Constitution to meet in Convention at   on the   Day of   in the Year   and that the said Convention consisting of Delegates from at least   States should have full power to appoint and publish a Day as early as may be and appoint a Place for commencing proceedings under this Constitution; that after such appointment and publication, the Legislatures of the several states should elect Members of the Senate and direct the Election of Members

3. Both Farrand and Madison reported this vote as 8 in favor, 3 against, Georgia being listed in favor in both accounts.

of the House of Representatives: and that the Members of the Legislature should meet at the Time and place assigned by the said Convention, and should as soon as may be after their Meeting choose the president of the United States and proceed to execute this Constitution."

George Washington: Diary

Monday 6th.   Met, according to adjournment in Convention, & received the rept. of the Committee. Dined at Mr. Morris's and drank Tea at Mr. Meridiths.

TUESDAY, AUGUST 7, 1787

George Washington: Diary

Tuesday 7th. In convention. Dined at Mr. Morris's and spent the evening there also.

WEDNESDAY, AUGUST 8, 1787

GEORGE WASHINGTON: DIARY

Wednesday 8th.   In convention. Dined at the City Tavern and remained there till near ten oclock.

THURSDAY, AUGUST 9, 1787

Thursday 9th. In Convention. Dined at Mr. Swanwicks and spent the Afternn. in my own room—reading letters and accts. from home.

ELBRIDGE GERRY TO ANN GERRY

Philadela. Thursday Eveng. 9 oClock 9th Aug. 1787

I arrived here, my dearest Life, about an hour ago with Colo. Hamilton, whom I met at the Hook. We escaped a heavy thunder gust, which gave us Chase, about an hour before we reached the City. We had a cool ride, free from Dust, and I am not fatigued—How is my dearest Girl, her little pet, and family Friends? An answer to such questions as these, is more interesting to me than all the delusive prospects of pleasure or Happiness from other quarters. When I went to Bed last Evening, I began to reproach myself and have continued to do so ever since, for leaving behind my little *Comforter,* in the Absence of my lively Friends. I mean her portrait. How happened it to escape your Memory as well as mine? I think such another Accident will not soon happen to me. Miss Dally informs me she has some very good Hyson at 10/3 this Currency which is a Dollar and a half by the half Dozen—inclosed is a Sample and if it suits inform me in your next of what quantity to take. Miss Dally thinks it more difficult to preserve the Flavour of Hyson than of the black Tea. How shall it be preserved?

I have had some Conversation with Col. Hamilton, respecting the last bill drawn by Mr. Harrison, and as We are both at Miss Dally's, I shall have a good Opportunity to perfect it soon. He expects to return in a Week to New York and I hope to send it by him. I likewise entered into the Merits of the other Bill, but found as your pappa has always said and as Colo. Hamilton himself acknowledged, tho he knew little or nothing of the Matter, he depends on Mr. Harrison for Information, but there must be other Dependance. I shall think upon the state of this Matter & write your pappa thereon. Adieu my only Source of Happiness, kiss our lovely little Girl for me whenever you kiss her for yourself and with my sincerest Regards to pappa Mamma and the Family believe me to be your ever

affectionate

E. Gerry

ALS (Sang Collection, Southern Illinois University)

215

FRIDAY, AUGUST 10, 1787

GEORGE WASHINGTON: DIARY

Friday 10th.   Dined (after coming out of Convention) at Mr. Binghams and drank Tea there. Spent the evening at my lodings.

ELBRIDGE GERRY TO ANN GERRY

Philadelphia 10th August 1787

I called, my lovely Girl, on Mrs. Carney after Dinner for the Articles left in her closet, and she made a particular Enquiry for yourself and the baby. She was glad to hear you were both well and wished to see you but said you had acted judiciously in not returning this Month, for it has been very sickly since We left the City with Young Children, a great Number of whom had dyed. There was scarcely a Day she said passed without her seeing some carried by her Door—I then went to Mrs. Bond, who was very particular in her Enquiries about Yourself and Miss Gerry, as well as her young Ladies and Mr. Bond. She had heard from them of the Attentions paid them in New York, and inquired whether they had called often on you. I told her, not, and that you had complained of it. She was very friendly and desired me to call frequently and in a familiar Manner, as We had done before. Fanny is in the Country, and Mrs. Cadwallader is well, but I did not see her. She is preparing to exchange her House for her Mamma's and they are to remove soon. The president, Major Butler, Colo. Langdon, Governor Rutledge and a number of others made very particular Enquiry for You and send their Compliments—inclosed are three Letters which I found here for You—Mr. Warren's was under Cover to me, which was the Cause of it's being opened. I had forgot to mention that Mrs. Bond was pleased to hear You had remained in New York, saying, the City was very unfavorable at present for Children. Thus my dearest Life, what We have adopted with Respect to your remaining in New York, appears to be fortunate as it relates to our darling Infant. I have not had Time to call on any of the high orders as yet, and I think I shall not be able to devote much Time to unnecessary and unprofitable Etiquette.

Adieu my dearest Life, may the best of Heaven's Blessings ever attend you and yours the valuable pledge of your Affection, and with my usual regards to our Friends of the Family and be assured I am ever your affectionate E. Gerry

Aug '11   I am favoured my Love with yours of the 9th to which I shall reply in my next—You make no Mention of Miss Bonds, have they called on you since I left New York. I fancy when they return, I shall make myself scarce.

ALS (Sang Collection, Southern Illinois University)

SATURDAY, AUGUST 11, 1787

GEORGE WASHINGTON: DIARY

Saturday 11th.   In Convention. Dined at the Club at Springsbury and after Ten returnd. home.

SUNDAY, AUGUST 12, 1787

GEORGE WASHINGTON: DIARY

Sunday 12th. Dined at Bush hill with Mr. William Hamilton. Spent the evening at home writing letters.

RICHARD DOBBS SPAIGHT TO JAMES IREDELL[1]

Philadelphia, August 12th, 1787.

Dear Sir:

—The Convention having agreed upon the outlines of a plan of government for the United States, referred it to a small committee to detail: that committee have reported, and the plan is now under consideration. I am in hopes we shall be able to get through it by the 1st or 15th of September.

It is not probable that the United States will in future be so ideal as to risk their happiness upon the unanimity of the whole; and thereby put it in the power of one or two States to defeat the most salutary propositions, and prevent the Union from rising out of that contemptible situation to which it is at present reduced. There is no man of reflection, who has maturely considered what must and will result from the weakness of our present Federal Government, and the tyrannical and unjust proceedings of most of the State governments, if longer persevered in, but must sincerely wish for a strong and efficient National Government. We may naturally suppose that all those persons who are possessed of popularity in the different States, and which they make use of, not for the public benefit, but for their private emolument, will oppose any system of this kind.

ELBRIDGE GERRY TO SAMUEL GERRY

Philadelphia 12 Aug 1787

Dear

I am favoured with yours of July 8th and since the Receipt of it have been to New York to accompany Mrs. Gerry and her baby, with whom

---

1. Farrand (3:68) omitted the final two sentences, which are printed from Griffith J. McRee, *The Life and Correspondence of James Iredell,* 2 vols. (New York, 1857–58), 2:168.

this City did not very well agree. Indeed the Convention adjourned for about ten Days and We improved the Opportunity to take an airing. I have left them there by the Advice of all her Friends, as the Heat of Philadelphia in the Month of August might prove injurious to our Infant. . . . The Convention will probably agree in a Constitution which will have some Force, but I am not at Liberty yet to make any Communications.

My Regards to Mrs. Gerry, your Family and all our Friends and be assured I am ever yours sincerely

E. Gerry.

ALS (Massachusetts Historical Society)

MONDAY, AUGUST 13, 1787

GEORGE WASHINGTON: DIARY

Monday 13th.   In Convention. Dined at Mr. Morris's, and drank Tea with Mrs. Bache, at the Presidents.

TUESDAY, AUGUST 14, 1787

The Members of the Legislature shall be inelligible to any Office to which pay is annexed except in the Army Navy or foreign Ambassies; and in case of such appointment and during the time of Service they shall Vacate their Seats.

PHOTOSTAT (Library of Congress)

GEORGE WASHINGTON: DIARY

Tuesday 14th.   In Convention. Dined, drank Tea, and spent the evening at home.

ELBRIDGE GERRY TO ANN GERRY

Tuesday Evening Phila. 14th Augt.
I am very anxious for the Health of my dearest Girl and her lovely Infant in consequence of your letter of the 12th recd this Day. Let me intreat You, upon the Receipt hereof, to ride every Day with the Baby, until You are both recovered. The Morning before the Heat comes on, is the best Time: but your Arrangement must be such as to reduce it to a Certainty You will be in before the Heat rises [?]. Should you neglect it in the Morning be Sure to ride in the Evening, for nothing will serve either of you so much as Exercise: and if You find the least Difficulty about a Carriage, hire a Hackney.

What a question You have proposed respecting your little Image— whether I should not have thot you vain in proposing that I should take it? Should I at this period think you vain for supposing You have my sincerest Affection? For supposing that I am never happy without You? For supposing when you are with me, my Joys are doubled and Sorrows divided? Would you entertain then a Doubt that in your absence your

1. The eligibility of legislators for offices in other branches of government was extensively debated on this date as well as on September 1 and 3 (Farrand, 2:283–90, 484, 489–92). The present motion, from the Pierce Butler papers, appears to be in Butler's hand.

Miniature would be the best Relief next to that of reading your letters and knowing this, knowing that my Happiness would be promoted by seeing it, how could You be supposed vain in rendering me such an act of Kindness? I know and revere You my life for your Delicacy, but have you not in this extended it a little too far?

Mr. Martin I saw at Convention: he rode from Trenton in the forenoon and had nearly fainted when he dismounted, on account of the Heat. I called on Mrs. Martin this Evening but did not find her at her Lodgings. This City is now and has been for several Days excessive hot. Your Bill shall be honored for the Bodricks[?]. The Tea I shall not take, but shall comply with your Wishes, if I should find any better.

I think you conducted perfectly right with respect to your Uncle. Would it not be best lest Child Should not be accurate in delivering your Message, to send him a line informing him of your Reasons for not accepting a partial payment, and that You had thus communicated them to prevent Mistakes or any misconstructions?

I was writing to you on Sunday Morning, but I should have Spent the Day in Festivity, had I known it had been your Birth Day. God Grant my lovely Nancy, You may Live to see birth Days repeated, until Satiated with the Happiness of this Life. You ardently pant for that which is more compleat and permanent.

Colonel Hamilton returns to New York tomorrow Morning. I have with him gone thro the Bill for settling the residuary Estate of Mary Walters, having made some material Alteration. Others proposed, he thinks it best to communicate on principles of Delicacy to Mr. Harrison before he adopts them; and having taken the Bill with your pappa's Notes and the Will to New York, he has promised me to see your pappa and Mrs. Harrison on arriving there and to make the necessary Alterations. I have sent by him a pamphlet on female Education. I should write your pappa had you not mentioned his Absence but you will communicate this on his Return.

I was on Sunday Evening at Mrs. Cadwalladers with Major Butler and General Wayne. Mrs. Bond was also there and the Ladies made very particular enquiry about you and the Baby. They desired me to be frequent in my Visits and to give their Regards to you. Wayne says he saw Mrs. Reed in South Carolina; that she has lost her Colour entirely and has a sallow Appearance; and that Reed having frequently boasted there of his powers in Gallantry is chagrined exceedingly at having no prospects favourable to their Wishes. The Miss Bonds have wrote to their Mamma desiring her to give Information to their Brother that the Weather is too hot for him to return here at present: but their Sister observed on it, that they could not expect a Continuance of such Attention and did not view them in the proper light.

I was last Evening at Mrs. Morris: who was very particular and so was Mr. Morris about you and the Baby. General Mifflin inquired this Morning whether you was in Town, as he heard different Stories about it and Mrs. Mifflin wished to call on you. I informed him you was not and altho I have a great Respect for Mrs. Mifflin I certainly shall not call on her, because this is too much like Philadelphia Hospitality. I am very sure it is his Maneuvre not hers. Adieu my dearest Life, my Regards as usual to the Family, kiss little poppet heartily for both of us & be assured I am ever

yours affectionately   E. Gerry

ALS (Sang Collection, Southern Illinois University)

WEDNESDAY, AUGUST 15, 1787

GEORGE WASHINGTON: DIARY

Wednesday 15th.   The same—as yesterday.

THURSDAY, AUGUST 16, 1787

GEORGE WASHINGTON: DIARY

Thursday 16th. In Convention. Dined at Mr. Pollocks & spent the evening in my chamber.

THOMAS MCKEAN TO WILLIAM ATLEE

. . . The Convention is still sitting; nothing transpires. I am tired feasting with them. Some say, they will continue together about two more weeks, others say two months. . . .

ALS (Library of Congress)

FRIDAY, AUGUST 17, 1787

Friday 17th.   In Convention. Dined and drank Tea at Mr. Powells.

ELBRIDGE GERRY TO ANN GERRY

Fryday Philada. 17th Aug. 87

My dearest Girl

   I was at the City Tavern the last Evening, at the Time of Mr. King's arrival & read your letter with the four inclosed. I am with You very much greived at the Accounts Mr. Warren gives of Mrs. Russell and wish You would write her on every Opportunity. Inclosed is a line to the postmaster respecting the postage, which being either a Mistake or Imposition, must be refunded. I am extremely pleased with the Letter from our lovely Friend in Dublin and shall inclose my answer to you by the earliest opportunity. I feel very much for Mrs. Knox, and the affection which we mutually feel for our Infant must produce Sympathy for the Loss of hers. I anticipated your Intentions of riding, or rather the necessity of the measure, in my last and I think it will be necessary to guard against the Coolness and dampness of Mornings and Evenings, and also of the house when washed, which is very apt to injure adult persons, much more Infants. The baby should not be carried in a Room the day it is washed. I have a Servant recommended to me, but he does not suit. He cannot Drive, and seems to be fearful of doing too much. Some Members of the convention are very impatient, but I do not think it will rise before three Weeks. I am done thinking of the Miss Bonds; they are quite giddy and will require Time to recover their senses. Inclosed is a letter from your Brother Robert, whose Accounts of the hurricane are very distressing. I have called four times on Mrs. Martin, without finding her at home. Mr. Hazzelhurst inquired for you a day or two since and apologized for not knowing You was in Town. He and Mrs. and Miss Hazzlehurst called at your lodgings as soon as they heard of it, but you was gone. He is an englishman, and whether this is philadelphia economy or not, I will not undertake to determine but by his frankness am disposed to think otherwise. One of the letters you inclosed was from Mr. Fayerweather, who says, Mr. Prentice has put into the Barn 100 bushells at least of good rye, and that the hay, corn, buckwheat and apple trees are very promising. Mrs. Miss and Mr. Jack Fayerweather, with all the neighbours desired their best respects to yourself and Miss Thompson. Adieu my dearest Life, take Care of yourself, our lovely infant I know will be faithfully attended. Kiss her always for me and yourself and with my sincere Regards to all your Family be assured I am ever your most affectionate E. Gerry

Was the cover of the letter stamped with the Word "Boston"; if not it was put on in New York. Desire your Brother to deliver the Letter to the postmaster and receive his answer: and if it should be in the negative, to inform him I shall consider this a gross Imposition and inform of it to proper Authority.

ALS (Sang Collection, Southern Illinois University)

SATURDAY, AUGUST 18, 1787

GEORGE WASHINGTON: DIARY

Saturday 18th.   In Convention. Dined at Chief Justice McKeans. Spent the afternoon & evening at my lodgings.

GEORGE WASHINGTON: ANECDOTE

In response to Gerry's motion of this day that no standing army exceed 3,000 men (Farrand, II, 329), Washington is alleged to have suggested a counter-motion that "no foreign enemy should invade the United States at any time, with more than three thousand troops."

(Paul Wilstach, *Patriots off Their Pedestals* [reprint ed., Freeport, N.Y., 1970], 29)

SUNDAY, AUGUST 19, 1787

GEORGE WASHINGTON: DIARY

Sunday 19th.   In company with Mr. Powell rode up to the white Marsh. Traversed my old Incampment, and contemplated on the dangers which threatned the American Army at that place. Dined at German town. Visited Mr. Blair McClenegan. Drank Tea at Mr. Peters's and returned to Philadelphia in the evening.

ROGER SHERMAN TO HENRY GIBBS

Philadelphia Aug. 19th 1787

. . . I hope the Convention will rise by the last of this month, but it is uncertain. . . .

ALS (Yale University Library)

MONDAY, AUGUST 20, 1787

PIERCE BUTLER: MOTION[1]

And to make all Laws, not repugnant to this Constitution that may be necessary for carrying into execution the foregoing powers and such other powers as may be vested by this Constitution in the Legislature of the United States.

P. Butler

PHOTOSTAT (Library of Congress)

GEORGE WASHINGTON: DIARY

Monday 20th. In Convention. Dined, drank tea and spent the evening at Mr. Morris.

NATHANIEL GORHAM TO NATHAN DANE

Philadelphia Aug. 20 1787

Dear Sir

. . . The Proprietors of a large library in this place have complimented us with the use of it. We sometimes saunter there for amusement. Among other books are large treatises on Heraldry. Mr. King and I have sometimes diverted ourselves in looking for the coats of Arms of most of our Acquaintances.[2] Among others we found the name of Dane, as per the inclosed Sheet. Believe me to be very sincerely Yours.

N. Gorham

ALS (New England Historic Genealogical Society)

---

1. Madison indicated that the "necessary and proper" clause, contained in the Committee of Detail report of August 6, was considered and approved on this day. The present motion, written and signed by Butler, but not introduced, was apparently prepared as a substitute for the Committee of Detail language (Farrand, 2:344–45).

2. As noted above (July 7), King also diverted himself by borrowing from the Library Company of Philadelphia "Grosse's Voyages 2 vols. and Andrews' letters on France." Luther Martin borrowed "Jones' Asiatic Poems."

TUESDAY, AUGUST 21, 1787

MOTIONS[1]

I.

The Legislature shall fulfill the Engagements[2] of the United States and consider themselves equaly bound as Congress now are to the Creditors of the same.

II.

All demands either of States or Individuals against the United States shall be as good and valid under this present Government as the former and all the duties and authority of Congress in this behalf shall devolve upon this Legislature.

PHOTOSTAT (Library of Congress)

GEORGE WASHINGTON: DIARY

Tuesday 21st.   Did the like this day also.

JOHN FITCH TO WILLIAM SAMUEL JOHNSON

Philadelphia 21 August 1787

Honored Sir:

Gratitude compells me to return you my sincere thanks for the honor you did me yesterday in calling to see my works, as the Countenance of such exalted Characters must give energy to any undertaking. I humbly beg leave thro' yourself to return my thanks to the Honourable Gentlemen that accompanied you and pray the further countenance and patronage of

1. The extent of the new government's obligations to pay its debts and those contracted by the states and Congress during the Confederation period was debated between August 18 and 25. The two motions printed here—the first in Butler's hand, the second in a hand unidentified—were apparently prepared during this period, probably between August 21 and August 25 (Farrand, 2:325–26, 355ff.). They are among the Butler Papers in the Library of Congress.

2. The superscription "foreign" was added before this word, apparently at a different time.

yourself and those Worthy Gentlemen in bringing to perfection so great an undertaking as I now have on hand. Pardon me Sir for saying no more than that I am.

Your most Devoted and very Humble Servant
John Fitch

ALS (Connecticut Historical Society)

ELBRIDGE GERRY TO ANN GERRY

Philadelphia 21st August 78

I made the same Mistake my dearest Girl respecting the post that You did, and went myself to the Stage House, but could not find an Opportunity to transmit a letter. I am happy to hear that you & our dear infant are well, God grant that You may continue so: I was really uneasy at not hearing from You on friday or Saturday. I was at Mrs. Bonds on Sunday evening where I found Mrs. Cadwallader. They interrogated me on my not calling oftener on them and were very kind in every respect particularly in their inquiries about you and the baby. I perfectly agree with you in your observations on the conduct of certain persons. I think their friends, was it known would be much displeased with them: I mentioned in my last that I had received my little friend and Companion, who presents herself to my view every morning and evening regularly for a kiss.

We cannot fortell or forsee the Decrees of Omnipotence respecting our existence, that is a matter which he wisely conceals from mortals: but I do not expect a long life, my constitution appears not to be formed for it, and such as it is, constant attention of one kind or another pray on it: but if anything makes life in the least desirable it is you, my dearest girl and our lovely offspring. Detached from your comforts, life to me Would be a source of evils. When troubles occur now, I reflect that they are of no consequence, compared with the happiness resulting from my little family. This opens a prospect which satisfies every Desire. Your pappa is in the Instance you mention too sudden; he desired me to see *Hamilton* and Doctor Johnson and I saw them both. Hamilton was disposed to all the alterations proposed and made several: but as some required an alteration of the State of Facts in consequence of your pappa's minutes, Hamilton said he would have that done in New York as soon as he arrived, first consulting your pappa and seeing him with Harrison. He thot that as Harrison drew the Bill, delicacy required such a mode of proceeding, and indeed I should have conducted in the same manner had the case been my own. I think it would be best for your pappa to meet them, and after they have made the alteration, I will consult Doctor Johnson, if he will send the Bill and Will. I see their design of procrastination, but these things have their course, and cannot be too much hastened. Who married Miss Sukey Van horn? Do I know him? I am as sick of being here as You can conceive. Most of the Time I am at Home or in convention. I do not think in a Week I am ten hours any where else. We meet now at ten and sit till four: but entre nous, I do not expect to give my voice to the measures. Tell your mamma and the young ladies I am surprized to hear such Accounts of them: what is the matter with your brother. Kellus appears to be very industrious. He lived with Stevenson, his wife's Mother was named Fischer, but is now married to John Cuyler who as well as Stevenson live in the Bowery. Is Mr. Osgood's Man really sick? I desired your pappa to request You to take care of him. I would have you hire a coach when you want one. Major Butler informs me of Mrs. Butlers arrival at Newport in 48 hours: she desired particularly her compliments and mentioned our letters as acts of friendship and politeness. Inclosed is the letter from our lovely Friend at Dublin and the answer which you will seal and send to her: also your brother Roberts Letter. Adieu my dearest Life, kiss heartily our dear little poppet for me, and with my regards to your mamma and all the family be assured I am ever your sincere and affectionate

E. Gerry

ALS (Sang Collection, Southern Illinois University)

WEDNESDAY, AUGUST 22, 1787

GEORGE WASHINGTON: DIARY

Wednesday 22d.   In Convention. Dined at Mr. Morris's farm at the Hills. Visited at Mr. Powells in the Afternoon.

THURSDAY, AUGUST 23, 1787

Thursday 23d.   In Convention. Dined, drank Tea & spent the evening at Mr. Morris's.

WILLIAM PATERSON TO OLIVER ELLSWORTH

> New Brunswick,
> 23d. August, 1787.

What are the Convention about? When will they rise? Will they agree upon a System energetick and effectual, or will they break up without doing any Thing to the Purpose? Full of Disputation and noisy as the Wind, it is said, that you are afraid of the very Windows, and have a Man planted under them to prevent the Secrets and Doings from flying out. The Business, however, is detailed, I hope you will not have as much Alteration upon the Detail, as there was in getting the Principles of the System, if you should, Patridge himself, if Patridge was alive, would not be able to foretell the Time of your rising. I wish you much Speed, and that you may be full of good Works, the first mainly for my own Sake, for I dread going down again to Philada.—

My Compliments to all your Fellow-Labourers under the Same Roof—

Farrand, 4:73

JAMES McHENRY TO PEGGY McHENRY

> Philadelphia 23 August 1787

My dear Peggy

It is altogether uncertain when the Convention will rise; but it is likely to be about three weeks hence. . . .

Your uncle has at length assigned his effects to his creditors; but I understand he does not intend to avail himself of the bankrupt act which I think he ought to do. . . .

PHOTOSTAT (Library of Congress)

WILLIAM SAMUEL JOHNSON TO JOHN FITCH

Thursday Afternoon 23d August

Dr. Johnson presents his Compliments to Mr. Fitch and assures him that the Exhibition yesterday[1] gave the Gentlemen present much satisfaction. He himself, and he doubts not the other Gentlemen, will always be happy to give him every Countenance and encouragement in their Power, which his Ingenuity and Industry entitles him to.

ALS (Library of Congress)

1. At least two members of the Convention—James Wilson and Robert Morris— were financial backers of Fitch. He demonstrated his steamboat on the Delaware River on August 22 before (by his account) almost all of the Convention members. On September 5 Fitch wrote Edmund Randolph, inviting the "Honorable Members of the Convention to make a short Voyage in the Boat," which would "be ready the beginning of next week." Apparently, no collective cruise occurred, but Oliver Ellsworth had gone aboard Fitch's boat before he departed the Convention on August 23 (Fitch to Randolph, September 5, 1787, Library of Congress; Franklin B. Dexter, ed., *The Literary Diary of Ezra Stiles*, 3 vols. [New York, 1901], 3:279).

FRIDAY, AUGUST 24, 1787

GEORGE WASHINGTON: DIARY

Friday 24th.   Did the same this day.

SATURDAY, AUGUST 25, 1787

MOTION[1]

No Regulation of Commerce or Revenue shall extend to giving the Ports of One State any preference to those of another State. Nor to oblige Vessels bound to or from one State, to pay any Toll or Duty in any other but the State they may have cleared out for. Neither shall they meet with any Stopage Molestation or Hindrance from the Ports or Batteries of any other State. The Legislature of the different States shall have full power to Establish such ports of Entry and Clearance in their Individual States as they may think proper.

PHOTOSTAT (Library of Congress)

GEORGE WASHINGTON: DIARY

Saturday 25th.   In Convention. Dined with the Club at Springsbury & spent the afternoon at my lodgings.

WILLIAM LIVINGSTON TO JOHN TABOR KEMPE

Philadelphia 25 August 1787

Sir

I received your letter of the 11th of April a few days before I set out the second time for this place as a member of the federal convention of the United States. Having left that Body for a week to adjust my private affairs which were rather deranged when I joined it as I had been previously a

---

1. On this day motions were introduced prohibiting preferential commercial regulations and governing the establishment of ports of entry. These "several propositions" were referred, the same day, to a committee which reported, August 28, a resolution resembling the first part of the motion printed here. This motion must, therefore, have been submitted to or generated by the committee, of which Butler was a member, on or shortly after August 25. The motion appears to be in Butler's hand; another draft motion, almost identical but in another hand, is in the Butler papers (Farrand, 2:417–18, 437).

month at Burlington with our Legislature and went from thence to the Convention without returning home it was impossible for me to enter upon the agreeable task of serving you.

TR (Massachusetts Historical Society)

SUNDAY, AUGUST 26, 1787

GEORGE WASHINGTON: DIARY

Sunday 26th.   Rode into the Country for exercise 8 or 10 miles. Dined at the Hills and spent the evening in my chamber writing letters.

JAMES McHENRY TO PEGGY McHENRY

Philadelphia 26 August 1787

My dear Peggy.

. . . I am now going to drink tea at your aunts after which I propose to spend half an hour in the state house walks, and then return home to finish the evening with the poetic and ingenious Haley. I am very much pleased with this writer and wish that I could send you all that he has published, but I do not believe that his works are to be had in town. . . .

PHOTOSTAT (Library of Congress)

ELBRIDGE GERRY TO ANN GERRY

Phila. 26 August

In consequence my dearest Life of your Letter of the 22d I have paid off Kellus and he goes this day for New York. He behaved very well while with me, but is totally unqualified for a house Servant. He proposes to wait on you with recommendations, but I am doubtful whether he understands anything of coachmanship. If he does, I would risque his drinking unless you think it is hazardous: indeed a driver never should be subject to a failing of this kind: and I suspect he is too much in this way, because one of his recommendations says, "he is *generally* sober"—you can therefore direct him to call when I return to N. York. I fear my dearest Girl, You do not exercise eno. This Season never agrees with You, I very well know, but was you to ride, bath in the Evening and leave off tea, I think you would find yourself better. You mistook my meaning with respect to my Lodgings: I meant my situation as a delegate was uneasy: I am exceedingly distrest at the proceedings of the Convention being apprehensive, and almost sure they will if not altered materially lay the foundation of a civil War. This entre nous. I hope you will meet with a [indecipherable] to your liking: the Stays I have and propose to send them by Vans whom you will notice. I sent a letter every post Day last week, those dated the 17th were sent on Monday: and yet you seemed to think I did not write as often as usual. Have the letters miscarried? I am unhappy that any low Spiritedness of mine should have so distressed my dearest nancy. On Monday & tuesday I was fatigued and rather unwell, but am recruited since. I never was more sick of any thing than I am of conventioneering: had I known what would have happened, nothing would have induced me to come here. I am and must be patient a little longer. Inclosed is another letter to our dublin friend, and an account of a hurricane which begun in Marlboro in Massachusetts and extended to weston, about 6 or 8 Miles from our House. Mr. Codman is here and says there are no hopes of Mrs. Russel and Miss Lever is in the same Way: he says she is very much emaciated and appears to be in a deep decline. I am very much afraid that She has been imprudent and if it is the case I shall pity her exceedingly. Mr. Vance says Mr. Tracy is still out, and that a Widow Lady of Newburyport Mrs. Amory put all her property into his hands amounting to about £10,000 our Currency, and is obliged to take her [three indecipherable words] from the want of property. But these are such delicate Subjects they will not bear mentioning unless between ourselves. [Name indecipherable] is returned and made a good Voyage: he accidentally put into some port where his cargo was wanted & made an expeditious and good sale. I dined at Mr. Morris' on Thursday, and he and Mrs. Morris made particular Enquiry. The Attentions to the convention ladies seems nearly at an End. I do not know but what it will be a pleasing reflection that we have not fatigued our philadelphia friends. I am very much concerned for your mamma. What is her complaint? Engage her to return with us to Massachusetts if possible. I think the Air will be a service to her. I long to see you my dearest Life & our little charmer as you justly call her [indecipherable phrase]. Kiss her for me so long as you can make it agreeable to her and be assured I am at all Times and on every occasion.

Yours affectionately   E. Gerry

ALS (Sang Collection, Southern Illinois University)

ABRAHAM LANSING TO ABRAHAM YATES

August 26 1787

Dear Sir

The Judge and my Brother have attended the Circuit in Montgomery County, from which place the former returned but two Days and will in the Morning go to Washington County to hold a Court. I find but little Inclination in either of them to repair again to Philadelphia and from their

General Observations I believe they will not go. Early in the Commencement of the Business at Philadelphia, my Brother informed me that he was
in sentiment with a respectable *Minority* of that Body, but that they had
no prospect of succeeding in the Measures proposed and that he was at a
stand whether it would not be proper for him to leave them. This Circumstance convinces me the more that they will not again attend. Mr.
Hamilton will consequently be disappointed and chagrined. We have reports here that Mr. Paine (Common Sense) is employed to write in favor
of the British form of Government and that the system which will be
recommended to the States will be similar to that Constitution the Kingly
part excepted. Your Intercourse with the high prerogative Gentlemen will
enable you to learn at Least the outlines of the Government which we are
in their Ideas to adopt or sink into Oblivion. The situation of our Country
is critical and truly alarming. If we once get fairly in Confusion it is hard
to say where we will stop. . . .

ALS (New York Public Library)

MONDAY, AUGUST 27, 1787

[JOHN BLAIR?][1]: DRAFT RESOLUTION

The Judicial power of the United States, shall be vested in one (or more) Supreme Court(s of Law, Equity or Admiralty and one Court to be established and sit at the place where Congress shall sit) ⟨and in such Courts of Admiralty as Congress shall establish in any of the States⟩—and also (one) ⟨in⟩ Court⟨s⟩ of Admiralty to be established (in each State—the Judges of which Courts shall hold their offices during good behaviour and shall at stated times receive for their Services a compensation which shall not be diminished during their Continuance in office—and no such Judge shall be capable of holding or exercising by himself or others, any other office under the United States or any of them—Nor have during—nor shall be appointed to any other such office whose emoluments are of greater value—within three years after a resignation of his office as Judge) ⟨in such of the States as Congress shall direct⟩—

The Jurisdiction of the Supreme Courts shall extend to all Cases in Law & Equity (and admiralty and maritime Jurisdiction) arising under this Constitution,—the Laws of the United States and Treaties made or which shall be made under their Authority; to all Cases affecting Ambassadors, other public Ministers and Consuls; to all Cases of Admiralty and Maritime Jurisdiction; to Controversies to which the United States shall be a party, to controversies between two or more States; between *Citizens of the Same State* ⟨Persons⟩ claiming Lands under Grants of different States, and between *a State and the Citizens thereof* and foreign States, Citizens or Subjects.

In all Cases affecting Ambassadors, other public Ministers and Consuls—and those in which a state shall be a party ⟨and Suits between persons claiming Lands under Grants of different States⟩ the Supreme Court shall have original jurisdiction—And in all the other Cases before mentioned the Supreme Courts shall have appellate Jurisdiction as to Law only—except in Cases of Equity and Admiralty and Maritime Jurisdiction in

1. The attribution to Blair, on the basis of what evidence is unknown, was made by an unidentified hand in Mason's papers in the Library of Congress. Farrand was evidently unwilling to accept the attribution. Parts crossed out in the original are indicated by parentheses; Mason's emendations are enclosed in angle brackets.

which last mentioned Cases the Supreme Court shall have appellate Jurisdiction, both as to Law and Fact—

In all Cases of Admiralty and Maritime Jurisdiction, the Admiralty Courts appointed by (the) Congress shall have original Jurisdiction, and an Appeal may be made to the Supreme Court of Congress for any Sum and in such manner as Congress may by law direct.

In all other Cases not otherwise provided for the *Superior* State Courts shall have original Jurisdiction, and an Appeal may be made to the Supreme ⟨Federal⟩ Court (of Congress) in all Cases where the Subject in Controversy—or the Decree or Judgment of the State Court shall be of the value of one thousand Dollars and in Cases of less value the Appeal shall be to the High Court of Appeals, Court of Errors or other Supreme Court of the State where the Suit shall be tryed—

The Trial of all Crimes, except in the Case of impeachment shall be in the Superior [Court] of that State where the offence shall have [been] committed in such manner as the Congress shall by Law direct, except that the Trial shall be by a Jury—But when the Crime shall not have been committed within any one of the United States the trial shall be at such place and in such Manner as Congress shall by law direct, except that such Trial shall also be a Jury.

Farrand, 4:54–56

George Washington: Diary

Monday 27th.   In Convention. Dined at Mr. Morris's and drank Tea at Mr. Powells.

TUESDAY, AUGUST 28, 1787

Wheresoever any person bound to service or labour in any state, shall flee into another state (it shall be lawful for the person entitled to such service or labour to reclaim and recover him) he shall not be thereby discharged from such service or labour: but the legislatures of the several states shall make provision for the recovery of such person.

PHOTOSTAT (Library of Congress)

George Washington: Diary

Tuesday 28th.   In Convention. Dined, drank Tea, and spent the evening at Mr. Morris's.

James McHenry to Peggy McHenry

Philadelphia, 28 Augt. 1787

My dear Peggy

It is extremely distressing to me to be under the necessity to remain a day longer in this place, where I find no enjoyments whatever and am even without the satisfaction of knowing that what I am assisting in will meet the approbation of those who sent me hither. The only consolation which arises to me is from a hope that my stay will be of shorter duration than I have suggested, when I look to home to repay me for the sacrifice I am making of my happiness. . . .

PHOTOSTAT (Library of Congress)

---

1. This motion, in the Pierce Butler papers though not in Butler's hand, was related to his and Charles Pinckney's effort, August 28, "to require fugitive slaves and servants to be delivered up like criminals." Butler withdrew the proposal "in order that some particular provision might be made apart from this article." The next day he successfully moved the adoption of a fugitive slave clause, which with some alteration was included in article 4, section 2, of the Constitution (Farrand, 2:443, 453–54).

246

WEDNESDAY, AUGUST 29, 1787

GEORGE WASHINGTON: DIARY

Wednesday 29th. Did the same as yesterday.

ELBRIDGE GERRY TO ANN GERRY

Wednesday Aug. 29

What is the Cause my Dearest Love that you are of late so liable to fainting? I am quite distressed about it. If you do not find relief soon, I shall quit the convention, and let their proceedings take their chance. Indeed I have been a Spectator for some time; for I am very different in political principles from my colleagues. I am very well but sick of being here; indeed I ardently long to meet my dear nancy. I think we shall not be here longer than a fortnight, and if it was possible I would leave this place immediately. I wrote three or four letters last week, and this is the fourth this Week, including one that accompanies the Stays. I am very sure I did not send a letter without franking it, and think the cover must have been taken off. There are a set of beings here capable of any kind of villainy to answer their purposes and I think they need not open this letter, to know my opinion of them: but if that measure is necessary, they have my permission. I think they have intercepted some before, and that a person who is a notorious turn-coat knows the contents. If he should open this he will know who I mean, by his interrogating me whether I had heard from a particular friend. I will seal with my Cypher in future. Adieu my dearest Girl, let me hear that you are happy and I may bid defiance to any injuries from politics. Kiss our little darling, give my regards to all Friends and be assured I am your most affectionate

E. Gerry

If you conclud to take the silk or as much of it as is wanted I will not look farther.

ALS (Sang Collection, Southern Illinois University)

ABRAHAM YATES, JR., TO JEREMIAH VAN RENSSELAER
AND HENRY ACTHANDT

New York 29 August 1787

Mr. King was here the beginning of the Week before last told me the Convention would he supposed Report by the first of September, last Week it was reported (in the Congress Room) that a Misunderstanding had happe'd In this Convention, that they were now so far from agreeing that it would be a doubt whether they would agree in time so as that this Congress can take up the Matter—Since I have been informed that there is an additional Difficulty Ariseing from the Massachusetts Members, all along four have attended, one of the four (I Suppose a high flier) is gone home, the Others Refusing to agree to what was Intended to be reportd.

These are Information I have Picked up from the Members of Congress and I begin to Suspect that the Secrecy has a Stronger operation upon me (my Sentiments being so well known) as upon others that Differ. Upon the whole I belive You had better not make this public as coming from me but to keep it among the frnds it may be good information to Yates and Lansing.

Farrand, 4:74

THURSDAY, AUGUST 30, 1787

August the 30th

Objections to the Constitution as far as it has Advanced

   1st. No privilige is given to the House of Representatives, which by the way are too few, in disposition of money; by way of counter ballance to the permenent condition of the Senate, in the circumstances of duration, power, & smallness of Number.

   2d. The expulsion of members of the Legislature is not sufficiently Checked.

   3d. The inequality of Voices in the Senate is too great.

   4th. The power of Raising Armies is too unlimited.

   5th. The sweeping Clause absorbs every thing almost by Construction.

   6th. No Restriction is made on a Navigation Act and certain Regulations of Commerce.

   7th. The Executive is One.

   8th. The power of pardon is Unlimited.

   9th. The appointment to Office will produce too great influence in the Executive.

   10th. The Jurisdiction of the Judiciary will swallow up the Judiciaries of the States.

   11th. Duties on Exports are forbiden but with the assent of the General Legislature of the U.S.

PHOTOSTAT (Library of Congress)

GEORGE WASHINGTON: DIARY

Thursday 30th.   Again the same.

   1. From the Pierce Butler papers and in Butler's hand, but evidently copied from a document prepared by another delegate, for the objections contain remonstrances against provisions—a single executive—which Butler strongly favored. Many of the objections appear with amplification in George Mason's statement of September 15, leading to the assumption that they were formulated by the Virginia delegate (Farrand, 1:88–89, 2:637–40).

BENJAMIN RUSH TO TIMOTHY PICKERING

August 30, 1787.

The new federal government like a new Continental waggon will overset our State dung cart, with all its dirty contents (reverend, and irreverent) and thereby restore order and happiness to Pennsylvania. From the conversations of the Members of the Convention, there is reason to believe the foederal Constitution will be wise—vigorous—safe—free—& full of dignity.—General Washington it is said will be placed at the head of the new Government, or in the stile of my simile, will drive the new waggon.

Farrand, 4:75

JOHN DICKINSON TO POLLY DICKINSON

August 30, 1787

. . . It is expected, we shall finish about the middle of September, when I hope, the sight of you and our dear dear Children in Health will give inexpressable Delight to

Your truly affectionate
John Dickinson

ALS (Historical Society of Pennsylvania)

FRIDAY, AUGUST 31, 1787

GEORGE MASON: ALTERATIONS PROPOSED[1]

The Council of State, instead of being formed out of the Officers of the great Departments—to consist of not less than five, nor more than seven Members, to be constituted and appointed by Law; or by 2/3ds. of the Senate,[2] with a duration & Rotation of Office, similar to that of the Senate.

The Objects of the National Government to be expressly defined, instead of indefinite powers, under an arbitrary Constructions of general Clauses.

Laws disapproved by the Executive, not to be reinacted, but by a Majority of 2/3ds. instead of 3/4ths. of the Legislature.

No Laws, in the Nature of a Navigation Act, to be passed, but by a Majority of 2/3ds. of the Legislature.

The Duties imposed upon Imports, by the National Government, to be the same in all the States.[3]

The Legislature to be restrained from establishing perpetual Revenue.

Laws for raising or appropriating Revenue, or fixing the Salleries of Officers, to originate in the House of Representatives.

1. From the Pierce Butler papers. A briefer version of this document—the last two articles missing, the order different—in James Madison's hand, dated at the bottom edge of the page, August 31, 1787, is in the Madison Papers, Library of Congress. See Farrand, 4:56–57. On the back of the document Madison wrote: "The within paper communicated to Js. Madison Jr. by Docr. McHenry March 16 1788 with a note subjoined that it was given by Mr. Mason to one of the Maryland deputation for their consideration—with information that if the alterations could be obtained the system would be unexceptionable. Their concurrence and assistance to carry them was requested." A longer version of this document, missing the last article but in other respects virtually identical to the one printed here, has been found in the Dickinson Papers at the Historical Society of Pennsylvania. Since Dickinson and Butler were both members of the so-called Committee on Postponed Parts, appointed on August 31, Mason apparently prepared this document for distribution to members of that committee.

2. Dickinson draft: "or to consist of six Members, to be appointed by 2/3 of the Senate."

3. Marginal note: "since adopted."

The Members of both Houses to be ineligible to Offices under the National Government; except to Commands in the Army or Navy; their Seats to be vacated by accepting such Commands, and to be ineligible during their continuance.

The President of the united States to be ineligible a second Time.

The power of making Treaties, appointing Ambassadors &c. to be in the Senate, with the Concurrence of the Council of State—or vice versa.

The Appointment of all Offices, established by the Legislature, to be in the Executive, with the Concurrence of the Senate, or vice versa.

The power of granting pardons in the Executive not to extend to Impeachments, or to Treason—nor to preventing or staying process before Conviction & to be so expressly defined, as not, by any Construction to apply to persons convicted under the Laws & Authority of the Respective States.

The following is the Substance of a Clause, which was offered & miscarried in the Convention; it will come in very properly in the 5th. Section of the IV Article referred for reconsideration after the word *except*—"Bills for raising Money for the purposes of Revenue, or for appropriating the same, or for fixing the Salleries of the Officers of Government, shall originate in the House of Representatives, & shall not be so altered or amended by the Senate as to encrease or diminish the Sum to be raised, or change the Mode of raising, or to Object of its' Appropriation."

PHOTOSTAT (Library of Congress)

PIERCE BUTLER: NOTES[4]

Money Bills	The Clause restraining the origination of Money Bills—rejected.
Add. 1 Clause Art. 7	To pay the Debts and provide for the Common Defense and General Welfare.
	The Clause in the Report of the Committee of five limiting the duration of Tax Acts and money appropriations—rejected.

4. These notes appear to have been produced in the Committee on Postponed Parts, appointed on August 31, of which Butler was a member. They are in his hand.

Trade. Art. 7th Sect 1st   To regulate with foreign Nations, among the several States and with Indian Tribes. No Person shall be eligible to the Office of President who shall not have arrived at the Age of 30 Years neither shall any person be so eligible who shall not be a natural born Citizen of the United States, excepting those who now are or at the time of the Adoption of this Constitution shall be a Citizen of the said States any one of whom may be President, provided that at the time of his Election He shall have been an Inhabitant for fourteen Years.

PHOTOSTAT (Library of Congress)

GEORGE WASHINGTON: DIARY

Friday 31st.   In Convention. Dined at Mr. Morris's and with a Party went to Lansdale & drank Tea with Mr. & Mrs. Penn.

SATURDAY, SEPTEMBER 1, 1787

GEORGE WASHINGTON: DIARY

Saturday 1st.   Dined at Mr. Morris after coming out of Convention and drank Tea there.

ELBRIDGE GERRY TO ANN GERRY

Saturday 1 Sep.

I am distressed my dearest Girl exceedingly, at the information in yours of the 29th and the notice of your indisposition, and shall prepare myself to leave this city on the arrival of the next post unless you are better: indeed I would not remain here two hours was I not under a necessity of staying to prevent my colleagues from saying that I broke up the representation, and that they were averse to an arbitrary System of Government, for such it is at present, and such they must give their voice to unless it meets with considerable alterations. I think it probable that the Convention will rise in ten days, but in case of my absence my dearest Life I think it will be proper and indeed necessary for you to take Rhubarb two or three evenings successively, and drink gruel morning and evening with cold camomile tea when thirsty, to remove that Sickness & pain in your Stomach. Likewise have a chicken boiled every day and drink the broth without fat on it or much thickenning, taking care that it is not weak and that it is seasoned with such herbs as you like. I am glad you have quitted tea, but milk is not good for the Bile, which afflicts you at present. I am very happy to hear our little darling is so thriving and wish most ardently to have the same good tidings respecting yourself. It has been very warm here, but I have not Suffered much. As to Kellus I am done thinking of him: I have had two others offering their Service Since he went away, but Servants in general are a pack of such idle fellows, that without the best recommendations I am not disposed to take any of them. I sent you two letters for Miss Stanford and you mention the receipt of only one. The silk is not a good bargain by any means. I will desire Miss Dally to look out for some here and will shop myself. What quantity is sufficient for a suit.

Sunday

Yesterday I dined with General Pinckney and Mrs. Pinckney made particular inquiry for you and the baby. There was considerable company, and she was very agreable and attentive. The General is as we always thot the cleverest being alive. I love him better every time I meet him. Mrs. Pinckney says Mrs. Butler proposes to return to New York from Newport, having been there some time without being introduced to a person. I am sorry for this, but she should not have gone or remained there without letters to some of the citizens. Mrs. Rimbaugh landed at New York; did you hear of it or was her stay too short for you to know it or for her to know you was there? She had an infant about the age of ours, which died on the passage. It was ill when they left Charleston and she had hopes by the voyage of saving it. I have not seen her, but had this from Mrs. Pinckney. Don't omit what I have recommended for restoring your health, as I am persuaded there is no necessity for you taking nauseous draughts of physicians, and they generally make their patients invalids. Give my warmest Regards to your mamma, sisters brother & pappa if he has returned; kiss our delightful little darling plentifully for me and be assured I am ever

Yours most affectionately

E. Gerry

ALS (Sang Collection, Southern Illinois University)

SUNDAY, SEPTEMBER 2, 1787

GEORGE WASHINGTON: DIARY

Sunday 2d.   Rode to Mr. Bartrams and other places in the Country, dined & drank Tea at Grays ferry and returned to the City in the evening.

WILLIAM SAMUEL JOHNSON TO ANNE JOHNSON

                    Philadelphia Sunday Evening 2d. September 1787
My Dearest
    I am much obliged to you for your kind offer to meet me at N. York and I wish very heartily I could now tell you with any certainty when I may probably be so happy as to arrive there, but we meet with so many unforseen delays that I can yet fix no time with any degree of precision, tho I still hope it may be in about a fortnight. . . .

ALS (Connecticut Historical Society)

RICHARD DOBBS SPAIGHT TO JOHN GRAY BLOUNT

                    Philadelphia 2 September 1787
Dear Sir
    I have for a long time past flattered myself that every post would bring me a letter from you in answer to those I have wrote you but have not as yet been favored with a single line. My situation here is extremely distressing as I expected when I came away only to stay six weeks or two months at farthest. I made a money provision merely for that term, and out of that, forty one dollars still remain in the hands of Mr. Blackledge who was to send them after me, but I have not heard from him since I left No. Carolina. I have now overstayed this term. I counted upon two months and shall be here till tomorrow week when I hope to get away provided I can get money to pay off my accounts here and bear my expences home. While I have no other means of doing than by borrowing and no other way of doing that, than to get some friend to lend me his name to a note for thirty days and get it discounted at the bank and depend for the payment of it on the remittance I expect you will make for me. You will therefore do me an essential service by remitting on the best terms you can

such monies as you have received upon my account as speedily as possible. I suppose you will send the remittance to Stuart and Bars. I will then leave directions with them to whom to pay it.

The Convention will I imagine finish their business by next saturday in that case if I can be supplied with cash I shall leave this the monday following.

I am with regard & esteem

Your most Obt. Ser^t.
Rich^d. Dobbs Spaight

ALS (North Carolina Division of Archives and History)

MONDAY, SEPTEMBER 3, 1787

George Washington: Diary

Monday 3d. In Convention. Visited a Machine at Doctr. Franklins (called a mangle) for pressing, in place of Ironing, clothes from the wash. Which Machine from the facility with which it dispatches business is well calculated for Table cloths & such Articles as have not pleats & irregular foldings and would be very useful in all large families. Dined, drank Tea, & spent the evening at Mr. Morris's.

Nicholas Gilman to John Sullivan

Philadelphia September 3 1787

. . . It is respecting the domestic debt. I find many of the States are making provisions to buy in their Quotas of the final Settlements and I most ardently wish that the Towns in New Hampshire may be so far awake to a sense of their Interest as to part with their property freely in order to purchase their several Quotas of the public Securities now in circulation while they are to be had at the present low rate; which is in this place, at two shillings and six pence in the pound. If they suffer the present opportunity to pass and we should be so fortunate as to have an efficient Government, they will be obliged to buy them of Brokers, Hawkers, Speculators and Jockeys, at six or perhaps at eight times their present value. I know your Excellency is well aware of the danger the people are in of suffering through their unwillingness to pay taxes, but perhaps if they were fully sensible of the measures that are pursuing in other States, it might operate as a new incentive to an immediate exertion.

ALS (New Hampshire Division of Records)

TUESDAY, SEPTEMBER 4, 1787

PIERCE BUTLER: NOTES ON DEBATES

Pinckney. To be acquainted with the talents of the person elected. He would not vote for a good Man unless He thought He would be elected but he would vote for any Man that would be likely to turn out the President. No Sir[1]

GEORGE WASHINGTON: DIARY

Tuesday. 4th.   In Convention. Dined &ca. at Mr. Morris's.

WILLIAM LIVINGSTON TO JOHN JAY

September 4, 1787
. . . The mountains will bring forth before long, but as they will go longer than any the best man and wisest upon earth would have calculated, it is less to be feared that the birth will be such a fetus as a ridiculous mouse, than a monstrum horrendum ingens. . . .

ALS (Columbia University Library)

---

1. Pinckney expressed doubts on both September 4 and 5 about the abilities of presidential electors to acquire sufficient knowledge of the candidates; thus his remarks, recorded by Butler, could have been made on either day (Farrand, 2:501, 511).

WEDNESDAY, SEPTEMBER 5, 1787

GEORGE WASHINGTON: DIARY

Wednesday 5th.   In Convention. Dined at Mrs. Houses & drank Tea at Mr. Binghams.

THURSDAY, SEPTEMBER 6, 1787

GEORGE WASHINGTON: DIARY

Thursday 6th.   In Convention. Dined at Doctr. Hutchinson's and spent the afternoon and evening at Mr. Morris's.

FRIDAY, SEPTEMBER 7, 1787

JAMES MADISON: MOTION

But no Treaty (of peace)[1] shall be made without the concurrence of the House of Representatives, by which the territorial boundaries of the U.S. may be contracted, or by which the common rights of *navigation* or *fishery* recognized to the U. States by the late treaty of peace, or accruing to them by virtue of the laws of nations may be abridged[2]

Farrand, 4:58

GEORGE WASHINGTON: DIARY

Friday 7th.   In Convention. Dined and spent the afternoon at home (except when riding a few Miles).

---

1. Words in parentheses crossed out.

2. Note added in John C. Payne's hand: "The subject was then debated, but the motion does not appear to have been made."

SATURDAY, SEPTEMBER 8, 1787

GEORGE WASHINGTON: DIARY

Saturday 8th.   In Convention. Dined at Springsbury with the Club and spent the evening at my lodgings.

ALEXANDER HAMILTON TO MR. DUCHE

Philadelphia, Sept. 8, 1787

I am very sorry that the situation of affairs here will not permit me to tell you what I want. I can not without indiscretion add anything to what I have already said.

According to all appearances the Convention will conclude toward the middle of the week. Up to now nothing has been communicated to the public about its operations.

You can tell the Marquis de la Fayette something which will bring him the greatest pleasure, that is, there is every reason to believe that if the new Constitution is adopted his friend General Washington will be the Chief.

I am etc.

MICROFILM COPY (Archives of the French Foreign Ministry, Consular Correspondence, 909)

SUNDAY, SEPTEMBER 9, 1787

George Washington: Diary

Sunday 9th.   Dined at Mr. Morris's after making a visit to Mr. Gardoqui who as he says came from New York on a visit to me.

Jonathan Dayton to Elias Dayton

Philadelphia, September 9, 1787
. . . We have happily so far finished our business, as to be employed in giving it its last polish and preparing it for the public information. This, I conclude, may be done in three or four days, at which time the public curiosity and our desire of returning to our respective homes will equally be gratified. Give this information to Mr. Boudinot who is very desirous, I suppose from his letter, of hearing. . . .

ALS (Harvard University)

James McHenry to Peggy McHenry

Philadelphia, Sunday, 9 Sept. 1787
. . . It is likely the convention will finish their business in about eight days. . . .

PHOTOSTAT (Library of Congress)

Elbridge Gerry to Ann Gerry

Philadelphia 9th September
Sunday Evening
I have received, my dearest Girl, your letter of the 5th and it is impossible to say what time we shall rise this week, some say not 'till the latter end, others about the middle. I am myself of opinion that Thursday will finish the Business to which I have every prospect at present of giving my negative. I am very happy indeed that you are better and hope you will not be troubled with a return of your complaints, which have very much distressed me. I am clearly of your opinion respecting the taste for dress in this City and your choice my dearest love is always conclusive with me.

I only give you this information, which never can injure before we form our determination. I have not seen any silks here yet that I like and unless I find one we will take that which you mention. I called on Mr. Gardoqui who arrived here yesterday, this evening but found him not at home. Miss Ross daughter of Mr. Ross who dined with us at Mr. Bonds and sister to Miss Ross whom Mr. Vaughan wants to address, a young lady about 18 was buried this evening. She came to town this day week with Miss Nixon and Miss West who had spent several days at Mr. Ross's, and returned home in the evening. The next day she was seized with a violent fever and delirium which continued till yesterday morning, when she expired. She was remarkably gay the day week before she died and was a fine sprightly Girl, as I am informed, a serious momento this, not to be too solicitous about events of any kind. I intended this evening to call on Miss Bonds but I am growing more and more indifferent about an acquaintance that seems to have very little friendship for its foundation. I have found only one piece to pattern your curtains: it may do to make a counter of this and to take yours for repairing the curtain unless you think the black streak will be much seen. Oh how I long to be with you, our little frolicksome pet and friends at New York: when will the time arrive. Adieu my dearest Love, kiss the little child and give my sincere regards to all the family and

believe me ever your most affectionate
E. Gerry

I think your answer to this will find me here.

ALS (Massachusetts Historical Society)

GEORGE WASHINGTON TO GEORGE AUGUSTINE WASHINGTON

Philadelphia, Septr. 9th 1787

Dear George,

This acknowledgment of your letter of the 2d of this Month is probably the last letter that I shall write you from this place, as the probability is that the Convention will have compleated the business which brought the delegates together in the course of this Week. God grant I may not be disappointed in this expectation, as I am quite homesick. . . .

ALS (John Rylands Library)

MONDAY, SEPTEMBER 10, 1787

GEORGE WASHINGTON: DIARY

Monday. 10th.   In Convention. Dined at Mr. Morris's & drank Tea there.

ELBRIDGE GERRY TO SAMUEL PURVIANCE

                                    Philadelphia 10th September 1787
My dear Sir
    . . . The Convention will probably rise in a day or two, but the Injunction to Secrecy still remains. . . .

ALS (Huntington Library)

TUESDAY, SEPTEMBER 11, 1787

GEORGE WASHINGTON: DIARY

Tuesday 11th.   In Convention. Dined at home in a large Company with Mr. Gardoqui. Drank Tea and spent the evening there.

WILLIAM LIVINGSTON TO JOHN JAY

September 11, 1787

. . . But my hopes of returning by the time expected are a little clouded by reason of there being certain creatures in this world that are more pleased with their own speeches than they can prevail upon any body else to be. . . .

ALS (Columbia University Library)

WEDNESDAY, SEPTEMBER 12, 1787

GEORGE WASHINGTON: DIARY

Wednesday 12th.   In Convention. Dined at the Presidents and drank Tea at Mr. Pines.

THURSDAY, SEPTEMBER 13, 1787[1]

GEORGE MASON: SUGGESTED REVISIONS OF COMMITTEE OF STYLE REPORT

refused

In the beginning of the 4th. Clause of the 3d. Section of the 1st. Article—Strike out the words—*the Vice president of the united States* and instead of them insert—a vice-president of the United States shall be chosen in the manner hereinafter directed who

refused

In the 3d. Clause of the 5th. Section of the 1st. Article, after the words *such parts* add—of the Journals of the Senate.—

agreed to

At the end of the same Clause add—and a regular Statement & Account of the Receipts & Expenditure of all public money shall be published from time to time[2]

refused

In the 8th. Section of the 1st. Article to the Beginning of the Clause, before the words *To provide for organizing arming & disciplining the Militia*—add—That the Liberties of the People may be the better secured against the Danger of regular Troops or standing Armys in time of Peace

refused

In the 3rd. Clause of the 9th. Section of the 1st. Article strike out the words—nor any ex post facto Law

agreed

In the 4th. Clause of the same Article after the words *Census*—add—or Enumeration.—

refused

In the 1st. Clause of the 10th. Section of the same Article strike out ex post facto Laws.—& after the words *obligation of* insert—previous

In the latter End of the 3d. Clause of the 2d. Article—Enquire of the Committee about the Senate chusing the vice president

In the 7th. Clause of the 1st. Section of the 2d. Article—strike out the words—*during the period for which he shall have been elected*—and instead of them insert—so as in any manner to affect the person in office at the time of such Encrease or Diminution—

1. The dating follows that in Robert Rutland, ed., *The Papers of George Mason*, 3 vols. (Chapel Hill, 1970), 3:983–85, rather than Farrand, who placed this document at September 15. The document could, in fact, have been composed any time between September 13 and 15.

2. "From time to time" is in Washington's hand.

At the end of the 1st. Clause of the 2d. Section of the 2d. Article—

add the words—or Treason; but he may grant Reprieves in Cases of Treason, until the End of the next ensuing Session of Congress

agreed At the End of the 2d. Clause of the 2d. Sec: of the 2d. Article add—and which shall be established by Law

*but the Congress may by Law vest the Appointment of such inferior officers as they think proper in the president alone— in the Courts of Law, or the Heads of Departments

Section 4th. of the same Article—Inconsistency between this & the 7th. Clause of the 3d. Section of the 1st. Article—Amend by inserting after the word *Office,* the words—and disqualified from holding or enjoying—any office of Honour—Trust or Profit under the United States.—

Article 3d. Sec: 1. before the word *diminished*—insert—encreased or—

In the 2d. Clause of the 2d. Sec: of the 3d. Article—strike out the word *Fact*—and insert—Equity—

In the 3d. Sec: of the 3d. Article—*Corruption of Blood* inaccurately expressed; and no Exception or Provision for the wife—who may be innocent, & ought not to be involv'd in Ruin from the Guilt of the Husband—

Sec: 2. Article 4th. The Citizens of one State having an Estate in another, have not secured to them the right of removing their property as in the 4th.—Article of the Confederation*

Article 5th. By this Article Congress only have the Power of proposing Amendments at any future time to this Constitution, & shou'd it prove ever so oppressive, the whole people of America can't make, or even propose Alterations to it; a Doctrine utterly subversive of the fundamental Principles of the Rights & Liberties of the people

In the 9th. Sec: of the 1st. Article after the Clause no Tax or Duty shall be laid on Articles exported from any State

disagreed   Insert

No Law in the Nature of a Navigation Act shall be passed before the year 1808 without the Assent of two thirds of the members present in each House

not proposed *Amend by adding the following Clause

and any Citizen having an Estate in two or more States shall have a Right to remove his property from one State to the other

Farrand, 4:59–61

GEORGE WASHINGTON: DIARY

Thursday 13th.   Attended Convention. Dined at the Vice Presidents Chas. Biddles. Drank Tea at Mr. Powells.

FRIDAY, SEPTEMBER 14, 1787

MOTION[1]

provd that no Monopoly be granted or trading Co. established

PHOTOSTAT (Library of Congress)

GEORGE WASHINGTON: DIARY

Friday 14th.   Attended Convention. Dined at the City Tavern, at an entertainmt. given on my acct. by the City light Horse. Spent the evening at Mr. Meridiths.

---

1. This motion, in an unidentified hand in the Pierce Butler Papers, may have been prepared on September 14 or 15, when both George Mason and Elbridge Gerry expressed apprehensions that the power to regulate trade could be construed to permit the creation of "mercantile monopolies" (Farrand, 2:616, 633).

SATURDAY, SEPTEMBER 15, 1787

GEORGE WASHINGTON: DIARY

Saturday 15th. Concluded the business of Convention, all to signing the proceedings; to effect which the House sat till 6 Oclock; and adjourned till Monday that the Constitution which it was proposed to offer to the People might be engrossed and a number of printed copies struck off. Dined at Mr. Morris's & spent the evening there.

Mr. Gardoqui set off for his return to New York this forenoon.

THOMAS FITZSIMONS TO NOAH WEBSTER

Philadelphia, September 15, 1787

Dear Sir:

I shall make you no apology, for addressing myself to you upon the present occasion, because you must be especially interested with me in the event, and having contributed my mite to the service of our common country, I have some right to call upon others for assistance. I consider the present moment as the crisis that will determine whether we are to benefit by the revolution we have obtained, or whether we shall become a prey to foreign influence and domestic violence. The business of the convention is nearly at an end and a few days will bring before the people of America the constitution prepared for their future government. That it is the best which human wisdom could devise, I mean not to assert; but I trust it will be found consistent with the principles of liberty and calculated to unite and bind together the members of a great country. It is already too evident that there are people prepared to oppose it, even before they are acquainted with the outline, and it is easy to see that if unreasonable jealousies are disseminated, its Adoption may be at least protracted. In my mind, to delay is to destroy. There are so many interests, foreign and domestic, opposed to order and good government in America, as to warrant an apprehension of their interfering, if time is given for cabal and intrigue. . . .

TR (Yale University)

JOHN DICKINSON TO GEORGE READ

September 15

Dear Sir,

Yesterday I was prevented by a severe Headache from attending in Convention, and I am now setting off for Wilmington.

Some person mentioned to Me, that the Members were to give an Entertainment to the Gentlemen of the Town, from whom we have received Civilities. I therefore beg that You will apply the enclosed Bank bill for Me to that Use.

I am Sir
Your sincere Friend
John Dickinson

ALS (Delaware Hall of Records)

SUNDAY, SEPTEMBER 16, 1787

GEORGE WASHINGTON: DIARY

Sunday 16th. Wrote many letters in the forenoon. Dined with Mr. & Mrs. Morris at the Hills & returned to town in the Eveng.

JAMES McHENRY TO PEGGY McHENRY

Philadelphia 16 September 1787

My dear Peggy.

   Yesterday evening the plan of government passed by an unanimous vote, and tomorrow we shall determine the mode to promulgate it and then put an end to the existence of the convention. . . . .

PHOTOSTAT (Library of Congress)

MONDAY, SEPTEMBER 17, 1787

GEORGE WASHINGTON: DIARY

Monday 17th.   Met in Convention when the Constitution received the Unanimous assent of 11 States and Colo. Hamilton's from New York (the only delegate from thence in Convention) and was subscribed to by every Member present except Govr. Randolph and Colo. Mason from Virginia & Mr. Gerry from Massachusetts. The business being thus closed, the Members adjourned to the City Tavern, dined together and took a cordial leave of each other—after which I returned to my lodgings—did some business with, and received the papers from the secretary of the Convention, and retired to meditate on the momentous wk. which had been executed, after not less than five, for a large part of the time Six, and sometimes 7 hours sitting every day, sundays & the ten days adjournment to give a Comee. opportunity & time to arrange the business for more than four Months.

THURSDAY, SEPTEMBER 20, 1787

September 20, 1787

Congress assembled. . .

"In Convention Wedy. Sept. 5th. 1787 *Resolved,* That the United States in Congress be requested to allow and cause to be paid to the Secretary and other Officers of this Convention such sums in proportion to their respective times of service as are allowed to the Secretary and similar Officers of Congress.

Ordered that the Secretary make out and transmit to the treasury Office of the United States an account for the said services and for the incidental expenses of this Convention.

G. Washington, Presidt."

Board of Treasury to take Order to settle with and pay the Officers and incidental charges mentioned in the resolution of the Convention, conformable to the recommendation therein contained.[1]

Farrand, 4:76–77

1. At this point Farrand published the following footnote:

In a statement of Expenditures of the Civil List from 1st July to the 30th September 1787, signed by Joseph Nourse, Register, there are the following entries for the expenses of the Convention as paid by Congress.

CONGRESS

Sept. 21 William Jackson, esqr. late Secretary to the Foederal Convention for his Salary during the sitting thereof agreably to an Act of Congress of 20th September 1787	
4 months at 2600 dollars per annum is	866.60
Septemr. 21 To William Jackson esqr. Secretary to the Foederal Convention for the allowance made by Act of Congress of 20th Septr. 1787	
to the door keeper 4 months at 400 dollars per annum	133.30
to the Messenger 4 months at 300 dollars per annum	100.00
to the Clerks employed to transcribe and engross	30.00
Sept. 21 Stationary purchased for the use of the Foederal Convention paid therefor	36.00

SEPTEMBER 29, 1787

CHARLES COTESWORTH PINCKNEY TO MATTHEW RIDLEY

New York Sepr. 29. 1787

Dear Sir Matthew:

Yesterday Congress passed the Constitution agreed on by the Federal Convention, and resolved to transmitt it to the several states for the assent and ratification of State Conventions to be chosen in each state. This is done that it may be paramount to all state Constitutions and that all laws made in pursuance thereof may be the supreme Law of the Land. A Gentleman who is going to London has promised to take charge of this Letter, and to put it into the post there; as I understand you pay no inland postage I shall enclose an authentic Copy of the Constitution, which both as a Philosopher and a Politician you may wish to peruse. I do not suppose it will meet your entire approbation, but when you consider the different Interests and Habits of the several states and that this plan of government was the result of mutual concession and Amity, it will account for the introduction of some clauses that may appear to you exceptionable. You should read the Letter from the Convention to Congress before you read the Constitution, as we have there briefly stated our reasons for having made it such as it is. I make no doubt that it will be very soon adopted by a large Majority of the states; and I shall set out for Carolina tomorrow that I may be present when it is considered by our state. . . .

ALS (Northumberland County Record Office)

OCTOBER 30, 1787

NATHANIEL GORHAM TO BENJAMIN FRANKLIN

Boston Oct. 30th, 1787

The speech you made in Convention just before the close of the business & I think the last day of our siting, was in the opinion of every one who heard you—exceedingly well calculated to correct that possitive attachment which men are too apt to have for their own ideas.—I am sure that it is a temper such as that speach inculcates which prevents war & blood shed—the one I allude to is that where you observe on the French Lady who thought herself always in the right.

The request I would therefore with all respectful deference make you is that you would be so kind as to furnish me with a copy of it for the purpose of publishing it, provided you do not think it improper. . . .

I will take care to do it in such manner as not to wound your delivery of sentiments.

On the whole I submit the matter to your superior judgment—being anxious & desirous that you may be of the same mind with me on this subject—

Farrand, 4:78

NOVEMBER 3, 1787

RUFUS KING AND NATHANIEL GORHAM: RESPONSE TO ELBRIDGE GERRY'S OBJECTIONS[1]

The provision in the report of the Convention authorises one Rep. for every 30,000 Inhab. (taken comformably to the Census) ascertained as is there proposed—from the best materials that have been collected the united States at this Time contain 3 mils. of Inhab. comprehending all the Free Inhabitants & 3/5 only of the Slaves—this number wd. give 100 Rep— it is true that the first house will consist of only 65 Members, but the Congress must cause the Numbers of Inhab. to be taken within 3 yrs, and may do it within one—If the present Numbers will give 100 Reps. and the Opinion is well founded which we take to be the Case, that the people of america double in 25 years, then in 25 years the Number of Reps may be 200, in 50 years 400, in 75 years 800, and in One Century 1600—it is true that the (Compact) Rept. does not make it *necessary* that the Members shall be thus increased, in a direct proportion with the increase of the Inhab. but only declares that they shall not *exceed* one for every thirty thousand; they may be less, they may be in that proportion, but they cannot be more numerous—this indeed appears to us a sufficient provision to produce such a Repn. of the people in the house of Reps as will completely and safely accomplish the objects of their Appointment.

The 2d objection (made by Mr. G.) "that the people have no security for the right of Election" is in our Judgment as destitute of foundation as the first—Mr. Gerry admits the right of Election to be well deposited. He agrees that only the Electors of Representatives to the most numerous Br. of the state Legislature ought to be Electors of Representatives to the federal Govt. and then asserts that the exercise of this Right vested by the Rept. in the Electors is not secured—we are at a loss to know how Mr. Gerry would support this assertion or where the Report is defective on this point—the Time place & manner of electing Representatives must in the first instance be prescribed by the state Legislatures, but the Congress may make or alter the regulations on this Subject, possibly Mr. G. may ground

1. Farrand printed an extract of this document under the date January 24, 1788 (2:368). In the document printed here, we have followed Farrand's style of enclosing in parentheses parts of the text that were crossed out in the original.

his Objection upon this authority's being vested in Congress—we wish to submit our remarks on this clause to your candid consideration—we agree and have always contended that the people ought to enjoy the exclusive right of appointing their Rep. but we also hold it an important principle that as it is of consequence to the Freedom of the people that they should possess the right of Election so it is essential to the preservation & Existence of the Government that the people should be bound to exercise it for this reason in the Constitution of Massachusetts not only the persons are clearly designated and their Qualifications ascertained, who may vote for Representatives, but the Genl. Court have a right to compel the Electors to exercise their rights of elections, and thereby to preserve the Government from Dissolution—

If the Time place and manner of electing Representatives to the General Court was left entirely to the several Towns in the Commonwealth and if the constitution gave no power to the Genl. Court to require and compel the Towns to Elect Representatives, there wd. be a manifest defect in the Constitution, (and an omission in the Instrument of Government,) which agreeably to the Course of human Affairs (would) might in a short period subvert the Government—Town after Town from disaffection or other motives might refuse to elect Representatives, Counties & larger districts might combine against sending members to the General Court, (they might be disposed to divide the state, set up for separate states, and the Government might be in this silent manner be totally overthrown) and in this silent manner the Govt might be wholly destroyed—If these remarks are just as applying to this State and prove the propriety of vesting as the Constitution has done a power in the Genl. Court to compel the Electors to exercise their right of Election, they are equally just in Relation to Congress, and equally prove the propriety of vesting in that assembly a power to compel the Electors of the federal Representatives to exercise their rights and for that purpose if necessary to make Regulations concerning the Time place & manner of electing members of the H. of Reps—

It may be said that the State Legislatures are more capable of regulating this subject than the Congress; that Congress may fix improper places, inconvenient Times, and a manner of electing contrary to the usual practice of the several States, it is not a very probable supposition that a law of this Nature shd. be enacted by the Congress but let the supposition be ever so probable as applied to cong. it is thirteen Times more probable that some one of the States may make these inconvenient Regulations than that Congress should enact them Congress will be interested to preserve the United States entire and to prevent a dismemberment—the individual States may some of them grow rich & powerful; and as the great members of the antient Confederacies have heretofore done, they may be desirous of becoming wholly independent of the Union and therefore may either omit to form any Regulations or Laws, concerning the Time place & manner of electing federal Rep. or they may fix on improper places, inconvenient Times, & a manner of Electing wholly disagreeable to the people. Should either of these cases take place, and no power be vested in Congress to revise their Laws or to provide other Regulations, the Union might be dismembered and dissolved, without a constitutional power to prevent it. But this revisionary power being vested in Congress, the States will make wise & prudent regulations on the Subject of Elections, they will do all that is necessary to keep up a Representation of the People; because they know that in case of omission the Congress will make the necessary provision for this Object—[2]

"Some of the powers of the Legis. are ambiguous & others indefinite & dangerous"—this clause contains an imputation so very general that no reply in detail can be attempted without commenting on every sentence wh. forms the Grant of powers to Congress—Most of the sentences are transcribed from the present confederation, and we can only observe that it was the intention and honest desire of the Convention to use those expressions that were most easy to be understood and lest equivocal in their meaning; and we flatter ourselves they have not been intirely disappointed—we believe that the powers are closely defined, the expressions as free from ambiguity as the convention could form them, and we never could have assented to the Report had We supposed the Danger Mr. G. predicts—

The Executive is blended with & will have an undue influence over the Legislature—The same objection might be made agt. the constitution of this State, the executive & legislative powers are connected in the same manner by our constitution as they are said by Mr. G. to be blended in the Rept. of the Convention—when the Govr. objects to a Bill, it cannot become a law unless 2/3 of both branches afterwards concur in enacting it, the same must be done by the Congress provided the president objects— but as experience has not proved that our Executive has an undue influence over the Legislature—we cannot think the objection well founded.

"The judicial Department will be oppressive" a concise examination of the Report on this Subject may refute this unsupported Objection—The president with consent of the Senate will appoint the Judges—the Govr. with advice of Council appoints the Judges of this State—the Senate are in this instance in the nature of a Council to the President and if we have no reason to complain of the manner in wh. the Judges in this Commonwealth are appointed, from the great similarity in the two cases there seems to be no Ground of complaint agt. the manner of appointing the federal Judges—the Judicial Department is divided in to a supreme and inferior

2. Marginal note: "R. Island required by Cong. & refused to send Delegates."

Courts—in a few enumerated instances the supreme Court have original & final Jurisdiction—in all the other cases which fall within the federal Judicial, the supreme court may or may not have appellate Jurisdiction as congress shall direct—for the appellate Jurisdiction of the supreme court is subject to such exceptions and regulations as Congress may think proper to establish or in other words Congress may determine what causes shall be finally tried in the inferior Courts, and in what causes appeals shall be allowed to the Supreme Court—But it may be said that in a triffling controversy between a Citizen of M. & N.H. or between the U.S. & a Citizen of any individual state, or in any of the cases where the Supreme Court have not original Jurisdiction, that either of the parties may carry the case by appeal from the inferior Court before the Supreme Court, and that the place of their Sessions may be at one extreme of the Union, and thereby the Department may become highly oppressive—The same Objection may be raised against the Judicial Department as established in our Constitution—Because the General Court may erect a supreme Court, Courts of common pleas, & Justices Courts it may be objected, that in a small cause cognizable by a Justice of the peace of the County of Lincoln between an inhabitant of Cumberland and an inhabitant of Lincoln, or in an excise or impost Cause between an Inhabitant of Lincoln & the Commonwealth, that either of the parties may appeal from the Court of Justice to the S.C. and that their Sessions may be fixed by the G. Court in Berkshire another extreme of the State; & thus the State Judicial may become oppressive—We again refute a remark made on a former occasion that as experience has not shewn this Oppression of the Judicial under the Constitution of this State, and as the General Court have from Time to Time made such laws as have prevented such oppression, we cannot but suppose that the Members of the federal Government will be actuated by motives equally pure, and that they will enact laws in like manner tending to the ease & happiness of the People.

Distinction *between the Power* to make a law & the law When made (It is proper on this Subject to observe, that there is a distinction between the power to make a law & the law itself the report of the convention in this instance partakes of both in some instances it is a law, and in others merely an authority in pursuance of which Congress may enact Laws)

Treaties of &c may be formed by the President wt. advice of 2/3 of a Quorum of senate (It is not improbable upon mature reflection that you will be of Opinion that) the clause as it stands in the report is two 3d. of the senators present—The Senate have power over their own members and can compel their attendance—if the senators are all present, then no Treaty can be formed without the Consent of Nine States or Eighteen Senators, and of the President—Under the present Confedn. Treaties of the highest importance can be formed by the Delegates of Nine States without the concurrence of any other person, so that if the Senators attend the Duties of their Office, and they may be compelled, instead of its being more easy as Mr. G. suggests to form Treaties it in Fact may be much more difficult than under the present Confederation, and in our Judgment the public Security will not only be increased, but the Objects of Treaties will far more probably be obtained by the powers of forming them being vested in the Prest. & 2/3 of the present Senators than by (their) remaining as is provided in the present Confedn. The Report requires the joint consent of both branches of Congress together with the Concurrence of the Presidt. to declare war—this is preferable to vesting that power in the President & Senate—and as war is not to be desired and always a great calamity, by increasing the Checks, the measure will be difficult—but as peace is forever to be desired, and can be alone obtained by Treaty it seemed preferable to trust it with the President & Senate—

When the constitution vests in the Legislature "full power & authority to make and ordain all manner of wholesome & reasonable Orders, laws Statues, ordinances, directions & instructions" as is the case with the Consn. of this State (Cap. 1, Ar. 1. Sect. 4.), a Declaration or Bill of Rights seems proper, But when the powers vested are explicitly defined both as to quantity & the manner of their Exercise a Dec[larati]on or Bill of Rights is certainly unnecessary & improper—

John Kaminski and Gaspare Saladino, eds., *The Documentary History of the Ratification of the Constitution* (Madison, 1981), 13:550–55.

DECEMBER 2, 1787

DANIEL CARROLL TO BENJAMIN FRANKLIN

Annapolis Dec. 2d. 1787

I am afraid you will think that I have transgressed on your act of kindness, when I inform you that I have been compelled to make use of your observations delivered in the Committee of Convention on the subject of Representation, & those delivered on the 17th of Sept.—the House of Delegates having pass'd a Resolve requesting the attendance of their Deputies to give them information of the proceedings in Convention, Messrs. McHenry, Jenifer, Martin & myself attended. . . .

Altho' Mr. McHenry distinguis'd himself on this occasion, beyond the most sanguine hopes of his friends, and the expectations of the adverse party, such motives were imputed to many of the Members, to Gl. Washington and yourself by name, and such a misrepresentation made, that I found myself compelled to let Mr. McHenry *read* your first speech already mention'd, and to *read* myself that delivered on the 17th of Sept. after having giving a *just* relation in what manner they were receiv'd by me, & that I did it at the risk of your displeasure, for the public Good.

I have not communicated these speeches to any but Messrs. Th. Johnson Mr. Carroll of Carrollton and my Brother untill this occasion, nor have I suffered any copy to be taken nor will not *without your permission* to persons *I can depend on* to be used occasionally for the same purpose I have done it, or will do any thing else with them you may require.

Farrand, 4:79

ROGER SHERMAN TO———

New Haven, December 8th, 1787

Dear Sir

I am informed that you wish to know my opinion with respect to the new Constitution lately formed by the federal Convention, and the objections made against it.

I suppose it is the general opinion that the present government of the United States is not sufficient to give them credit and respectability abroad or security at home. But little Faith or confidence can be placed in a government that has only power to enter into engagements, but no power to fulfil them.

To form a just opinion of the new constitution it should be considered, whether the powers to be thereby vested in the federal government are sufficient, and only such as are necessary to secure the common interests of the States; and whether the exercise of those powers is placed in safe hands. In every government there is a trust, which may be abused; but the greatest security against abuse is, that the interest of those in whom the powers of government are vested is the same as that of the people they govern, and that they are dependent on the suffrage of the people for their appointment to, and continuance in office. This is a much greater security than a declaration of rights, or restraining clauses upon paper.

The rights of the people under the new constitution will be secured by a representation in proportion to their numbers in one branch of the legislature, and the rights of the particular State governments by their equal representation in the other branch.

The President, Vice President and Senators, tho' chosen for fixed periods, are re eligible as often as the electors shall think proper, which will be a very great security for their fidelity in office, and will likewise give much greater stability and energy to government than an exclusion by rotation. . . . The greatest possible security that a people can have for their civil rights and liberties, is, that no laws can be made to bind them, nor any taxes be imposed upon them without their consent by representatives chosen by themselves. This was the great point contended for in our contest with Great Britain; and will not this be fully secured to us under the new constitution?

Declarations of rights in England were charters granted by Princes, or acts of Parliament made to limit the prerogatives of the crown, but not abridge the powers of the legislature. These observations duly considered will obviate most of the objections that have been made against the constitution. The powers vested in the federal government are only such as respect the common interests of the Union, and are particularly defined, so that each State retains its sovereignty in what respects its own internal government, and a right to exercise every power of a sovereign State not delegated to the United States. And tho' the general government in matters within its jurisdiction is paramount to the constitutions and laws of the particular States, yet all acts of the Congress not warranted by the constitution would be void. Nor could they be enforced contrary to the sense of a majority of the States. One excellency of the constitution is that when the government of the United States acts within its proper bounds it will be the interest of the legislatures of the particular States to support it, but when it overleaps those bounds and interferes with the rights of the State governments, they will be powerful enough to check it; but distinction between their jurisdictions will be so obvious, that there will be no great danger of interference.

The unanimity of the convention is a remarkable circumstance in favour of the constitution, that all the States present concurred in it, and all the members but three out of forty two signed it, and Governor Randolph, declared, that tho' he did not think fit to sign it, he had no fixed determination to oppose it, nor have I heard that he has since made any opposition to it. The other two Honorable Gentlemen whom I esteem for their patriotism and good sense have published their objections, which deserve some notice; and I think the foregoing observations on the principles of the constitution must evince that their fears are groundless. The peoples right of election is doubly secured, the legislatures of the particular States have right to regulate it, and if they should fail to do it properly, it may be done by Congress, and what possible motive can either have to injure the people in the exercise of that right. The qualifications of the electors are to remain as fixed by the State constitutions. It is objected that the number of representatives will be too small, but it is my opinion that it will be quite large enough if extended as far as the constitution will admit. The present number in both branches will consist of ninety one members which is the same number that the States have a right to elect under the confederation, and I have heard no complaint that the number is not sufficient to give information, of the circumstances of the States and to transact the general affairs of the Union; nor have any of the States thought fit to keep up the full representation that they are entitled to nor will the additional powers of Congress make it necessary to increase the number of members. They will have the additional powers of regulating commerce, establishing a uniform rule of naturalization, and laws on the subject of bankruptcies, and to provide for the punishment of counterfeiting coins and securities of the united States, and to prescribe a uniform mode of organizing, arming and training the militia under the authority of the several States, and to promote the progress of science by securing to persons for a limited time the benefit of their writings and inventions. The other powers are the same as Congress have under the articles of Confederation with this difference, that they will have authority to carry into effect, what they have now a right to require to be done by the States.

It was thought necessary in order to carry into effect the laws of the Union, and to preserve justice and harmony among the States, to extend the judicial powers of the confederacy. They cannot be extended beyond the enumerated cases, but may be limited by Congress, and doubtless will be restricted to such cases of importance and magnitude as cannot safely be trusted to the final decision of the courts of the particular States. The Supreme court may have a circuit through all the States to make the trials as convenient, and as little expensive to the parties as may be; and the trial by jury will doubtless be allowed in Cases proper for that mode of trial, nor will the people in general be at all affected by the judiciary of the United States, perhaps not one to an hundred of the citizens will ever have a cause that can come within its jurisdiction, for all causes between citizens of the same States, except where they claim lands under grants of different States, must be finally decided by the Courts of the State to which they belong.

The power of making war and raising and supporting armies is now vested in Congress who are not restrained from keeping up armies in time of peace, but by the new constitution no appropriation of money for that purpose can be in force longer than two years. But the security is that the power is in the legislature who are the representatives of the people and can have no motive to keep up armies unnecessarily. In order to [be] a well regulated government, the legislature should be dependant on the people, and be vested with a plenitude of power, for all the purposes for which it is instituted, to be exercised for the public good, as occasion may require. Powers are dangerous only when trusted in officers not under the control of the laws; but by the new constitution, Congress are vested with power to make all laws which shall be necessary and proper for carrying into execution, all the powers vested in the government of the United States, or in any department or officer thereof. . . .

TR (Yale University Library)

DECEMBER 15, 1787

NATHANIEL GORHAM TO BENJAMIN FRANKLIN

Charles Town Dec. 15, 1787

Your esteemed favour covering your observations I duly recd. . . . and had them (excepting a few lines) published; some very good Friends to our common Country supposed they might without injury to the performance be omitted—and as you was so obliging as to submit it in some to my disposition I ventured to do it—

Farrand, 4:80

DECEMBER 23, 1787

RUFUS KING TO JEREMIAH WADSWORTH

. . . [Mason] is now united with Patrick Henry in an attempt to prejudice the system, by suggesting to the proposed Convention a mode of effecting amendments. I understand that the Speaker of their Senate and the Speaker of the Representatives are to be authorized to open a Correspondence with the several *States* on the subject of the Constitution; to propose *to them* that their Conventions should suggest amendments and that a second Convention should be assembled at Philadelphia for the purpose of reconsidering the system, examining the proposed amendments, and reporting a revised Plan to be submitted for ratification to the State Conventions. This was the Plan of Governor Randolph in the federal Convention, but the idea met with an almost unanimous Disapprobation in that Assembly. . . .

ALS (Wadsworth Atheneum)

JUNE 3, 1788

[LUTHER MARTIN?]¹, OBSERVATIONS

Constitution as agreed to by the Convention at Philadelphia, until within a few days of their rising.

I. WE, the people, of the States of New-Hampshire, Massachusetts, Rhode-Island and Providence Plantations, Connecticut, N. York, New-Jersey, Pennsylvania, Delaware, Maryland, Virginia, North-Carolina, South-Carolina and Georgia, do ordain, declare and establish the following Constitution for ourselves and posterity.

Constitution as altered a few days before the Convention rose, and as now offered to the United States.

We, the people, of the United States, in order to form a more perfect union, establish justice, ensure domestic tranquillity, provide for the common defence, promote the *general welfare* and secure the blessings of liberty to ourselves and posterity, do ordain and establish this Constitution for the United States of America.

ART. I,

The style of this Government shall be *the United States* of America.

Struck out.

REMARKS.

As the Constitution was first agreed to, it exhibits the people as already associated in *politic* capacities, as the people of New-Hampshire, Massachusetts Bay, &c. and, of course maintaining those governments; and although they in that *corporate* capacity establish the following Constitution for themselves and their posterity, yet still it is done with respect to the governments *then* existing, and not by any means throwing off the existing

1. Martin published his *Genuine Information* in the December 28, 1787–February 8, 1788 issue of Hayes's *Maryland Gazette* and continued to publish Convention documents in that paper during the first half of 1788 (he evidently placed the New Jersey plan in the February 15, 1788 issue). The observations in the June 3 issue of the *Gazette* can be attributed to Martin because the commentaries on the contrasting sections of the Committee of Detail report and the Constitution as adopted repeat several of his characteristic objections to the Constitution, especially his alarm at its apparent supersession of the state bills of rights.

compacts, and acting *as unassociated individuals*.—As altered, every appearance of the *existing* governments, under their respective Constitutions, is relinquished, the very names struck out, general purposes and powers given extending to every purpose of the social compact, and then *this Constitution* including all these purposes, is made the Constitution of the United States, without any reserve of the several States and their Constitutions then existing; and then this Constitution enacted for these unlimited purposes, we afterwards find is expressly declared paramount to *all Constitutions*, and laws existing in the States.—It is said the alterations of nine States being sufficient to render it binding required this. It is nonsense, for if only nine States *agree* they are no more the people of the United States, than they are the people of the *disagreeing* States by name; but why put in those general and unlimited purposes and powers, and why strike out the first article containing the style of the government, which is that of a *confederacy*, and could only operate to resist the idea of one great consolidated government?

ART. V.

The times, places, and manner of holding elections of the members of each house, shall be prescribed by the legislature of each State, but their provisions, concerning them, may at any time be *altered* by the legislature of the United States.

The times, places, and manner of holding elections for senators and representatives shall be prescribed in each State by the legislature thereof; but the Congress may at any time by law, *make*, or alter such regulations, except as to the places of chusing senators.

REMARKS.

The insertion of the word *make*, gives Congress an *original* power in this business, which could only be necessary in case the States are at some period to lose all existence; for the word *altering* as it at first stood, would extend to every necessary purpose, supposing the States continued in their existence.

ART V.

Sect. The legislature of the United States, shall have power to lay and collect taxes, duties, imposts and exises.

The Congress shall have power to lay and collect taxes, duties, imposts and exises, to pay the debts, and *provide for the common defence and general welfare* of the United States.

REMARKS.

The original Constitution was very clear and express, cautiously avoiding the conferring of general powers, or powers in general terms, which amounts to the same thing—If these last powers are construed to extend to explain purposes to which money is to be applied, they are unnecessary; for the clause declaring and defining the manner of appropriation is sufficient—but the grammatical construction is a general grant of power—

and in every view supposing it was intended to give a general and undefined power, I know of no manner so effectual as this giving them money for this general and undefined purpose.

To *call forth the aid* of the militia to execute the laws of the union, *enforce treaties*, suppress insurrections, and repel invasions.

To *provide* for calling forth the militia to execute the *laws* of the union, suppress insurrections and repel invasions—To provide for organizing, arming and disciplining the militia, and governing such part of them as may be employed in the service of the United States, reserving to the States respectively, the appointment of the officers and the authority of training the militia according to the discipline prescribed by Congress.

REMARKS.

As the Constitution stood at first, *to call forth the aid, &c.* it was in the style of *requisition*, in which all *original* power remained with the State.—The word PROVIDE gives an *original* power; lest the *providing* which must mean making provisions or laws for organizing, arming, disciplining and governing the militia, gives a compleat power, and subjects the yeomanry of this country, at any, and all times, to *martial* law, which is not restrained in this Constitution, as it is in Great-Britain.—The *infering treatise*[2] is indeed struck out—but treaties being by a subsequent clause made *laws* of the land it became unnecessary, as they may be called to execute *treaties* as *laws*—and the compleat power over militia being given Congress, the States can have no defence left to support their rights, if they have any.

No *navigation* act shall be passed without the consent of *two-thirds* of the members present in each house.

Struck out entirely, and it ought to be a *sine qua non* with the *southern States*.

ART. X.

The Executive power, &c. but shall not be elected a second time.

The ineligibility struck out.

ART. XI.

The Judicial power of the United States, shall be vested in one Supreme Court, and in such inferior Courts as shall, *when necessary*, from time to time, be constituted by the legislature of the U. States.

The Judicial power of the United States, shall be vested in one Supreme Court, and in such inferior Courts as Congress may from time to time ordain and establish.

2. Obviously a printer's error; "inserting treaties" were probably the words as Martin originally wrote them.

Sect. 3. The jurisdiction of the   The *Judicial power* shall extend,
Supreme Court, &c.   &c.

REMARKS.

The manifest idea of the first Constitution was to confine the jurisdiction of the United States to one general supreme court, with an appeal from the State courts in particular cases—although, *if necessary* (which was then only explained to extend to *revenue* cases) they might establish some inferior courts, but no jurisdiction was assigned them by the Constitution, but by the alteration all the powers of jurisdiction are extended to all inferior federal courts, which will render them very numerous of course, and lay the foundation of swallowing up the State jurisdictions.

ART. VII.

The *acts of the legislature of the United States,* made in pursuance of this Constitution, and all *treaties* made under the authority of the United States, shall be the supreme law of *the several States,* and the judges of the several States shall be bound thereby in their decisions; any thing in the Constitutions or laws of the several States to the contrary notwithstanding.

This Constitution and the laws of the United States, which shall be made in pursuance thereof, and all treaties made, or *which shall be made,* under the authority of the United States, shall be the supreme *law of the land,* and the judges *in* every State shall be bound thereby; any thing in the Constitution or laws of any State to the contrary notwithstanding.

REMARKS.

A careful attention to the change in this clause will serve as a clue to all the other changes—in the clause as it first stood, only the acts of the legislature in pursuance of defined Constitution, which admitted of no general expression, were to be construed paramount to the Constitution and laws—As it is altered—an undefined Constitution with full general powers is declared to supercede all the State Constitutions and whether in part, or in what part, or whether in toto, no man can presume to say—secondly, by inserting after treaties made these words *and shall be made* the Constitution has an expost facto force, which is contrary to those very principles it seems anxious to establish—but thirdly, the original clause, clearly demonstrated that it was the intention of the Convention to execute this new Constitution by means, and thro' the intervention of the States, as it says—they shall be the supreme law of the *several States,* and the judges of the several States, but the alteration into supreme law of *the land,* and the judges *in* the several States, discover plainly the design of erecting one consolidating government universally pervading the land, and to be executed independant of the States and of course from necessity and on purpose abolishing them gradually, if it is not absolutely done by the very first alteration.—

Besides this, an appeal was then given both as to *law and fact*, at that late stage of the business, which effectually destroys the trial by jury in civil cases and may elude it in criminal cases—the establishment of the trial by jury in criminal cases only was not so important whilst it was intended to execute the Constitution thro' the medium of the State courts—nor would a bill of rights have been so essential as the bills of rights of the several States and rights incorporated in the Constitutions of the several States, would have been binding on the State courts, where not expressly done away by the new Constitution, but the executing the laws of Congress by national courts, who cannot be bound by these bills of rights totally reverses the subject. Almost all the objections to the proposed Constitution are grounded on these alterations, effected contrary to the sense of the Convention until within a few days of the end of their session.

The Maryland Gazette; or, The Baltimore Advertiser, June 3, 1788

HUGH WILLIAMSON TO JOHN GRAY BLOUNT

New York 3rd June 1788

. . . We all admire the beautiful Trope of Col. Mason at the Court House in the County where he was elected. You may have been taught said he to respect the Characters of the Members of the late Convention. You may have supposed that they were an assemblage of great Men. There is nothing less true. From the Eastern States there were Knaves and Fools from the States Southward of Virginia They were a parcel of Coxcombs and from the middle States Office Hunters not a few. . . .

ALS (North Carolina Division of Archives and History)

AUGUST 10, 1788

CHARLES PINCKNEY TO MATTHEW CAREY

Charleston August 10, 1788.

I would with pleasure send you a copy of my system on which those Observations are founded—(or rather it was a *speech at opening the system* & erroneously termed Observations) but I have not one.—the original being laid before the convention, & the copy I gave to a gentleman at the northward.—If you think the copy of the system is indispensable to the publication, I am sorry it is not in my power to procure it for you.—The System was very like the one afterwards adopted with this important addition—that it proposed to give to the federal government an absolute Negative on all the laws of the States.

Farrand, 4:80

OCTOBER 1788

JAMES MADISON: REMARKS ON JEFFERSON'S DRAFT OF A CONSTITUTION

A revisionary power is meant as a check to precipitate, to unjust, and to unconstitutional laws. These important ends would it is conceded be more effectually secured, without disarming the Legislature of its requisite authority, by requiring bills to be separately communicated to the Exec: & Judicy depts. If either of these object, let ⅔, if both ¼ of each House be necessary to overrule the objection; and if either or both protest agst. a bill as violating the Constitution, let it moreover be suspended notwithstanding the overruling proportion of the Assembly, until there shall have been a subsequent election of the H. of Ds and a re-passage of the bill by ⅔ or ¼ of both Houses, as the case may be. It sd not be allowed the Judges or the Executive to pronounce a law thus enacted unconstitul & invalid.

In the State Constitutions & indeed in the Fedl. one also, no provision is made for the case of a disagreement in expounding them; and as the Courts are generally the last in making their decision, it results to them, by refusing or not refusing to execute a law, to stamp it with its final character. This makes the Judiciary Dept. paramount in fact to the Legislature, which was never intended, and can never be proper.[1]

Farrand, 4:81

---

1. This paragraph, omitted by Farrand, is printed from Robert Rutland, ed., *The Papers of James Madison*, 15 vols. (Charlottesville, 1962–), 11:293.

MARCH 28, 1790

JAMES MADISON TO TENCH COXE

Your idea of appropriating a district of territory to the encouragement of important inventions is new and worthy of consideration. I can not but apprehend however that the clause in the constitution which forbids patents for that purpose will lie equally in the way of your expedient. Congress seem to be tied down to the single mode of encouraging inventions by granting the exclusive benefit of them for a limited time, and therefore to have no more power to give a further encouragement out of a fund of land than a fund of money. This fetter on the National Legislature tho' an unfortunate one, was a deliberate one. The Latitude of authority now wished for was strongly urged and expressly rejected. . . .

ALS (Library of Congress)

JAMES MADISON TO EDMUND PENDLETON

If Congress can do whatever in their *discretion* can be *done by money*, and will promote the *general welfare*, the Government is no longer a limited one possessing enumerated powers, but an indefinite one subject to particular exceptions. It is to be remarked that the phrase out of which this doctrine is elaborated, is copied from the old articles of Confederation, where it was always understood as nothing more than a general caption to the specified powers, and it is a fact that it was preferred in the new instrument for that very reason as less liable than any other to misconstruction. Remaining always & most Affecly yours

ALS (Library of Congress)

JANUARY 16, 1802

JOHN DICKINSON TO GEORGE LOGAN

Wilmington the 16th of the 1st Month 1802

. . . In the first section of the second Article it is said—"Each State shall appoint, in such Manner as the legislature thereof may direct, a Number of Electors equal to the whole Number of Senators and Representatives, to which the state may be entitled in the Congress" etc.

After the word "Electors" should be inserted these words—"to be chosen by the people," which will be agreeable to the true Meaning of the Constitution. This is manifest from a fair Interpretation of the whole Instrument by comparing the different parts and from the most reputable contemporary Exposition of it.

As I was one of the Convention who framed the Constitution, I can affirm, that the Intention of that Assembly was that the Electors should be chosen by the People and not appointed by the Legislatures of the States.

There was a Committee of one delegate from each state appointed by the Convention, to consider of and report the most adviseable Mode of chusing the President. I do not pretend to be exact as to words, as I write from Recollection.

I was the Member from Delaware. One Morning the Committee met in the Library Room of the State House, and went upon the Business. I was much indisposed during the whole Time of the Convention. I did not come into the Committee till late, and found the members upon their Feet.

When I came in, they were pleased to read to Me their Minutes, containing a Report to this purpose, if I remember rightly—that the President should be chosen by the Legislature. The particulars I forget.

I observed, that the Powers which we had agreed to vest in the President, were so many and so great, that I did not think, the people would be willing to deposit them with him, unless they themselves would be more immediately concerned in his Election—that from what had passed in Convention respecting the Magnitude and accumulation of those powers, We might easily judge what Impressions might be made on the Public Mind, unfavorable to the Constitution We were framing—that if this single Article should be rejected, the whole would be lost, and the States would have to work to go over again under vast Disadvantages—that the only true and safe Principle on which these powers could be committed to an Individual, was—that he should be in a strict sense of the Expression, *the Man of the People*—besides, that an Election by the Legislature, would form an improper Dependence and Connection.

Having thus expressed my sentiments, Governieur Morris immediately said—"Come, Gentlemen, let us sit down again, and converse further on this subject." We then all sat down, and after some conference, James Maddison took a Pen and Paper, and sketched out a Mode for Electing the President agreeable to the present provision. To this we assented and reported accordingly. These two Gentlemen, I dare say, recollect these Circumstances.

The full Exercise of this momentous Right being positively secured to the People, by Terms that will admit of no Controvercy, it should be further provided, that the Electors of the President, should be chosen by those of the people in each State, who shall have the Qualifications requisite for Electors of the most numerous Branch of the State Legislature. Perhaps, it may also be adviseable, to provide for the Case of two or more persons voted for as Electors of the President having an Equality of Votes.

I have a heartfelt Pleasure in trusting, that the practice of appointing the Electors of the President by the Legislature of any States, will be for ever abolished. Whatever advantages we Republicans derive at present from such a practise, which tho devised by our Opponents has, like all the rest of their Contrivances, turned against them, Yet—we ought with a Magnanimous Integrity to cast them away from us, and putting our Trust in Divine protection, with singleness of Heart, make Truth, Justice, and the Happiness of our Country, the only Objects of our political Attentions. . . .

By the Constitution it was designed, that the President should entirely owe his Elevation to the will of the people directly declared through their Organs the Electors. This was a broad and solid Base for him to stand upon. There was no Cloud interposed between him and the people, to Obscure Objects. The electors having performed their ephemeral Duty, melt at once into the common Mass. No *standing* Body or Bodies whatever, can consider the President as their *Creature,* and an unbecoming Connection between him and the Legislatures of the several states is utterly prevented.

The Constitution evidently contemplates a Repartition of Legislative, Executive, and Judicial Powers: But, what a strange Departure from this simple Principle appears, when we see the Legislatures of the several states creating the President of the Union—which they as absolutely do, by appointing his Electors, as if they themselves elected him—and also creating the Senate vested with such large legislative, executive, and judicial Authority. They not specifying who is Voted for a President, and who is Vice President may cause Confusion. . . .

ALS (Historical Society of Pennsylvania)

AUGUST [1804?]

WILLIAM SAMUEL JOHNSON TO ————

Stratford August

Dear Sir

As I have no correspondent at Boston I presume the honor you did me last autumn to call upon me on your return from New York will be a sufficient apology for my acquainting you with a fact which my friends think I ought to communicate to some gentleman of the Mass. Legislature

In their excellant remonstrance to Congress on the surprising introduction of Louisiana into the union they observe that on enquiry they could not discover that the subject had ever been contemplated by the convention. That it was not actually mentioned in the convention is true, but the subject occurred to me in my comparing the government we were about to form with existing & antient republic's. & particularly that of Holland, which I observed had acquired territory but did not admit it into their union but governed it as a subordinate territory. And this as far as I can discover was the case with all the antient republic's, and Rome we know in this manner governed almost the whole of the then known world, by her proconsuls; though indeed she had the indiscretion to admit all Italy to the priviledges of the city & thereby sowed the seeds of her ruin. I then thought to mention the subject in the convention, but first, as was usual in every case committed the matter to my colleagues & stated the question to them in this manner viz. suppose G.B. should make war upon us & in the course of such war we should conquer Nova Scotia & retain it at a peace could this territory be admitted into the union? They both answered without hesitation, by no means it might be held & governed as a subordinate territory. Shall we make it a question before the convention as a subject for their deliberation? They both agreed it was a matter so obvious that it was not worth the while to trouble the convention with it. However I made it a subject of conversation among all the little parties of the members I was conversant with for some time after and I believe mentioned it on several committees but in no instance did I find any Gentleman who thought there would be any grounds for such an admission; or occasion for any provision of the convention with regard to it. For as is remarked in your remonstrance, it was the universal sense that our greatest danger of failure was from the great extent of the union so that I cannot doubt but had the subject been stated to the convention there would have been an unanimous vote against such an admission into the union, so that I was very much surprised when I saw the measure proposed in Congress & astonished when it was adopted. And give me leave to submit to your consideration whether the tenure in its very nature does not forbid it. Louisiana was held by France an absolute government as a subordinate territory in full & absolute dominion at the will of the sovereign, it was conveyed by that sovereign to the sovereign of the United States of America & vested in the sovereignty of the union in the same manner. Congress is not that sovereign (though some of its members at times act & speak as if they were so) but the agent of sovereignty with special limitations. Louisiana *is not a free & independant state* it is the property of the union the people are not citizens but subjects of the U.S. but *the subject of the* U.S. the objects & materials of our union were sovereign, free & independant states. Is it possible then that such a subordinate territory so holden could be united to a body so consisting of sovereign and independant States. (Would it not be more a juncture a union of the dead with the living) or had Congress power to take this property from the sovereigns & first to declare it a free and independant state & thus bring it into the union? I think not. Tis true there is a provision of the constitution that Congress may make new States—but out of what are they to make them? The subject before the convention & about which the provision was made was only free & independant states; it therefore amounted only to a power to divide the largest states & so modify parts of the union in point of government as should be most convenient & beneficial to the people. I am not sure this idea is not too metyphisical to be of any use but if ever the part I have stated or the idea relative to the tenure of Louisiana has any solidity in it you & your Friends (Blessed be God) a strong corps of intellect & wisdom united under a chief magistrate (*whom I have the honor to* know to be a Gentleman) of tried wisdom, integrity, & firmness will know how to apply them. . . .

TR (Connecticut Historical Society)

NOVEMBER 30, 1806

In a conversation this day with Abraham Baldwin a senator from Georgia— & a member of the Convention who formed the Constitution of the United States—he said that, Genl. Washington at that time, in a morning's walk, told him he did not expect the constitution would exist more than 20 years.

He said, That the convention was more than once upon the point of dissolving without agreeing upon any system. Many believed they had no authority to report a new system, but only propose amendments to the old articles of Confederation. Some were for a government of energy embracing many objects of legislation—but others to have a more limited authority & to extend to fewer objects. All were better pleased with it when the propositions were reduced to form & connected together than they expected. All the members present, except three signed it—these were Elbridge Gerry of Massachusetts, George Mason & Edmund Randolph of Virginia.

Mr. Baldwin observed That after the instrument was engrossed & ready to be signed, Genl. Washington then President of the convention rose, with his pen in his hand—& observed, That his duty as presiding officer, & his inclination had united in preventing him from taking an active part in the interesting debates of that body—That doubts might exist whether *he approved* of the instrument, or only signed it by order of the Convention—he tho't it his duty to remove these doubts by explicitly declaring That tho' he did not consider it a perfect system—yet he approved of it as a man, & as a delegate from Virginia.—There was however one feature in it he wished, even at this late hour, might be changed—It was the only favor he had, or would ask of the Convention—That was the representation of the States—40,000 souls he tho't too high a number for a representative.—A state, who has from 70 to 100 representatives in its Legislature, will if this principle is retained have not more than 2, 3, or 4 representatives in the House of Representatives in Congress. This principle, to him, appeared antirepublican—He wished the convention would strike out 40, & insert 30,000—To this the Convention unanimously agreed.

(Everett S. Brown, ed., *William Plumer's Memorandum of Proceedings in the United States Senate 1803–1807* [New York, 1923], 518–19)

JULY 26, 1810

THOMAS JEFFERSON TO JAMES MADISON

Dear Sir   Monticello July 26. 10
   Your's of the 17th and that by the last mail are received. I have carefully
searched among my papers for that of Hamilton which is the subject of
your letter, but certainly have it not. If I ever had it (which I should
doubt) I must have returned it. I say I doubt having had it because I find
it in your Conventional debates under the date of June 18 where it is copied
at full length, being so entered I presume in your original manuscript.
Having it in that, I do not suppose I should have wanted his original. I
presume you have your MS. of the debates with you. If you have not,
drop me a line and I will copy it from my copy. . . .

ALS (Library of Congress)

OCTOBER 16, 1818

JOHN QUINCY ADAMS TO WILLIAM JACKSON

October 16, 1818

Sir,

By a Resolution of Congress at their last Session, the Journals of the Convention which formed the Constitution of the United States, have been directed to be published, together with such documents relating to their proceedings as are in possession of the Government.

In the month of March 1796 the volume containing the Journal of the Convention, and that containing their proceedings while in Committee of the Whole, with another containing statements of the yeas and nays taken, on various questions, and nine separate papers of little consequence, were deposited in the Department of State, by President Washington, and these are all the documents possessed by the Government coming within the scope of the Resolution directing the publication.

The Volume containing the Journal closes with the proceedings of Friday 14th September 1817 [i.e., 1787]. The Journal of Saturday, the 15th and of Monday the 17th of September, are therefore not included in it, and if published without further addition, it will leave the proceedings of the Convention incomplete.

I have thought it therefore advisable, to apply to you as the Secretary of that Convention to enquire, whether you have in your possession, or can direct me to any other source from which could be obtained any papers by which the journal of the two deficient days can be completed. And also, whether you have copies of any other papers, relating to the proceedings of the Convention, which you would have the goodness to communicate to be added to the publication.

Governor Bloomfield, some months since transmitted to me several papers, which came to his possession as Executor to Mr. Brearly, one of the Members of the Convention. Among them are Copies of sundry Resolutions offered to the Convention on the 15th of June 1787 by Mr. Patterson. And of a plan of a Constitution of the United States proposed by Colonel Hamilton.

The Resolutions offered by Mr. Patterson, are referred to in the Journal of 15th June 1787, but no Copy of them was among the papers deposited by President Washington in the Department of State. There is no reference in the Journal to the plan proposed by Colonel Hamilton; but the Journal notices a plan for a constitution proposed by Mr. Charles Pinckney, no Copy of which is among any of the papers which we possess.

As it is desirable that the publication should be made as soon as possible, your answer at as early a moment, as may suit your convenience, will confer an obligation.

I am with much Respect, Sir, your very humble Servt.

John Quincy Adams

ALS (Yale University Library)

OCTOBER 19, 1818

WILLIAM JACKSON TO JOHN QUINCY ADAMS

Philadelphia, October 19th, 1818

I had the honor of receiving your letter of the 16th instant, this morning; and I regret that the means of complying with your request, as it regards any documents connected with the proceedings of the Convention, which formed the Constitution of the United States, are not within my power— Every Document, relative thereto, having been delivered to President Washington on the day when I left Philadelphia for New York, to present the Constitution to Congress.

It is almost impossible, in the lapse of thirty years, to state occurrences with accuracy; but I am inclined to believe that the Convention adjourned from friday, the 14th of September 1787 to Monday the 17th, and on that day no other transaction passed in Convention, than to sign the Constitution and the letter to Congress.

There is no Person so capable of giving correct answers to your several enquiries as President Madison, who was certainly among the most efficient Members of the Convention.

I expect to have the honor of paying my respects to you before the Meeting of Congress, and should anything occur to improve my recollection of the facts, to which you refer, it shall be faithfully communicated.

Farrand, 4:81–82

OCTOBER 21, 1818

Philadelphia, October 21st., 1818.

Being desirous to render the reply, which I had the honor of making to your letter of the 16th instant, as satisfactory as the remote period and circumstances, to which it refers, will admit, I have conversed with Messrs. Butler and Ingersoll, who were Members of the Convention, and are now resident in this city.—They corroborate my recollection of the adjournment from friday the 14th of September 1787 to Monday the 17th, for the purpose of preparing the Constitution for signature—and Mr. Ingersoll adds that Dr. Franklin, Mr. G. Morris and himself were the Committee appointed on the 17th to draught the letter to Congress, and that no other business, besides signing the Constitution and that Letter, was transacted on that day.

That the Constitution of the United States, as agreed on by the Convention, was the result of numerous concessions to what was deemed the nearest approach to the general interest, is manifested by many of its provisions, and the brief notice of other Plans, that were not acted on, was a necessary consequence of the same conciliatory disposition. It was, indeed, cause of felicitation to the best men in that respectable Assembly, that its proceedings were conducted and closed in a spirit of unanimity and accommodation, honorable to individuals and highly beneficial to the Public.

Farrand, 4:82–83

JULY 6, 1821

July 6, 1821

Sir

In compliance with your wishes, which you did me the honor to communicate yesterday, I have made the necessary examinations to ascertain whether any of the documents referred to in the original book of notes made by the late Chief Justice Yates, of the proceedings of the General Convention of the U.S. had been received with the book, and I am firmly persuaded I received none.

When I obtained the book from Mrs. Yates, the widow of the Chief Justice, I expressly stipulated to transcribe it, and furnish her with a copy in a month, which was accordingly done, and from the shortness of the intervening time, I am perfectly satisfied a copy of *all* I received, was delivered to her—as to furnish a copy of every part was in the spirit, if not in the express terms, of the stipulation; and it could not possibly have escaped the recollection of that lady, her family, and myself, if any had been omitted.

At the time I became possessed of the notes, it was of some personal interest to me to have them in my power, though to acquire the copyright never was my intention, and it was reserved to Mrs. Yates. While copying the notes I was tempted to add marginal notes, explanatory or corrective to the text, the matter of which might have been extracted from my own notes, made on the same occasion, but I refrained from doing so, and made the transcript verbatim, without the least mutilation or other alteration.

After the copy had been completed it was carefully compared with the original, and, as I have no doubt of its correctness, I think I may venture to vouch for its accuracy.

I am, Sir, respectfully, your
obedient servant,

John Lansing, Jr.

Albany Argus, August 24, 1821

JUNE 27, 1823

JAMES MADISON TO THOMAS JEFFERSON

Montpellier, June 27, 1823

Believing as I do that the General Convention regarded a provision within the Constitution for deciding in a peaceable & regular mode all cases arising in the course of its operation, as essential to an adequate System of Govt. that it intended the Authority vested in the Judicial Department as a final resort in relation to the States, for cases resulting to it in the exercise of its functions, (the concurrence of the Senate chosen by the State Legislatures, in appointing the Judges, and the oaths & official tenures of these, with the surveillance of public Opinion, being relied on as guarantying their impartiality); and that this intention is expressed by the articles declaring that the federal Constitution & laws shall be the supreme law of the land, and that the Judicial Power of the U.S. shall extend to all cases arising under them: . . . thus believing I have never yielded my original opinion indicated in the "Federalist" No. 39 to the ingenious reasonings of Col: Taylor agst. this construction of the Constitution.

Farrand, 4:83–84

FEBRUARY 11, 1824

James Madison to Robert S. Garnett

Montpellier, Feb. 11, 1824.

The general terms or phrases used in the introductory propositions, and now a source of so much constructive ingenuity, were never meant to be inserted in their loose form in the text of the Constitution. Like resolutions preliminary to legal enactments it was understood by all, that they were to be reduced by proper limitations and specifications, into the form in which they were to be final and operative; as was actually done in the progress of the session.

Farrand, 4:84

AUGUST 1824

JAMES MADISON TO PETER S. DUPONCEAU

Montpellier Aug. 1824.
A characteristic peculiarity of the Govt. of the U. States is, that its powers consist of special grants taken from the general mass of power, whereas other Govts. possess the general mass with special exceptions only. Such being the plan of the Constitution, it cannot well be supposed that the Body which framed it with so much deliberation, and with so manifest a purpose of specifying its objects, and defining its boundaries, would, if intending that the Common Law shd. be a part of the national code, have omitted to express or distinctly indicate the intention; when so many far inferior provisions are so carefully inserted, and such appears to have been the public view taken of the Instrument, whether we recur to the period of its ratification by the States, or to the federal practice under it.

Farrand, 4:85

Timothy Pickering: Memorandum

Major William Jackson   Philadelphia, Aug. 11, 1827

A letter of the 7th instant from Wm. Coleman stated to me the request of Mrs. Hamilton, that I would call on Major Jackson (who was Secretary of the Convention that formed the Constitution of the United States) who could "import some interesting and important intelligence respecting the agency of Hamilton in forming the Constitution, etc. etc. Mrs. Hamilton went to him a few years ago for the purpose of obtaining it, but was told by the Major that he was still under an injunction of secrecy; as he had promised General Hamilton in his life time, not to breach the seal which contained the deposit left with him, till twenty years should have elapsed; · the time has now expired; and Major Jackson, at her request, will doubtless deliver them to you."

Having called twice at Major Jackson's house, without finding him at home, he this morning called on me. I read to him that part of Coleman's letter above quoted: when he answered, that Mrs. Hamilton was entirely mistaken, as to the confidential intelligence he was supposed to possess: and then stated to me.

That after, by mutual concessions, the Constitution had been adopted in the Convention, General Washington (who had been its President) spoke to him to this effect: "Major Jackson, you have been observed to be constantly taking notes of what passed in the Convention, during the discussions of the numerous propositions presented for consideration; but it would be wholly improper to publish them: and I must therefore desire you not to suffer them to be made public while you live." Upon which, Jackson says he pledged himself to Washington, this his request should be sacredly observed.

I asked Jackson, of what those notes consisted? He answered—of the speeches of members of the Convention: that altho' he did not write any usual short-hand yet, by putting a single letter for short words, and a syllable for long ones, he was able to keep pace with speakers who uttered their words with the deliberation usual in debate. I then asked him if from these abreviations he had written out the speeches at full length, as it could be done only by himself? He answered—*"That he was doing it."* You will at once reflect, that the fortieth year since the Convention finished its labours, is nearly elapsed: whence it is to be apprehended that those speeches may remain locked up forever, in the Major's abreviations. Some years have passed away since his Political Register (i.e., newspaper) became defunct; and subsequently Major Jackson has had no business or employ-ment, public or private. At any rate, you see, that no information con-cerning Hamilton can be derived from him. . . .

AD (Massachusetts Historical Society)

JANUARY 14, 1828

TIMOTHY PICKERING TO JOHN LOWELL

. . . James Wilson (afterwards Judge Wilson) was a member of the National Convention by whom the Constitution was formed. In conversation with him, above thirty years ago, he told me, that after the entire instrument had been agreed on, in its existing form, the final revision of it was committed to him in regard to *grammatical accuracy* or *correctness of style* (such is the impression in my memory); certainly not to introduce a single idea. This philological office comprehended, of course, what related to punctuation: but whether in the instance in question, Wilson found a semicolon after excises, or substituted it in place of a comma, or found it without any marked pause can never be known. Whether punctuation ought ever to govern the construction of any writing, it does not belong to me to decide; but it certainly gives facility to an understanding of its meaning. . . .[1]

ALS (Massachusetts Historical Society)

1. In a draft of this letter, dated January 9, 1828, Pickering wrote that Wilson "once told me, that after all the articles and parts of it had been agreed on, arranged, and in its present form adopted and fixed, its final revision, in regard to correctness of style, was committed to him" (Pickering Papers, Massachusetts Historical Society). In a letter to John Marshall, March 10, 1828, Pickering stated that Wilson "once told me, that after the Constitution had been finally settled, it was committed to him to be critically examined respecting its style in order that the instrument might appear with the most perfect precision and accuracy of language" (ibid.).

OCTOBER 30, 1828

JAMES MADISON TO JOSEPH C. CABELL

October 30, 1828

2. A history of that clause, as traced in the printed journal of the Federal Convention, will throw light on the subject.

It appears that the clause, as it originally stood, simply expressed "a power to lay taxes, duties, imposts, and excises," without pointing out the objects; and, of course, leaving them applicable in carrying into effect the other specified powers. It appears, farther, that a solicitude to prevent any constructive danger to the validity of public debts contracted under the superseded form of government, led to the addition of the words "to pay the debts."

This phraseology having the appearance of an appropriation limited to the payment of debts, an express appropriation was added "for the expenses of the Government," &c.

But even this was considered as short of the object for which taxes, duties, imposts, and excise might be required; and the more comprehensive provision was made by substituting "for expenses of Government" the terms of the old Confederation, viz.: and provide for the common defence and general welfare, making duties and imposts, as well as taxes and excises, applicable not only to payment of debts, but to the common defence and general welfare.

Farrand, 4:85–86

[1833]

JAMES MADISON TO ———

It seems to be forgotten, that the abuses committed within the individual States previous to the present Constitution, by interested or misguided majorities, were among the prominent causes of its adoption, and particularly led to the provision contained in it which prohibits paper emissions and the violations of contracts, and which gives an appellate supremacy to the judicial department of the U.S. Those who framed and ratified the Constitution believed that as power was less likely to be abused by majorities in representative Govts. than in democracies, where the people assembled in mass, and less likely in the larger than in the smaller communities, under a representative Govt. inferred also, that by dividing the powers of Govt. and thereby enlarging the practicable sphere of government, unjust majorities would be formed with still more difficulty, and be therefore the less to be dreaded, . . .

Farrand, 4:86–87

APRIL 19, 1835

EXTRACT FROM JAMES MADISON'S WILL

April 19, 1835.

Considering the peculiarity and magnitude of the occasion which produced the convention at Philadelphia in 1787, the Characters who composed it, the Constitution which resulted from their deliberation, it's effects during a trial of so many years on the prosperity of the people living under it, and the interest it has inspired among the friends of free Government, it is not an unreasonable inference that a careful and extended report of the proceedings and discussions of that body, which were with closed doors, by a member who was constant in his attendance, will be particularly gratifying to the people of the United States, and to all who take an interest in the progress of political science and the cause of true liberty. It is my desire that the report as made by me should be published . . .

Farrand, 4:87

JUNE 9, 1856

EDWARD COLES: HISTORY OF THE ORDINANCE OF 1787

. . . This brings to my recollection what I was told by Mr. Madison, and which I do not remember ever to have seen in print. The Old Congress held its sessions in 1787 in New York while at the same time the convention which made the constitution of the United States held its sessions at Philadelphia. Many individuals were members of both bodies, and thus were enabled to know what was passing in each, each setting with closed doors and in secret sessions. The distracting question of slavery was agitating and retarding the labours of both, and led to conferences and inter-communications of the members, which resulted in a compromise by which the northern or anti-slavery portion of the country agreed to incorporate into the Ordinance and Constitution the provision to restore fugitive slaves; and this mutual and concurrent action was the cause of the similarity of the provision contained in both, and had its influence in creating the great unanimity by which the Ordinance passed, and also making the constitution the more acceptable to slaveholders. Among the first passed by the first Congress and approved by President Washington, August 7, 1789, was one to adopt the Ordinance to the new constitution of the United States. It thus received the sanction of Congress under the present constitution, as it had previously done of the Old Congress under the Articles of Confederation. . . .

AD (Historical Society of Pennsylvania)

GEORGE BANCROFT: ANECDOTE

When, on the seventeenth, Gouverneur Morris proposed a reconsideration of the resolution of the former day, no one would second his motion.

A few days later [July 23] the number of senators for each state was fixed at two, and each of these, as had been proposed by Gerry and seconded by Sherman, was personally to have one vote.

From the day when every doubt of the right of the smaller states to an equal vote in the senate was quieted, they—so I received it from the lips of Madison, and so it appears from the records—exceeded all others in zeal for granting powers to the general government. Ellsworth became one of its strongest pillars. Paterson of New Jersey was for the rest of his life a federalist of federalists.

Farrand, 4:88–89

UNDATED

WILLIAM SAMUEL JOHNSON: MEMORANDUM

The result of whose deliberations was that it was advisable and perhaps necessy to call a convention of the States in order to form a new Constitution, & this was appointed to meet at Philadelphia In the year (   ) wh. accordingly met in a very full convention, and of this convention I was appointed a member by the State. The debates at the convention were very long. & for a long time it remained in doubt whether we shd. be able to effect any thing. But knowing the necessy of doing something we finaly by mutual concession agreed upon the present constitution of the U.S.

Farrand, 4:88

UNDATED

In conversing with Dr. Franklin on the subject of the constitution, after it was published, the Doctor said to N.W. that he had agreed to the form of the constitution, although it had always been his opinion that the legislative body should consist of one house only. But said the Doctor, "I have all my life been changing my opinions on many subjects and in this case I have yielded my opinions to those of other men."

TR (Yale University Library)

Appendix:
The Weather during the Convention

"It turned out to be a very hot summer in Philadelphia."[1] So claim the authors of a recent monograph on the Convention. Writers have always watched Philadelphia's weather during the summer of 1787 and have, with few exceptions, described it as hot and oppressive, apparently because the heroic stature of the framers seems to require them to have conquered the elements as well as the political crisis in the nation. Farrand did not publish meteorological records for the summer of 1787; the closest approximation is an edition of William Samuel Johnson's laconic journal (III, 552–54). Research for the present supplement uncovered three detailed accounts of Philadelphia's summer weather which, because of the interest in the subject, are published in tabular form below.

The entries under Morris are from a diary at the Hagley Museum and Library kept by the Philadelphia brewer Thomas Morris. Jacob Hiltzheimer, owner of a livery stable and other businesses in Philadelphia, was a member of the Pennsylvania Assembly; his diary is at the American Philosophical Society. Peter Legaux was a French immigrant who owned a farm and practiced viticulture at Spring Mill, thirteen miles northwest of Philadelphia. A student of Jean Andre DeLuc, the Swiss-born geologist and meteorologist, Legaux kept detailed meteorological records from 1786 to 1827. His observations for 1787 were published at the end of each month's issue of the *Universal Asylum and Columbian Magazine,* a Philadelphia literary magazine, from which they are printed here. Only selected items from Legaux's records are used. His full records, published in the *Universal Asylum,* contain each day's mean temperature in Fahrenheit and Reaumur, barometric readings, wind directions, amounts of precipitation, and even the frequency of appearances of the aurora borealis. In using Legaux's readings it should be remembered that he gives *mean* temperature and that all his information was recorded at his farm, not in downtown

1. James and Christopher Collier, *Decision in Philadelphia: The Constitutional Convention of 1787* (New York, 1986), 74–75.

Philadelphia. Each month Legaux noted the highest and lowest temperature readings; these are included at the appropriate dates.

Using Legaux's and other records, David M. Ludlum of the American Weather History Center compiled the following statistics on Philadelphia's weather during the summer of 1787:

	Average temp.	Depart. normal	Maximum	Minimum	Rainfall	Depart. normal
May	62.0	+0.7	80.1	34.1	4.96	+0.92
June	70.7	+1.0	93.8	45.0	1.88	−2.11
July	72.4	−4.1	96.0	45.7	3.09	−0.97
Aug.	74.5	−0.4	95.0	50.0	5.18	+0.95
Sept.	64.7	−1.7	93.9	36.5	2.62	−1.02

Ludlum calculated "normal" temperature and rainfall by using the Pennsylvania Hospital Records, 1825–71. He concluded that "in general terms Philadelphia enjoyed a cool summer in 1787."[2] It is, perhaps, not without interest to compare these findings with a recent discovery that, despite the heat in which the imaginations of generations of writers have enveloped Philadelphia on July 4, 1776, Independence Day was also cool.[3]

2. Unpublished paper in author's possession. It is obvious, however, from letters in the new supplement that the impact of temperature was subjective; what to one person was hot was to another pleasant.

3. Paul H. Smith, "Time and Temperature: Philadelphia, July 4, 1776," *Quarterly Journal of the Library of Congress* 33 (October 1976): 297–98.

	Hiltzheimer	Morris	Legaux
May 14	Some Rain in the Morning	Cloudy and dull with driz'ling Rain at times	56.9°; Rainy
May 15	Some Rain in the Morning	Wind N.E. yet it cleared away at Night it was mild	63.2°; Overcast, fair
May 16	Clear & Pleasant	clear & serene Morning & so continued through the day 'tho the wind continued N.East	61°; Fog, very fair
May 17	Cloudy in forenoon, Clear in the Afternoon	foggy Morning, clear afterwards & pleasant, & in Evening a small Shower	66°; Fog, fair, thunder, rain
May 18	Clear in forenoon, in the afternoon . . . a gust coming on fast, . . . [later] it began to rain	some Rain afternoon, & a Gust a little before Noon	67.2°; Overcast, rain, thunder, storm
May 19	Clear Last Night, had a Smart Shower of Rain with Some Thunder	pleasant Weather	67.1°; Very fair
May 20	a Gust in the Afternoon	gusty & uncertain weather, with Thunder about Noon	67.2°; Very fair, rain, storm
May 21	Clear & Pleasant	Wind N.W. & cool	60°; Very fair
May 22	Rain, in the Afternoon	Wind N. & Rain, & in the Evening clear & cool	60°; Overcast, rainy, changeable
May 23	Cloudy, forenoon . . . afternoon had Several Showers of Rain	Wind southerly & pleasant	60.2°; Fair, rainy
May 24	Cloudy, a little Rain	it look'd very likely to rain in the Morning but clear'd away	64.8°; Overcast, wet, cloudy, fair
May 25	rain All Day	rain (& pretty much of it) fell nearly all day	59°; Overcast, rain

	Hiltzheimer	Morris	Legaux
May 26	Clear	cool & Wind N.W.	57.3°; Fair
May 27	Cloudy, after Drops of Rain in the Morning	pleasant 'tho cool for the Season & rather windy	54.5°; Overcast, cloudy, cold
May 28	Clear but not warme	weather ditto	54.7°; Fair
May 29	Clear forenoon	pleasant weather	59°; Fog, very fair
May 30	The Wind South east, Rain All Day	much Rain, wind S.East	58.8°; Overcast, rain
May 31	Cloudy and Cool enough to sit by the Fire	there was a smart Shower in the Morning, the weather soon after clear'd up & the rest of the day was fine	69.7°; Thunder, rain
June 1	Cloudy & Cool	pleasant but rather cool	69°; Overcast, cold, fair
June 2	Cloudy . . . Rain toward evening, and Still Cold enough to Sit by the Fire	cool Morning, & I think there must be frost. Fire seems necessary, & we have kept one in the Parlour Morng. & Eveng. & sometimes throughout the day for the most part of the Spring	53.3°; lowest temp. of June, 45°; Overcast, cold, fair
June 3	Cloudy, with some rain	cool Wind from N.E. with flying Clouds & Rain in the Morning; in the Evening it clear'd at N.W. & was (I had almost said) cold	54.8°; Rain, after fair, cold
June 4	Clear Cool enough to Sit by the Fire	clear & cool wind pretty high (Westerly)	57°; Fair, cold, windy
June 5	Clear & Pleasant in the forenoon	pleasant. . . . In the Evening it rained	63.2°; Fair, overcast, rain

June 6	Rain Most All day	dull Morning Wind N.E. & about 11 o'clock it began to rain & continued throughout the Day	59.2°; Fog, overcast, wet, rain
June 7	Rain	variable Weather, Showers frequent	64°; Idem.
June 8	Cloudy	Clear & fine weather, wind N.W. in the Morng. clouded over before Noon & so continued most of the day.	63.2°; Fair, cloudy
June 9	Clear & Pleasant	Very fine Haymaking weather	72.4°; Fair, warm
June 10	Clear & warme	warmer than of late	72.4°; Fog, sun, fair
June 11	Clear & warme	very pleasant	76°; Fair
June 12	Clear & warme	fine Hay weather	71°; Fog, after fair
June 13	Clear and Pleasant	warm weather, the Thermometer at Noon 80 degrees	73.5°; Fog, fair
June 14	Clear & Pleasant	Warm & dusty, Therm. 84	77°; Fair
June 15	Pleasant	Ditto . . . 86	81.3°; highest temp. of June, 93°; Fair
June 16		easterly wind & cooler, Thermometer 76	76.7°; Overcast, fair
June 17	Cloudy and a Very little rain		68°; Rain, clouds, fair

	Hiltzheimer	Morris	Legaux
June 18	In the afternoon . . . Shower of rain		77°; Rain fog, clouds and storm
June 19	Clear & warme	pleasant Weather	73.5°; Fair
June 20	Clear	very pleasant, Wind Easterly	76°; Fog, fair and clouds
June 21	two Small Showers of rain	Weather sultry with a smart Shower afternoon	72.4°; Fog, clouds, rain, storm
June 22	much Thunder & Lightning, last Night with Heavy rain	a heavy thundergust in last Night with Rain. This Day cool & pleasant	76.5°; Fair, warm
June 23	Clear & warme	The weather was pleasant	76°; Fair
June 24	little rain	a Shower afternoon 3 o'clock	75°; Fair, small rain
June 25	Rain in the Morning, as well as last Night. Pleasant in the afternoon	A good deal of Lightning & Thunder in last Night with Rain. It also rained smartly this Morning	77.3°; Fair, windy
June 26	Clear & Pleasant	pleasant	72°; Idem.
June 27	Clear & warme	Weather pleasant	78°; Rain, then fair
June 28	Clear and Pleasant forenoon	ditto	70.8°; Very fair
June 29	Cloudy, and a Very little rain in the Morning	wind N.E.	70.7°; Overcast, fair
June 30	Clear & warme	Weather warm	73.5°; Idem.

Date			
July 1	Cloudy. Rain several times, but Very little	pleasant for the Season	73.7°; Overcast
July 2	Cloudy Close & Very warme	Foggy Morng. hot Sun afterwards	79.2°; Fog, cloudy, warm
July 3		Very warm weather. Thermometer 90 degrees	85.8°; highest temp. of July, 96°; Very fair
July 4	Clear & warme	Wind N.West & pleasant for the Season	77.4°; Idem.
July 5	Clear & warme forenoon		74.8°; Fair, clouds
July 6	Very warme		76°; Very fair
July 7	Very warme		74.5°; Idem.
July 8	Very warme, a Small Springle of rain in the afternoon		79.2°; Idem., warm
July 9	Warme . . . after Night had Much Thunder, but Little rain		81°; Idem.
July 10	Very warme		76°; Idem.
July 11	Cloudy		75°; Overcast, then fair
July 12	Clear & warme		77°; Cloudy, fair
July 13	Clear and Cool, but Very Dusty		71.1°; Very fair, aur. bor.
July 14	Windy & Very Dusty		61.5°; lowest temp. of July, 45.7°; Idem.

	Hiltzheimer	Morris	Legaux
July 15			64°; Fair, overcast, rain
July 16	had a Smart Shower of rain Last Night, and an other to day at Noon		74.2°; Overcast, thunder, rain, fair
July 17	Clear & Pleasant		66.8°; Very fair
July 18	Clear & Pleasant		63.3°; Idem.
July 19	In the Afternoon had a Small Shower of rain	A small Shower after dinner	66.8°; Overcast
July 20	Clear	Wind N.East and cloudy in the Morning, afterward clear & pleasant Weather	68.5°; Clouds, rainy
July 21	Clear & Pleasant	weather the same	73°; Fair
July 22	Warme	Therm. 80: rather warmer than lately	72°; Overcast, fair
July 23	Very warme	warm Weather; Therm. 83. In the Evening threat'ned Rain but went over	75.4°; Fair
July 24	Very warme	Wind N.East in the Morning, but soon changed to S.West & clear'd away	77°; Overcast, wet, fair
July 25	had Several Showers of rain fore & afternoon	some Rain about Noon, Wind S.E., & a very fine refreshing Rain after Dinner, which continued most of the Afternoon	74.6°; Overcast, thunder, rain
July 26	Had a Smart Shower of rain in the Morning	Cloudy most of the Day & some Rain	64°; Rainy

Date			
July 27	Clear, Cool & Very Pleasant	Clear & very pleasant Weather cool for the Season, Rain in Evening . . . Wind N.East	71°; Cloudy
July 28	Cloudy		70.2°; Overcast
July 29	Rain Last Night, and some this Morning	Wind N.E. & cool. Cloudy without Rain	67.8°; Idem.
July 30	Cloudy and uncommonly Cool	wind N.E. & [ditto?]	67.2°; Idem.
July 31	Cloudy & Some rain, and Quite Cool at the time	Wind N.E. & more like Fall than Midsummer	66.5°; Idem.
August 1	Cloudy, Cool, & some Rain	Wind yet N.East with some Rain in the Morning & cloudy all day	65.7°; Rain
August 2	Clear, and Much Warmer	Wind veering around to S. West the Weather for the greater part of the day was clear & in the Sun warm. The Eveng. pleasant	74.7°; Fair, cloudy
August 3	Clear warme & Pleasant	Hot Sun	77°; highest temperature of August, 95°; Very fair and warm
August 4	Clear & warme		82.8°; Idem.
August 5	Very warme	Summer Weather, Therm. 82	79.8°; Idem.
August 6	Rain in the Morning, afternoon Very warme	Wind S.E. and rainy in the Morng. after 10 o'Clock clear & warm	73.8°; Rain, then fair

	Hiltzheimer	Morris	Legaux
August 7	Very Close & warme with a few Drops of rain at times	Foggy Morning, afterwards clear & warm	77°; Overcast, fair
August 8	Very Foggy and Close in the Morning. afterward, exceeding warme	The same	80°; Fog, fair, warm
August 9	Very close & warme, Several Showers of rain	Rain afternoon with much Lightning & Thunder at Night	79°; Overcast, rain, thunder
August 10	Much lightning last Night and heavy Rain, to Day Cloudy and Close with Several Showers of rain in the evening	Rain in last Night, & several Showers this day	76.6°; Cloudy, rainy
August 11	Clear & warme	clear & pleasant Weather for Summer	73.8°; Fair
August 12	Clear & Pleasant	Ditto, but hot in the Sun	79.2°; Idem.
August 13	Clear & warme	the same	78.4°; Idem.
August 14	Very warme	very warm. Therm. 85	82°;. Idem.
August 15	Warme forenoon	more Air & pleasanter than yesterday. Rain in Evening with Lightning & Thunder	84.8°; Idem, windy, storm, thunder
August 16	Clear Cool & Pleasant	pleasant out of the Sun	74.3°; Fair
August 17	Cloudy & Some rain	Pleasant Morning; cloudy Afternoon & some Rain	63°; Dew, overcast, rain

August 18	Clear and Pleasant	cool, airy & pleasant	74.8°; Cloudy, high wind, fair
August 19	Clear & Pleasant	weather moderate	68°; lowest temperature of August, 50°; Fair
August 20	Rain . . . Very hard Shower of rain at Night	Wind S.E. & cloudy, about 10 o'Clock it began to rain & continued violently through the day & Evening	67.8°; Rain
August 21	Cloudy Close & warme . . . a Smart Shower of rain at Night	cloudy at times with some Rain	79.2°; Fair, rain, thunder
August 22	Clear & Pleasant	seasonable weather	74°; Fair
August 23	Clear & warme	Wind N.W. & reasonably pleasant weather	74.8°; Idem.
August 24	Clear and Very Warme	weather hot	75°; Idem.
August 25	Clear & Very warme	hot weather. Therm. 85	81.3°; Very fair and warm
August 26	Cool & Pleasant	moderate weather, Wind N.W.	73.1°; Cloudy, windy
August 27	Rain	Wind N.E. cloudy & cool with Rain in the Morning	60°; Overcast, rain
August 28	Rain	wind easterly with small Rain	65.6°; Idem.
August 29	Clear	remarkably damp, close & unwholesome weather, some Rain with Lightning in the afternoon	80.2°; Very fair, thunder, and rain

	Hiltzheimer	Morris	Legaux
August 30	Little rain early in the Morning	rain in the Morng. very pleasant Evening	72.8°; Overcast
August 31	Clear & Pleasant	pleasant Weather, Wind N.W. & N.E.	64.3°; Fair, cloudy
September 1	Rain Most all Day	Wind easterly with constant Rain from 2 o'Clock P.M. until Evening	64.7°; Overcast, rain
September 2	Clear & Pleasant	dull till near Noon, when the Weather clear'd & was pleasant	68°; Overcast, windy
September 3	Clear & Pleasant	pleasant Weather	65.3°; Fair
September 4	Clear	Ditto	64.9°; Fair, then clouds
September 5	Clear in the Afternoon		73.5°; Fog, fair, clouds, overcast
September 6	Clear & Pleasant	wind N.W. & cool, out of the Sun	72.2°; Very fair
September 7	Clear & Pleasant	cool Morning & pleasant throughout	61°; Cloudy, then fair
September 8	Clear & Pleasant	Ditto	64°; Overcast
September 9	in the afternoon . . . it was	warm Sun	72.5°; Very fair, and warm
September 10	exceeding warme at the Same time, the wind being from the West, which was no Benefit to the room up Stairs	Therm. 82 degrees	74.2°; Overcast, windy, fair
September 11	Exceeding warme	Weather oppressively hot, Therm. 85 [?]	80.9°; highest temperature of September, 93.9°; Very fair

September 12	Very warme	hot weather Therm. 87½	80.1°; Idem.
September 13	Exceeding close & warme Last Night—this Morning had alittle rain	Rain in the Morning, & rather cooler all day than the three last	77°; Overcast, rain
September 14	Rain Last Night, Close & Very warme today at Night had Some thunder, with Much Lightning, and heavy rain	Rain in last Night, the day at Times clear & Sun powerful. In the Evening the wind to eastward of South, very heavy clouds to the North & N.West with much Lightning, the wind suddenly veer'd about to N.W. when the atmosphere for an Hour or more was almost a continued Blaze of Light but no very heavy Thunder, for a considerable Time it rained heavily; & blew violently from N.W. about 10 minutes	75.3°; Thick, rain, thunder storm
September 15	Cool and Pleasant	Wind N.W. & Weather cool & pleasant weather	64.7°; Overcast, windy
September 16	Cool & Pleasant		51.8°; Clouds, fair, but cold
September 17	Clear & Quite Cool	cool	48.8°; lowest temperature of September, 36.5°; Fair, cold, overcast

INDEX
BY CLAUSES OF THE CONSTITUTION

The references attached to the various clauses of the Constitution are intended to include every item in the preceding volumes explanatory of the development of those clauses and their embodiment in the Constitution. Owing to the character of the work many of the items are merely copies or repetitions of others. All such repetitions, together with items of slight importance or only indirectly bearing on the clause in question, have been enclosed in parentheses. Some clauses were in early drafts but were dropped out of the final draft of the Constitution; these may be traced through the General Index. As indicated in the introduction to this volume, references to its contents are entered after the letter "**S.**"

[PREAMBLE]

WE THE PEOPLE of the United States, in Order to form a more perfect Union, establish Justice, insure domestic Tranquility, provide for the common defence, promote the general Welfare, and secure the Blessings of Liberty to ourselves and our Posterity, do ordain and establish this Constitution for the United States of America.

I. 18, 20, (27), 30, (33, 35, 38, 39, 40, 41, 225), 228, (235), 242, (247), 322, (328, 334), 335, (344). **II.** (129), 134, 137, 150, 152, 163, 177, (193), 196, (209), 565, 590, 651. **III.** (146). **IV.** 5, 38, 39, 84. **S.** 183, 184, 313.

ARTICLE. I.

Section. 1. All legislative Powers . . . vested in a Congress . . . which shall consist of a Senate and House of Representatives.

I. 20, (27, 45), 48, (54, 55, 57, 60, 225), 228, (235, 291, 334), 336, (344, 349, 350, 353), 355, (362, 366). **II.** 129, (135, 138, 150), 152, (158), 163, 177, (193, 196), 200, 565, 590, 651. **III.** 23, 25, 26, 40, 110, (155, 169), 191, 297, (340), 359, 419, 517. **IV.** 39. **S.** 184.

Section. 2. [Clause 1]. The House of Representatives shall be composed of Members chosen every second Year by the People of the several States, and the Electors in each State shall have the Qualifications requisite for Electors of the most numerous Branch of the State Legislature.

I. 20, (27, 46), 48, (54, 55, 56, 60, 118), 124, (130), 132, (140, 142, 145, 147, 209), 214, (220, 225), 228, (235, 291, 300, 353), 358, (364, 367, 368). **II.** 129, (139), 151, 153, 163, 178, (194), 201, 206, 209, (213), 215, (225), 565, 590, 651. **III.** 128, 146, 247, 355. **IV.** 4, 40. **S.** 184.

[Clause 2]. No Person shall be a Representative who shall not have attained to the Age of twenty five Years, and been seven Years a Citizen of the United States, and who shall not, when elected, be an Inhabitant of that State in which he shall be chosen.

I. 20, (210), 215, (221, 370), 375, (379). **II.** (116), 121, 129, 134, (139), 153, 164, 178, 179, (213), 216, (225, 226), 230, (245), 251, (265), 267, (281), 565, 590, 651. **III.** 147, 255. **IV.** 4, 39. **S.** 184.

[Clause 3]. Representatives and direct Taxes shall be apportioned among the several States . . . according to their respective Numbers, which shall be determined by adding to the whole Number of free Persons . . . three fifths of all other Persons. The actual Enumeration shall be made within three Years after the first Meeting of the Congress of the United States, and within every subsequent Term of ten Years, in such Manner as they shall by Law direct. The Number of Representatives shall not exceed one for every thirty Thousand, . . . and until such enumeration shall be made, the State of New Hampshire shall be entitled to chuse, three, Massachusetts eight, . . . and Georgia three.

I. (31), 35, (39, 40, 163, 169), 176, (181, 184, 192), 196, (204, 207, 227), 229, (236), 243, (247), 436, (438, 442, 444), 445, (455, 458, 459, 460), 461, 470, (476, 479), 486, (523, 524), 526, (535–538), 540, (557), 559, (563), 566, 572, 573, (575), 578, 589, 591, (597, 598), 600, 603. **II.** 2, (12), 13, (15), 106, 130, 135, (138, 139), 153, 164, 168, 178, 182, (213), 219, (339), 350, (351, 352), 356, (365), 511, (547), 553, 563, 566, 571, 590, (605, 607, 610, 612, 621), 623, 633, 635, (636), 638, 644, (649), 651. **III.** 83, 99, 143, (146, 147, 152, 155), 159, (169, 174), 181, 197, (249), 253, 255, (260, 264, 333, 336), 342, 352, (358, 364), 365, 366, 399, 404, (416), 428, 440. **IV.** 4, 6, 39, 59, 75, 98. **S.** 184, 269.

[Clause 4]. When vacancies happen in the Representation from any State, the Executive Authority thereof shall issue Writs of Election to fill such Vacancies.

II. (140), 154, 164, 179, (227), 231, (243), 566, 591, 652. **IV.** 41. **S.** 185.

[Clause 5]. The House of Representatives shall chuse their Speaker and other Officers; and shall have the sole Power of Impeachment.

II. 136, (145), 154, 158, 159, 164, 165, 178, (227), 231, (243), 566, 591, 652. **IV.** 46. **S.** 189.

Section. 3. [Clause 1]. The Senate . . . composed of two Senators from

each State, chosen by the Legislature thereof, for six Years; and each
Senator shall have one Vote.

    I. 20, (28, 31), 35, (39, 40, 46), 51, (55), 58, (61, 148), 150, (156,
158, 160, 193), 201, (206, 211), 218, (221, 225, 227), 228, 230, (235,
236, 289, 291, 300, 309, 395), 404, 408, 412, (416, 418), 421, 430,
(435, 460), 468, 474, (477, 480), 482, 494, (502, 503, 507, 509), 510,
(516, 523, 524), 526, (535), 549, (553, 555). **II.** (1), 3, 5, (12), 14,
(16), 17, 19, (85), 94, 129, 131, 133, (135, 141), 154, 165, 179, (228),
231, (243), 291, 566, 591, 652. **III.** (99, 101, 133), 135, (151, 154,
155, 169, 177), 188, (194, 243, 249), 252, (264, 270), 304, 337, 355,
359, (400, 414, 416), 483, 498, 538, 554, 575. **IV.** 14, 15, 41, 42,
88, 100. **S.** 38, 186, 187, 322.

    [Clause 2]. [Rotation in Term] so that one third may be chosen
every second Year; and if Vacancies happen by Resignation, or otherwise,
during the Recess of the Legislature of any State, the Executive thereof
may make temporary Appointments until the next Meeting of the Legislature, which shall then fill such Vacancies.

    I. 309, (396), 408, 415, (418), 421, (430, 435, 511, 516), 520.
II. 129, (135, 141), 154, 165, 179, (227, 228), 231, 235, (242, 243),
566, 591, 610, 612, 652. **III.** 147, 337. **IV.** 6, 41, 42, 51, 100.
S. 186, 322.

    [Clause 3]. No Person shall be a Senator who shall not have at-
tained to the Age of thirty Years, and been nine Years a Citizen of the
United States, and who shall not, when elected, be an Inhabitant of that
State for which he shall be chosen.

    I. 20, (211), 217, (221, 228), 235, 395, (408, 415), 428, (433, 435).
II. (116), 121, 129, (134, 141), 155, 165, 179, (228), 235, (242, 243,
245), 248, (256, 266), 272, (281), 567, 591, 652. **III.** 147, 255.
IV. 41. **S.** 186.

    [Clause 4]. The Vice President . . . shall be President of the
Senate, but shall have no Vote, unless they be equally divided.

    II. (495), 498, (532), 536, 574, 592, (610), 612, 652. **III.** 147, 343,
400. **IV.** 59. **S.** 269.

    [Clause 5]. The Senate shall chuse their other Officers, and also
a President pro tempore, in the Absence of the Vice President, . . .

    II. 155, 158, 165, 179, (229), 239, (244, 495), 498, (532), 538,
567, 574, 592, 653.

    [Clause 6]. The Senate shall have the sole Power to try all Im-
peachments. When sitting for that Purpose, they shall be on Oath or
Affirmation. When the President of the United States is tried, the Chief
Justice shall preside: And no Person shall be convicted without the Concurrence of two thirds of the Members present.

    I. 22, 224, 231, (232, 237, 238), 244, (247, 292). **II.** (39, 46, 136,

145, 147, 157), 159, 172, 186, (367, 423, 430, 493, 495), 497, 498, 499, (532, 547), 552, 563, 572, 574, 592, (610), 612, 653. **III**. 148, 162, (250), 406, 528. **IV**. 46, 48. **S**. 189, 190.

[Clause 7]. Judgment in Cases of Impeachment shall not extend further than to removal from Office, and disqualification to hold and enjoy any Office of honor, Trust or Profit under the United States: but the Party convicted shall nevertheless be liable and subject to Indictment, Trial, Judgment and Punishment, according to Law.

II. 173, 187, (435), 438, 576, 592, 612, 653. **III**. 407. **IV**. 56. **S**. 210.

Section. 4. [Clause 1]. The Times, Places and Manner of holding Elections for Senators and Representatives, shall be prescribed in each State by the Legislature thereof; but the Congress may at any time by Law make or alter such Regulations, except as to the Places of chusing Senators.

II. 135, (139, 141), 153, 155, 165, 179, (229), 239, (244), 567, 592, 613, 653. **III**. 148, (195), 267, 311, (319), 344, (359). **IV**. 40, 41. **S**. 185.

[Clause 2]. The Congress shall assemble at least once in every Year, and such Meeting shall be on the first Monday in December, unless they shall by Law appoint a different Day.

II. 135, 163, 177, (193), 197, (206, 209), 565, 592, 653. **III**. 148. **IV**. 101.

Section. 5. [Clause 1]. Each House shall be the Judge of the Elections, Returns and Qualifications of its own Members, and a Majority of each shall constitute a Quorum to do Business; but a smaller Number may adjourn from day to day, and may be authorized to compel the Attendance of absent Members, in such Manner, and under such Penalties as each House may provide.

II. (140, 141), 155, 165, 166, 180, (245), 251, (256), 300, 305, 567, 592, 611, 653. **III**. 252. **IV**. 40, 42. **S**. 185, 186.

[Clause 2]. Each House may determine the Rules of its Proceedings, punish its Members for disorderly Behaviour, and, with the Concurrence of two thirds, expel a Member.

II. (140, 141, 142), 156, 158, 166, 180, (246), 254, (256), 567, 592, 653. **III**. 112. **IV**. 40, 41, 42, 43. **S**. 185, 186, 187.

[Clause 3]. Each House shall keep a Journal of its Proceedings, and from time to time publish the same, excepting such Parts as may in their Judgment require Secrecy; and the Yeas and Nays of the Members of either House on any question shall, at the Desire of one fifth of those Present, be entered on the Journal.

II. 156, 166, 180, (246), 254, (257), 259, (264), 568, 592, 613, 635, 653. **III**. 311, 326, 345. **IV**. 6, 59. **S**. 269.

[Clause 4]. Neither House . . . shall . . . adjourn for more than

three days, nor to any other Place than that in which the two Houses shall
be sitting.

II. (140, 142), 156, 158, 166, 180, (258), 260, (293), 568, 593,
654. **III.** 312. **IV.** 41, 43. **S.** 185, 186, 187.

Section. 6. [Clause 1]. The Senators and Representatives shall receive
a Compensation for their Services, to be ascertained by Law, and paid out
of the Treasury of the United States. They shall in all Cases, except Treason, Felony and Breach of the Peace, be privileged from Arrest during
their Attendance at the Session of their respective Houses, and in going to
and returning from the same; and for any Speech or Debate in either
House, they shall not be questioned in any other Place.

I. 20, (210, 211), 215, 219, (221, 222), 228, 229, (235, 369), 371,
(383), 385, 391, (418), 426, (433). **II.** 129, 135, (140, 141, 142), 156,
166, 180, (246), 254, (256, 282), 290, (293), 334, (341, 502), 564,
567, 568, 593, 633, (635), 654. **III.** 127, 148, (155), 194, 312, 384.
IV. 40, 42, 43. **S.** 185, 186, 187.

[Clause 2]. No Senator or Representative shall, during the Time
for which he was elected, be appointed to any civil Office under the
Authority of the United States, which shall have been created, or the
Emoluments whereof shall have been encreased during such time; and no
Person holding any Office under the United States, shall be a Member of
either House during his Continuance in Office.

I. 20, 21, (210, 211), 217, (219, 221, 222), 228, 229, (235, 370),
375, 379, (383), 386, 391, (419), 428, (434, 435), 513, (518). **II.** 129,
130, (140, 141), 155, 166, 180, (282), 283, (293), 483, (484, 486),
489, 568, 593, 613, 654. **III.** (148, 155), 200, 313, 354. **IV.** 4, 41,
42, 57. **S.** 185, 186, 252.

Section. 7. [Clause 1]. All Bills for raising Revenue shall originate in
the House of Representatives; but the Senate may propose or concur with
Amendments as on other Bills.

I. (224), 233, (238, 523, 524), 526, (535, 538), 543. **II.** 3, (12),
14, (16), 131, (144), 154, 164, 178, 191, 210, (214), 223, (226), 230,
232, (243, 258), 262, (264, 266), 273, (294), 297, (353), 357, 358,
(505), 508, 509, 514, (545), 552, 568, 593, 638, 654. **III.** 148, (156),
201, 265, 317, (356, 416). **IV.** 5, 23, 45, 57. **S.** 102, 189, 252.

[Clause 2]. Every Bill . . . shall [be subject to Veto of President
and reconsideration by Congress]. . . . If after such Reconsideration two
thirds . . . shall agree to pass the Bill . . . it shall become a Law. . . . If
any Bill shall not be returned by the President within ten Days (Sundays
excepted) after it shall have been presented to him, the Same shall be a
Law, in like Manner as if he had signed it, unless the Congress by their
Adjournment prevent its Return, in which Case it shall not be a Law.

I. 21, (28, 94), 97, (105, 107, 109), 110, (131), 138, (141, 144,

226), 230, (236, 292). **II.** (71), 73, 132, (135, 146), 160, 167, 181, 200, 294, 298, (302), 563, 568, (582), 585, (589), 593, 608, 654. **III.** (133, 148), 202, (385), 424, 494. **IV.** 3, 7, 16, 47, 57, 81. **S.** 49, 190, 251, 297.

[Clause 3]. Every Order, Resolution, or Vote . . . shall [be subject to Veto of President] according to the Rules and Limitations prescribed in the Case of a Bill.

II. (295), 301, (303), 304, 569, 594, 655. **IV.** 5.

Section. 8. The Congress shall have Power

I. 21, (47), 53, (56, 61, 225), 229, (236), 243, (247), 291. **II.** (14), 16, (21), 25, 131, (151), 321, (325). **III.** 99, 268, 526, 612, 615.

[Clause 1]. To lay and collect Taxes, Duties, Imposts and Excises, to pay the Debts and provide for the common Defence and general Welfare of the United States; but all Duties, Imposts and Excises shall be uniform throughout the United States;

I. 243, (247). **II.** 135, (142), 157, (158), 167, 181, 211, (303), 305, 308, (322), 326, (352), 355, 366, 378, (382), 392, (408, 410), 412, 414, 418, 434, (437), 470, (473), 481, 493, 495, (497, 499, 503), 529, 569, 571, 594, (610), 614, 655. **III.** 84, 99, 149, (156, 169), 203, 213, 309, 365, 379, 456, 477, 483, 518, 547. **IV.** 5, 7, 43, 57, 85, 86. **S.** 187, 251, 318.

[Clause 2]. To borrow Money on the credit of the United States;

II. (144), 168, 182, (303, 304), 308, (311), 569, 594, 655. **III.** 205. **IV.** 45. **S.** 188.

[Clause 3]. To regulate Commerce with foreign Nations, and among the several States, and with the Indian tribes;

I. 133, (142), 243, (247). **II.** 135, (143), 157, (158, 159), 167, 169, 181, 183, 191, 211, (304), 308, (321), 324, (366), 367, 374, (396), 400, (409), 417, (446), 449, 493, 495, (497, 499, 503), 504, 529, 563, 569, 595, (610), 625, 631, 633, (634, 635, 636), 639, 655. **III.** 128, 164, 168, 210, 303, 333, 367, 477, 478, 518, 547, 615. **IV.** 23, 35, 43, 44, 52, 57, 61, 100, 102, 103. **S.** 102, 117, 187, 188, 209, 251, 270.

[Clause 4]. To establish an uniform Rule of Naturalization, and uniform Laws on the subject of Bankruptcies throughout the United States;

I. 245, (247). **II.** (144), 158, 167, 182, (304), 308, (445), 447, 483, (484, 486), 489, 569, 570, 595, 655. **III.** 120, 359, 380, 548. **IV.** 45. **S.** 188.

[Clause 5]. To coin Money, regulate the Value thereof, and of foreign Coin, and fix the Standard of Weights and Measures;

II. 136, (143, 144), 159, 167, 182, (304), 308, (311), 569, 595, 655. **IV.** 44. **S.** 188.

[Clause 6]. To provide for the Punishment of counterfeiting the Securities and current Coin of the United States;

II. (144), 168, 182, (312), 315, 316, (320), 570, 595, 655. **IV.** 45, 52. **S.** 188, 209.

[Clause 7]. To establish Post Offices and post Roads;

I. 243, (247). **II.** 135, (144), 159, 168, 182, (303), 304, 308, (311), (322), 326, 328, 569, 595, 615, (620), 655. **IV.** 45. **S.** 188.

[Clause 8]. To promote the Progress of Science and useful Arts, by securing for limited Times to Authors and Inventors the exclusive Right to their respective Writings and Discoveries;

II. (321, 322), 325, (505), 509, 570, 595, 655. **III.** (122).

[Clause 9]. To constitute Tribunals inferior to the supreme Court;

I. (118), 125, (127, 226), 231, (237, 292). **II.** (38), 45, 133, (144), 168, 182, (313), 315, (320), 570, 595, 655. **III.** 206. **IV.** 44. **S.** 188.

[Clause 10]. To define and punish Piracies and Felonies committed on the high Seas, and Offences against the Law of Nations;

II. (143), 168, 182, (312), 315, (320), 570, 595, 614, 655. **III.** 332. **IV.** 44. **S.** 188.

[Clause 11]. To declare War, grant Letters of Marque and Reprisal, and make Rules concerning Captures on Land and Water;

I. 18, 244, (247), 292. **II.** (143, 144), 168, 182, (313), 315, 318, (320, 322), 326, 328, (333), 505, (508), 570, 595, 655. **III.** 250, 405. **IV.** 44. **S.** 188.

[Clause 12]. To raise and support Armies, but no Appropriation of Money to that Use shall be for a longer Term than two Years;

II. (143), 158, 168, 182, (323), 329, (333), 334, (341, 505), 508, 509, 563, 570, 595, 616, (633), 635, 640, 656. **III.** 207, 319. **IV.** 44, 59. **S.** 188, 269.

[Clause 13]. To provide and maintain a Navy;

II. (143), 158, 168, 182, (323), 330, (333), 570, 595, 656. **IV.** 44. **S.** 188.

[Clause 14]. To make Rules for the Government and Regulation of the land and naval Forces;

II. (323), 330, (333), 570, 595, 656. **IV.** 94.

[Clause 15]. To provide for calling forth the Militia to execute the Laws of the Union, suppress Insurrections, and repel Invasions;

I. 21, 47, 54, 61, 245, (247). **II.** 135, (144, 159), 168, 182, (337), 344, (382), 389, 570, 595, 656. **III.** 148, (157), 207, 285, 318, 527, 616. **IV.** 45. **S.** 188.

[Clause 16]. To provide for organizing, arming, and disciplining, the Militia, and for governing such Part of them as may be employed in the Service of the United States, reserving to the States respectively, the Appointment of the Officers, and the Authority of training the Militia according to the discipline prescribed by Congress;

I. (292). **II.** (135), 136, 159, 168, (323), 330, (352), 356, (368), 377, (380), 384, (394), 570, 595, (616), 656. **III.** 118, (157), 208, 259, (319), 370, 420.

[Clause 17]. To exercise exclusive Legislation . . . over . . . the Seat of the Government . . . and to exercise like Authority over all Places purchased by the Consent of the Legislature of the State in which the Same shall be, for the Erection of Forts, Magazines, Arsenals, dock-Yards, and other needful Buildings;

II. (117), 127, 261, (321), 325, (505, 506), 509, 510, 570, 595, 656. **III.** 122, 408. **IV.** 5.

[Clause 18]. To make all Laws which shall be necessary and proper for carrying into Execution the foregoing Powers, . . .

II. (144), 168, 182, (337), 344, 563, 570, 596, 633, (636), 640, 656. **III.** 239, 362. **IV.** 45, 56, 57. **S.** 189, 251.

Section. 9. [Clause 1]. The Migration or Importation of such Persons . . . shall not be prohibited by the Congress prior to the Year one thousand eight hundred and eight, but a Tax or duty may be imposed on such Importation, not exceeding ten dollars for each Person.

II. (95, 143), 169, 183, 220, (354), 364, (366), 369, (378, 396), 400, (408), 414, (446), 449, 571, 596, 610, 640, 656. **III.** 135, (149), 160, (165), 210, 253, 324, 334, 346, 355, 360, 361, 367, 376, 436, 438, 439, 442. **IV.** 5, 44. **S.** 187.

[Clause 2]. The Privilege of the Writ of Habeas Corpus shall not be suspended, unless when in Cases of Rebellion or Invasion the public Safety may require it.

II. (334), 341, (435), 438, 576, 596, 656. **III.** 122, (149, 157), 213, (290).

[Clause 3]. No Bill of Attainder or ex post facto Law shall be passed.

II. (368), 375, (378), 448, 571, 596, 610, (617), 640, 656. **III.** (165). **IV.** 59. **S.** 269.

[Clause 4]. No Capitation, or other direct, Tax shall be laid, unless in Proportion to the Census . . .

II. (143), 169, 183, 366, (374, 378, 396), 400, (409), 417, 572, 596, (610), 618, 656. **III.** 83, 149, 325, 360. **IV.** 43, 59, 100. **S.** 187, 269.

[Clause 5]. No Tax or Duty shall be laid on Articles exported from any State.

I. 286, 592. **II.** 95, (142, 143), 168, 183, (303), 305, (354), 359, (365), 374, 571, 596, 657. **III.** 135, 149, 365. **IV.** 5, 43. **S.** 187.

[Clause 6]. No Preference shall be given by any Regulation of

Commerce or Revenue to the Ports of one State over those of another: nor shall Vessels bound to, or from, one State, be obliged to enter, clear, or pay Duties in another.

II. 378, (410), 417, 420, (434), 437, (468), 470, (473), 480, 482, 571, 596, (610), 618, 657. **III**. 136, 149, (157), 213, 365.

[Clause 7]. No Money shall be drawn from the Treasury, but in Consequence of Appropriations made by Law; and a regular Statement and Account of the Receipts and Expenditures of all public Money shall be published from time to time.

I. (523), 524, (526), 538. **II**. (12), 14, (16), 154, 164, 178, 280, (505), 509, 545, (552), 568, 596, (610), 618, 657. **III**. (149), 311, 326. **IV**. 59. **S**. 269.

[Clause 8]. No Title of Nobility shall be granted by the United States: And no Person holding any Office of Profit or Trust under them, shall, without the Consent of the Congress, accept of any present, Emolument, Office, or Title, of any kind whatever, from any King, Prince, or foreign State.

II. 169, 183, (381), 389, (394, 435), 442, 572, 596, 657. **III**. 150, 327.

Section. 10. [Clause 1]. No State shall enter into any Treaty, Alliance, or Confederation; grant Letters of Marque and Reprisal; coin Money; emit Bills of Credit; make any Thing but gold and silver Coin a Tender in Payment of Debts; pass any Bill of Attainder, ex post facto Law, or Law impairing the Obligation of Contracts, or grant any Title of Nobility.

I. 26. **II**. 135, (144), 169, 187, (435, 437), 439, (444), 448, 577, 596, (610), 619, 636, 640, 657. **III**. 100, 150, 214, 328, 349, 495, 547, 548, 616. **IV**. 45, 59. **S**. 188, 269.

[Clause 2]. No State shall, without the Consent of the Congress, lay any Imposts or Duties on Imports or Exports, except what may be absolutely necessary for executing it's inspection Laws: and the net Produce of all Duties and Imposts, laid by any State on Imports or Exports, shall be for the Use of the Treasury of the United States; and all such Laws shall be subject to the Revision and Controul of the Congress.

II. 135, (143, 159), 169, 187, (435, 437), 441, 442, (444), 577, (583), 588, 597, (605), 607, 624, 640, 657. **III**. 215, 268, 328, 519, 547. **IV**. 43. **S**. 187.

[Clause 3]. No State shall, without the Consent of Congress, lay any Duty of Tonnage, keep Troops, or Ships of War in time of Peace, enter into any Agreement or Compact with another State, or with a foreign Power, or engage in War, unless actually invaded, or in such imminent Danger as will not admit of delay.

II. 135, 169, 187, (437), 442, 504, 577, 597, 625, 633, 634, 657. **III**. 548.

ARTICLE. II.

Section. 1. [Clause 1]. The Executive Power shall be vested in a President of the United States of America. He shall hold his Office during the term of four Years, . . .

I. 21, (28, 63), 64, (70, 72, 73, 78, 79), 88, (90, 92, 93), 96, (105, 106, 109, 225), 230, (236), 244, (247), 254, (261, 266, 272, 292). **II**. 22, (23, 29), 33, (50), 51, 52, 58, (97), 100, 102, (107), 112, (116), 118, 132, 134, (135, 145, 158, 160, 161), 171, 185, (396), 401, 404, 407, (493), 497, 500, (507), 511, (517), 525, 527, 572, 597, 657. **III**. (110), 127, 132, 169, 216, 255, (298), 329, (338), 346, (354). **IV**. 4, 17, 46, 57, 101. **S**. 50, 189, 252.

[Clauses 1–4]. Each State shall appoint, in such Manner as the Legislature thereof may direct, a Number of Electors, equal to the whole number of Senators and Representatives to which the State may be entitled in the Congress; but no Senator or Representative, or Person holding an Office of Trust or Profit under the United States, shall be appointed an Elector.

The Electors shall meet in their respective States, and vote by Ballot for two Persons, of whom one at least shall not be an Inhabitant of the same State with themselves. . . . The Person having the greatest Number of Votes shall be the President, if such Number be a Majority of the whole Number of Electors appointed; . . . and if no Person have a Majority, then from the five highest on the List the said House shall in like Manner chuse the President. But in chusing the President, the Votes shall be taken by States, the Representation from each State having one Vote; . . . In every Case, after the Choice of the President, the Person having the greatest Number of Votes of the Electors shall be the Vice President. . . .

I. 21, (28, 64), 68, (77), 80, (89, 91, 149), 156, (163), 168, (174), 175, (180, 226), 230, (236), 244, (247, 292). **II**. (22), 29, (50), 57, (60), 63, 69, (71), 73, (85), 95, (97), 98, 99, 105, (107), 108, 113, (116), 118, 134, (135, 145), 171, 185, 196, (397), 401, (406, 493), 497, 499, (503, 507), 511, (517), 521, (530, 532), 535, 572, 597, (621), 626, 658. **III**. 132, 150, (158), 166, 217, 329, 331, 364, 382, 394, 399, 400, 401, 402, 405, 422, 458, 459, 460, 461, 462, 464. **IV**. 3, 5, 46, 58, 60, 96, 102. **S**. 269.

[Clause 5]. No Person except a natural born Citizen, or a Citizen of the United States, at the time of the Adoption of this Constitution, shall be eligible to the Office of President; neither shall any Person be eligible to that Office who shall not have attained to the Age of thirty five Years, and been fourteen Years a Resident within the United States.

II. 116, (121, 134), (337), 344, 367, (494), 498, (532), 536, 574, 598, 659.

[Clause 6]. In Case of the Removal of the President from Office, . . . the Same shall devolve on the Vice President, and the Congress may by Law provide for the Case of Removal, Death, Resignation or Inability, both of the President and Vice President, declaring what Officer shall then act . . .

I. (292). **II.** (146), 172, 186, 402, 427, (495), 499, (532), 535, 573, 575, 598, 626, 659. **IV.** 47, 102. **S.** 190.

[Clause 7]. The President shall . . . receive for his Services, a Compensation, which shall neither be encreased nor diminished during the Period for which he shall have been elected, and he shall not receive within that Period any other Emolument from the United States, or any of them.

I. 21, (63, 77), 81, (89, 91), 230, (236), 244, (247). **II.** 61, (69), 116, (121), 132, (134, 146), 172, 185, (335), 341, 575, 599, 621, 626, (636), 659. **III.** 111, 332. **IV.** 46, 47, 60. **S.** 190, 269.

[Clause 8]. Before he enter on the Execution of his Office, he shall take the following Oath or Affirmation: . . .

II. (146), 172, 185, (422), 427, (432), 575, 599, 621, 659. **IV.** 47. **S.** 190.

Section. 2. [Clause 1]. The President shall be Commander in Chief of the Army and Navy of the United States, and of the Militia of the several States, when called into the actual Service of the United States; he may require the Opinion, in writing, of the principal Officer in each of the executive Departments, upon any Subject relating to the Duties of their respective Offices, and he shall have Power to grant Reprieves and Pardons for Offences against the United States, except in Cases of Impeachment.

I. (66, 70, 74, 111), 244, (247, 292). **II.** 135, (145, 146), 157, 158, 171, 185, 329, (335), 342, 367, (411), 419, (422), 426, (495), 499, (533), 541, (543), 564, 575, 599, 621, 626, (636), 639, 659. **III.** 111, 127, (158), 218, 302. **IV.** 16, 46, 47, 53, 60. **S.** 49, 189, 210, 270.

[Clause 2]. He shall have Power, by and with the Advice and Consent of the Senate, to make Treaties, provided two thirds of the Senators present concur; and he shall nominate, and by and with the Advice and Consent of the Senate, shall appoint Ambassadors, other public Ministers and Consuls, Judges of the supreme Court, and all other Officers of the United States, whose Appointments are not herein otherwise provided for, and which shall be established by Law: but the Congress may by Law vest the Appointment of such inferior Officers, as they think proper, in the President alone, in the Courts of Law, or in the Heads of Departments.

I. 21, (63), 67, (70, 116), 119, (126, 127), 128, (224, 226), 230, 232, (236, 238), 244, (247, 292, 300). **II.** 23, (33, 37), 41, (71), 80, 116, (121), 132, (134, 136, 143, 144, 145, 146), 155, 169, 171, (172), 183, 185, 297, (313), 319, (382), 389, 392, (395, 398), 405, (407, 411), 418, 420, (495), 498, (532), 538, 540, (544), 547, 550, 574,

599, (621), 627, 628, 639, 659. **III**. 127, 133, 150, (158, 162), 166, 218, (249, 251), 302, 306, (342), 347, 356, (357, 358), 370, 371, 373, 375, 385, 421, 424, 427. **IV**. 44, 45, 46, 47, 52, 53, 57, 58, 60. **S**. 188, 189, 190, 210, 252, 262, 270.

[Clause 3]. The President shall have Power to fill up all Vacancies that may happen during the Recess of the Senate, by granting Commissions which shall expire at the End of their next Session.

II. (533), 540, 574, 600, 660. **III**. 421.

Section. 3. He shall from time to time give to the Congress Information of the State of the Union, and recommend to their consideration such Measures as he shall judge necessary and expedient; he may, on extraordinary Occasions, convene both Houses, or either of them, and in Case of Disagreement between them, with Respect to the Time of Adjournment, he may adjourn them to such Time as he shall think proper; he shall receive Ambassadors and other public Ministers; he shall take Care that the Laws be faithfully executed, and shall Commission all the Officers of the United States.

I. 21, (63, 66), 67, (70, 226), 230, (236), 244, (247, 292). **II**. 23, (32), 116, (121), 132, (134, 145, 146), 158, 171, 185, (398), 404, (411), 419, 420, (547), 553, 574, 600, 660. **III**. 312, 616. **IV**. 46, 47, 53. **S**. 189, 190, 210.

Section. 4. The President, Vice President and all civil Officers of the United States, shall be removed from Office on Impeachment for, and conviction of, Treason, Bribery, or other high Crimes and Misdemeanors.

I. (78), 85, 90, (91, 92, 226), 230, (236), 244, (247, 292). **II**. 53, (61), 64, 116, (121), 132, (134, 145), 172, 186, (337, 344, 367, 422), 427, (495), 499, (545), 550, 575, 600, (612), (637), 660. **III**. 111, 219, 406. **IV**. 3, 46, 56, 60. **S**. 189, 210, 270.

ARTICLE III.

Section. 1. The judicial Power of the United States, shall be vested in one supreme Court, and in such inferior Courts as the Congress may from time to time ordain and establish. The Judges, both of the supreme and inferior Courts, shall hold their Offices during good Behaviour, and shall, at stated Times, receive for their Services, a Compensation, which shall not be diminished during their Continuance in Office.

I. 21, (28), 95, (104), 116, (118, 119), 124, (126, 127, 226), 230, (236), 238, 244, (247, 292). **II**. (37), 41, 44, (117), 122, 132, 136, (146), 172, 186, (312), 314, 315, (320), 335, (341, 422), 428, (432, 532), 538, 575, 600, 621, (637, 638), 660. **III**. (169), 220, 332, 371, 391, 616. **IV**. 23, 47, 54, 60. **S**. 102, 190, 244, 270.

Section. 2. [Clause 1]. The judicial Power shall extend to all Cases, in Law and Equity, arising under this Constitution, the Laws of the United States, and Treaties made, or which shall be made, under their Authority;—to all Cases affecting Ambassadors, other public Ministers and Consuls;—to all Cases of admiralty and maritime Jurisdiction;—to Controversies to which the United States shall be a Party;—to Controversies between two or more States;—between a State and Citizens of another State;—between Citizens of different States,—between Citizens of the same State claiming Lands under Grants of different States, and between a State, or the Citizens thereof, and foreign States, Citizens or Subjects.

I. 22, (28), 211, (220), 223, 231, (232, 237), 238, 243, 244, (247, 292), 317, (326, 333). **II**. (39), 46, 132, 135, (136, 144, 146), 157, (159), 160, 162, 170, 172, 183, 186, (335), 342, 367, (396), 400, (406, 422, 423, 425), 428, 430, (432), 576, 600, 621, 660. **III**. 117, 127, (156, 169), 220, (240), 299, 310, 330, 349, 407, 420, 616. **IV**. 44, 47, 48, 54, 55, 56, 61, 85, 96. **S**. 188, 190, 244, 245, 270.

[Clause 2]. In all Cases affecting Ambassadors, other public Ministers and Consuls, and those in which a State shall be Party, the supreme Court shall have original Jurisdiction. In all the other Cases . . . appellate Jurisdiction, both as to Law and Fact, . . .

I. 22, (28), 244, (247, 292). **II**. (147), 157, 173, 186, (424), 431, 432, (434), 437, (458, 459), 466, 576, 601, (637), 661. **III**. (156), 220, (273, 287, 299). **IV**. 48, 53, 61. **S**. 190, 210, 270.

[Clause 3]. The Trial of all Crimes, . . . shall be by Jury; . . .

II. (144), 173, 187, (433, 434), 438, (444), 576, 587, 601, 628, 635, 640, 661. **III**. 101, 150, 163, (167), 221, (250, 298), 309, 332, (349), 352, 616. **IV**. 45, 55, 94, 95. **S**. 189, 245.

Section. 3. Treason against the United States, shall consist only in levying War against them, or in adhering to their Enemies, giving them Aid and Comfort. No Person shall be convicted of Treason unless on the Testimony of two Witnesses to the same overt Act, or on Confession in open Court.

The Congress shall have Power to declare the Punishment of Treason, but no Attainder of Treason shall work Corruption of Blood, or Forfeiture except during the Life of the Person attainted.

I. 292, (300). **II**. 136, (144), 168, 182, (337), 345, 351, 564, 571, (580), 601, 626, 633, (636, 637), 639, 661. **III**. 127, (158), 163, 218, 223. **IV**. 5, 45, 60, 61. **S**. 189, 270.

ARTICLE. IV.

Section. 1. Full Faith and Credit shall be given in each State to the public Acts, Records, and judicial Proceedings of every other State. And the Congress may by general Laws prescribe the Manner in which such Acts, Records and Proceedings shall be proved, and the Effect thereof.

I. 245, (247). **II.** 135, 174, 188, (445), 447, (456), 483, (485, 486), 488, 577, 601, 661. **III.** 112.

Section. 2. [Clause 1]. The Citizens of each State shall be entitled to all Privileges and Immunities of Citizens in the several States.

II. 135, 173, 187, (437), 443, (456), 577, 601, (637), 662. **III.** 112, 445. **IV.** 61, 98. **S.** 270.

[Clause 2]. A Person charged in any State with Treason, Felony, or other Crime, who shall flee from Justice, and be found in another State, shall on Demand of the executive Authority of the State from which he fled, be delivered up, to be removed to the State having Jurisdiction of the Crime.

II. 135, 174, 187, (437), 443, (456), 577, 601, 621, 662. **III.** 112.

[Clause 3]. No Person held to Service or Labour in one State, under the Laws thereof, escaping into another, shall, in Consequence of any Law or Regulation therein, be discharged from such Service or Labour, but shall be delivered up on Claim of the Party to whom such Service or Labour may be due.

II. 443, (446), 453, 577, 601, 621, 628, 662. **III.** 84, 254, 325.

Section. 3. [Clause 1]. New States may be admitted by the Congress into this Union; but no new State shall be formed or erected within the Jurisdiction of any other State; nor any State be formed by the Junction of two or more States, or Parts of States, without the Consent of the Legislatures of the States concerned as well as of the Congress.

I. 22, (28), 117, (121, 126, 226), 231, (237), 245. **II.** 39, (46), 133, (136, 147, 151, 159), 173, 188, (446), 454, (457), 461, (470), 578, 602, (628), 662. **III.** 119, 223, 399, 404, 438. **IV.** 48, 49. **S.** 191.

[Clause 2]. The Congress shall have Power to dispose of and make all needful Rules and Regulations respecting the Territory or other Property belonging to the United States; and nothing in this Constitution shall be so construed as to Prejudice any Claims of the United States, or of any particular State.

I. 22, (28, 193), 202, (206). **II.** (321), 324, (458), 461, 466, 470, 578, 602, 662. **III.** 401, 404.

Section. 4. The United States shall guarantee to every State in this Union a Republican Form of Government, and shall protect each of them against Invasion; and on Application of the Legislature, or of the Executive (when the Legislature cannot be convened) against domestic Violence.

I. 22, (28, 117), 121, (126, 193), 202, 206, (227), 231, (237). **II.** (39), 47, 133, (137, 144, 148, 151), 159, 168, 174, 182, 188, 220, 222, (313), 316, (320, 459), 466, (470), 563, 578, 602, 621, (628), 662. **III.** 56, 256, 548. **IV.** 45, 49. **S.** 188, 191.

ARTICLE. V.

The Congress, whenever two thirds of both Houses shall deem it necessary, shall propose Amendments to this Constitution, or, on the Application of the Legislatures of two thirds of the several States, shall call a Convention for proposing Amendments, which, in either Case, shall be valid to all Intents and Purposes, as Part of this Constitution, when ratified by the Legislatures of three fourths of the several States, or by Conventions in three fourths thereof, . . . Provided that no Amendment which may be made prior to the Year One thousand eight hundred and eight shall in any Manner affect the first and fourth Clauses in the Ninth Section of the first Article; and that no State, without its Consent, shall be deprived of it's equal Suffrage in the Senate.

I. 22, (28, 117), 121, (126, 194), 202, (206, 227), 231, (237). **II.** 84, (87), 133, (136, 148, 152), 159, 174, 188, (461), 467, (555), 557, 578, 602, 629, (634), 662. **III.** 120, 126, 367, 400, 575. **IV.** 49, 61. **S.** 191, 192, 270.

ARTICLE. VI.

[Clause 1]. All Debts contracted and Engagements entered into, before the Adoption of this Constitution, shall be as valid against the United States under this Constitution, as under the Confederation.

I. 22, (28), 117, (121, 126, 227), 231, (237). **II.** 6, (39), 46, (322), 326, (352), 355, (368), 377, (382), 392, (394, 396), 400, (408), 412, 571, 603, 663. **III.** 171, 239, 259, 275, 297, 299, 308, 327, 360, 361, 366, 484, 493.

[Clause 2]. This Constitution, and the Laws of the United States which shall be made in Pursuance thereof; and all Treaties made, or which shall be made, under the Authority of the United States, shall be the supreme Law of the Land; and the Judges in every State shall be bound thereby, any Thing in the Constitution or Laws of any State to the Contrary notwithstanding.

I. 21, (28), 47, (54, 61, 131), 140, 150, (162), 164, (169, 171, 173, 179, 225), 229, (236), 243, 245, (247), 250, 256, (293), 318, 438, 447. **II.** (21), 22, 27, 132, (136, 144, 157), 169, 183, (381), 389, 390, (394, 409), 417, 440, 572, 589, 603, 639, 663. **III.** 56, 73, 119, 127, 133, (241), 273, 286, 347, 516, 523, 527, 538, 549. **IV.** 3, 4, 5, 45, 83. **S.** 189, 312.

[Clause 3]. The Senators and Representatives before mentioned, and the Members of the several State Legislatures, and all executive and judicial Officers, both of the United States and of the several States, shall be bound by Oath or Affirmation, to support this Constitution; but no religious Test shall ever be required as a Qualification to any Office or public Trust under the United States.

I. 22, (28, 117), 122, (126, 194), 203, (207, 227), 231, (237). **II**. (84), 87, 133, (146, 148, 151), 159, 174, 188, (335), 342, (461), 468, 579, 603, 663. **III**. 227, 293, 297, 310. **IV**. 47, 49. **S**. 190, 191.

Article. VII.

The Ratification of the Conventions of nine States, shall be sufficient for the Establishment of this Constitution between the States so ratifying the Same.

I. 22, (28, 118), 122, (126), 179, (183, 209), 214, (220, 227), 232, (237), 250, (258, 264, 274), 314, (335). **II**. (84), 88, (96), 133, (136, 148, 149, 151), 160, 174, 189, 211, 468, (471), 475, 482, (556), 559, 579, 603, 631, (634), 663. **III**. 14, (66), 68, 72, 125, 137, (159), 227, 242, (257, 273, 288), 299, 308, (351). **IV**. 49, 50. **S**. 192.

GENERAL INDEX

Everything embodied in the final draft of the Constitution is to be traced through the Index by Clauses of the Constitution; but this General Index also analyzes the material by topics, independent of that index.

References to items which are duplicative of other items are in parentheses; usually the reference not in parentheses is to Madison's Notes. References to the fourth volume which *correct* material in the earlier volumes are in square brackets immediately after the references to the corrected items. As explained in the introduction, references to this volume follow the letter "**S**."

in Hamilton plan, **1**. 291, (300), **3**. 619.

bicameral, discussed and voted in convention, **1**. (334), 336–344, (344–353), 354–358, (362–364, 366, 367).

as referred to committee of detail, **2**. 129.

in its notes, **2**. (138), 150, 152, 163, **4**. 39.

in its report (III), **2**. 177.

report voted, **2**. (193), 196, (200).

as referred to committee of style, **2**. 565.

in its report, **2**. 590.

in Constitution, **2**. 651.

preconvention project, **3**. 23, 25.

supposed attitude of eastern delegates, **3**. 26.

Otto on plan (June), **3**. 40.

L. Martin's objections (Nov.), **3**. (155), 191–197.

Baldwin on (Dec.), **3**. 169.

Franklin's opposition, **3**. 297.

Davie on (1788), **3**. 340.

anecdote of Washington's advocacy, **3**. 359.

Morris on (1811), **3**. 419.

Bill of rights, in Pinckney plan, **3**. 122, 609.

in Sherman's proposals, **3**. 616, **S**. 287.

propositions proposed and committed, **2**. (334, 335), 341.

proposal rejected, **2**. (582), 587, 588.

Gerry on lack, **2**. 633, **3**. 128, **S**. 284.

Mason on lack, **2**. 637, 640, **3**. 136.

Wilson (1787) on omission, **3**. 143, 161, 162.

C. C. Pinckney (1788) on omission, **3**. 256.

L. Martin's attitude (1788), **3**. 273, 288–291, **S**. 295.

in first ten amendments, **4**. 93–95.

general reservation of rights, **4**. 95.

against states, **4**. 98.

See also Arrest; Habeas corpus; Jury; Press; Speech.

Bills. *See* Legislation; Money bills.

Bills of attainder. *See* Attainder.

Bills of credit, in Pinckney plan, **3**. 117, 607.

in Sherman's proposals, **3**. 616.

avoidance of state, desired by Randolph, **1**. 26.

prohibition of state, in notes of committee of detail, **2**. (144), 169, **4**. 44, **S**. 188.

power of Congress, in its notes, **2**. 168.

power and prohibition in its report (VII. § 1, XIII), **2**. 182, 187.

power discussed and dropped, **2**. (303), 308–310, (311).

prohibition on states, made absolute, **2**. (435), 439, (444).

prohibition as referred to committee of style, **2**. 577.

in its report, **2**. 597.

in Constitution, **2**. 657.

McHenry's explanation (Nov.), **3**. 150.

L. Martin (Nov.) on attempt to preserve power, **3**. 205.

his objections to prohibition on states, **3**. 214.

Davie (1788) on prohibition, **3**. 349, 350.

See also Counterfeiting; Legal tender; Paper money.

Bills of exchange, power over protest of foreign, proposed and committed, **2**. (445), 447, 448.

Blackstone, *Sir* William, cited, **1**. 472.

Blair, John, delegate from Virginia, **3**. 558.

credentials, **3**. 559–562.

Pierce on, **3**. 95.

arrives, **3**. 20.

attendance, **1**. 1, (3, 5), **3**. 587.

opposes single executive, **1**. 97.

approves veto of state laws, **1**. 168.

approves general plan for executive, **2**. 121.

opposes House control of money bills, **2**. 280.

opposes export duties, **2**. 363.

opposes weakening veto, **2**. 587.

plan for judiciary, **S**. 244, 245.

signs Constitution, **2**. 664.

Bleeker, Leonard, charges against Hamilton, **3**. 369.

Bloomfield, Joseph, Brearley's papers, **1**. xii, **3**. 431.

Blount, William, delegate from North Carolina, **3**. 559.

credentials, **3**. 569, 570.

Blount, William (*continued*)

Pierce on, **3**. 95.

attendance, **1**. 334, (335), **3**. 587.

on signing Constitution, **2**. 645 *n*., 646.

signs it, **2**. 665.

letters: to Caswell (May) on attending, **3**. 29;

(July) on leaving for Congress, **3**. 57;

(Aug.) on return and hopes, **3**. 71;

(Sept.) report on Constitution, **3**. 83;

to Clay (June) on attending, **4**. 64, **S**. 70;

to brother (June) on conditions, **4**. 65 (2), **S**. 76;

(July) on progress and task, violates secrecy, **4**. 71, **S**. 174, 175.

Bolingbroke, Henry St. John, *viscount*, early rise in office, **1**. 375.

Bond, Phineas, letter (July) to Carmarthen on rumors, **3**. 52.

Bonded servants. *See* White servants.

Bonds. *See* Securities.

Borrow money, power of Congress. *See* Debt.

Boston, elections, **2**. 216.

Boundaries. *See* Territory.

Bounties, Williamson (1792) on sectionalism, **3**. 365.

See also Protection.

Bourne, Edward G., acknowledgment to, **1**. ix.

Boutell, Lewis H., on Sherman's proposals, **3**. 615.

Bowdoin, James, defeated for reelection, **2**. 57.

Bowen, Jabez, letter to Convention, **3**. 19.

Boyd, Julian P., acknowledgment to, **4**. ix.

Brearley, David, delegate from New Jersey, **3**. 557.

papers and notes, **1**. xii, 16 *n*., 443 *n*., 573 *n*., **2**. 181 *n*., 610 *n*., 621 *n*., 633 *n*., **3**. 431.

credentials, **3**. 563.

Pierce on, **3**. 90.

arrives, **3**. 22.

attendance, **1**. 1, (3, 5), **3**. 587.

opposes proportional representation, **1**. 175, 176, (181, 184, 191).

moves request for attendance of New Hampshire delegates, **1**. 481, (494).

committees: original apportionment, **1**. 558, (562);

remaining matters, **2**. 473, (481).

on election of President, **2**. 402, 403.

presents reports, **2**. 483, (484), 493, (496), [**4**. 5], **2**. 505, (508).

on amendment, **2**. 630.

signs Constitution, **2**. 664.

letters: to Dayton (June) urging attendance, **3**. 37;

(July) on progress, committee of detail, **4**. 72, **S**. 195, 196;

to Paterson (Aug.) on progress and urging return, **3**. 73.

Brent, Daniel, Smyth's charge against Adams, **3**. 456–458.

Broom, Jacob, delegate from Delaware, **3**. 558.

credentials, **3**. 574.

Pierce on, **3**. 93.

arrives, **3**. 22.

attendance, **1**. 1, (3, 5), **3**. 587.

on term of senators, **1**. 421.

on basis of representation, **1**. 570.

finality of compromise, **2**. 19.

on election of executive, **2**. 32, 57, 63, 103, 404.

on term of executive, **2**. 33.

on ineligibility of congressmen to office, **2**. 290.

on payment of congressmen, **2**. 291, 293.

on punishment for treason, **2**. 348.

favors veto of state laws, **2**. 390.

on correspondence of President with governors, **2**. 419.

signs Constitution, **2**. 664.

Brown, John, letter to Convention, **3**. 19.

Brown, Nicholas, letter to Convention, **3**. 19.

Brown, William, North Carolina naval officer, **3**. 14.

Bureau of Rolls and Library, *Documentary History of the Constitution*, **1**. xii *n*., xv *n*., **4**. x, 11.

Journal, **1**. xii, **4**. 11.

Burnett, Edmund C., acknowledgments to, **3**. 18 *n*., **4**. ix.

Butler, Pierce, delegate from South Carolina, **3**. 559.

credentials, **3**. 583.

Pierce on, **3**. 96.

Canals (*continued*)
  Madison: (1824) on refusal of power,
    3. 463;
    (1831) on possible grant, **3**. 494.
  T. W. Cobb (1825) on refusal of
    power, **3**. 464.
  See also Internal improvements.
Capital of United States, in Pinckney plan
    and pamphlet, **3**. 122, 609.
  separation from a state capital, dis-
    cussed, **2**. (117), 127, 128.
  stability and locality, discussed, **2**. 261,
    [**4**. 5].
  separate district, proposed, **2**. (321),
    325.
  reported and voted, **2**. (505, 506), 509,
    510.
  as referred to committee of style, **2**.
    570.
  in its report, **2**. 595.
  in Constitution, 2. 656.
  provision for temporary, **2**. 665.
  Dayton on (1804), **3**. 408.
Capitation tax, apportionment, in notes of
    committee of detail, **2**. (143), 169,
    4. 43, **S**. 187.
  in its report (VII. § 5), **2**. 183.
  recommitted, **2**. 366, (374, 378).
  reported unchanged, **2**. (396), 400.
  voted, **2**. (409), 417.
  temporary provision against amendment,
    proposed and voted, **2**. (555, 556),
    559.
  as referred to committee of style, **2**.
    572, 578.
  in its report, **2**. 596, 602.
  amended to include other direct tax, **2**.
    (610*n*.), 618.
  in Constitution, **2**. 656, 663.
  report of North Carolina delegates
    (Sept.), **3**. 83.
  McHenry's explanation (Nov.), **3**. 149.
  Madison (1788) on limitation on slaves,
    3. 325.
  Baldwin (1790) on same, **3**. 360.
  See also Direct taxation.
Captures on land and sea, jurisdiction
    over, in Virginia plan, **1**. 22.
  dropped, **1**. (211), 220.
  power to make rules, in notes of com-
    mittee of detail, **2**. (143), 168, **4**.
    44, **S**. 188.

  in its report (VII. § 1), **2**. 182.
  power voted, **2**. (313), 315.
  as referred to committee of style, **2**.
    570.
  in its report, **2**. 595.
  in Constitution, **2**. 655.
Carmarthen, Francis Osborne, *marquis* of,
    letter from Bond on Convention, **3**.
    52.
Carnegie Endowment for International
    Peace, edition of Madison's Notes, **4**.
    x, 11.
Carrington, Edward, on franking mail of
    delegates, **3**. 17.
  letters: (June) to Jefferson on prospects
    and probable plan, **3**. 37;
    (Sept.) to Madison on attitude of Vir-
    ginia delegates in Congress, **3**. 98;
  from Hamilton, **3**. 366.
Carroll, Charles, of Carrollton, elected
    delegate, **3**. 22, 35, 558.
  why he declined, **3**. 339.
Carroll, Daniel, delegate from Maryland,
    3. 558, **4**. 64, **S**. 47.
  credentials, **3**. 586.
  Pierce on, **3**. 93.
  attendance, **1**. 557, (559), **3**. 587.
  committees: original apportionment, **1**.
    558, (562);
    commercial regulations, **2**. 410, (418);
    remaining matters, **2**. 473, (481).
  on slave representation, **1**. 588 *n*.
  on protection of states, **2**. 48.
  on per capita vote in Senate, **2**. 95.
  on election of executive, **2**. 105, 402,
    404.
  on direct tax before census, **2**. 106,
    350.
  on qualifications of congressmen, **2**.
    125, 226, 272.
  meetings of Maryland delegates, **2**.
    190, 210.
  opposes mere amendment of Confedera-
    tion, **2**. 190.
  on control of money bills, **2**. 210, 280.
  on taxation and commercial powers,
    navigation acts, **2**. 211.
  on ratification, **2**. 212, 357, 469, 475,
    477.
  on quorum in Congress, **2**. 253, 305.
  on expulsion of congressmen, **2**. 254.
  on entering dissent in Senate, **2**. 255.

on capital, **2**. 262.

on payment of congressmen, **2**. 292.

on veto, **2**. 300.

opposes export duties, **2**. 308.

on ex post facto laws, **2**. 376.

on prohibiting commercial discrimina-
tions, **2**. 417, 468, 475, 481.

opposes associating governors in appointing power, **2**. 420.

on admission and western claims, **2**.
461, 465.

on address to the people, **2**. 622.

on state tonnage duties and harbor improvements, **2**. 625, (633, 634).

on change in ratio of representation, **2**.
644.

signs Constitution, **2**. 664.

letter (May) on attendance, **4**. 62, **S**.
61.

letter (1788) to Madison on Maryland
Antifederalist statements, **3**. 305.

correspondence (1788) on Mercer's list
of monarchical delegates, **3**. 306,
319–324.

before legislature, **4**. 79, **S**. 285.

Carroll, *Rev.* John, letters to, **3**. 322–
324.

Carthage, and provinces, **1**. 135.

commercial cause of wars, **1**. 307.

Rome, **1**. 448, (456).

Caswell, *Gov.* Richard, circular (March)
calling for trade statistics, **3**. 14.

correspondence with delegates on allowance, **3**. 17, 46, 52.

to Spaight on adequate powers and separation of powers, **3**. 63.

reports from delegates, **3**. 29, 46, 57,
64, 68, 70, 71, 72, 74, 83.

and delegateship, **3**. 559, 567, 570.

Caucus, King (1824) on presidential nomination, **3**. 462.

Census, provision proposed and discussed,
1. 201, (205, 208, 564), 570, 571,
(575, 576), 578–588.

time of first and periodicity, proposals
and votes, **1**. (576), 588, (589, 590),
594, 596.

provision voted, **1**. (591), 597, **2**. 14.

as referred to committee of detail, **2**.
131.

in its notes, **2**. (139), 153, 154, 168,
4. 39, **S**. 184.

in its report (VII. § 3), **2**. 183.

first, within three years, **2**. (339), 350.

amended report, voted, **2**. 352, (357).

as referred to committee of style, **2**.
571.

in its report, **2**. 590.

correction, **4**. 59, **S**. 269.

in Constitution, **2**. 651.

Chapman, Reynolds, letter from Madison,
3. 494.

Charlemagne, authority, **1**. 285, (307).

Charles II of England, Louis XIV, **2**. 69,
251.

Charters. *See* Corporations.

Chase, Samuel, and Maryland delegation,
3. 339.

Chatham, William Pitt, *earl* of, reference,
2. 104.

Chesterfield, Philip Dormer Stanhope, *earl*
of, cited, **1**. 254, (261, 270).

Chief Justice of the United States, and
proposed executive council, **2**. 335,
(342), 367.

succession to presidency, **2**. 427.

to preside over presidential impeachment
trials: reported, **2**. (495), 498;

voted, **2**. (532), 538;

as referred to committee of style, **2**.
574;

in its report, **2**. 592;

in Constitution, **2**. 653.

Childs, Francis, Lansing-Hamilton controversy, **3**. 353.

Cicero, reference, **1**. 308.

Cincinnati, Order of the, political control
feared, **2**. 114, 119.

attitude toward Union, **3**. 17, 43.

meeting (1787), **3**. 23, **S**. 9 *n*.

Citizen of New Haven (Roger Sherman),
extract, **3**. 354.

Citizenship. *See* next titles; Naturalization;
Privileges.

Citizenship, in fourteenth amendment, **4**.
95.

See also next titles.

Citizenship as qualification for President,
instructions to committee of detail, **2**.
(117), 121, 124.

report by special committee, **2**. 367.

native or at adoption of Constitution, reported, **2**. 498.

voted, **2**. (532), 536.

in Constitution, **2**. 657.

in Hamilton's unpresented plan, **3**. 629.

Randolph on (1788), **3**. 327.

Foreigners, federal jurisdiction over cases, in Virginia plan, **1**. 22.

dropped in committee of the whole, **1**. (223, 232), 238.

in New Jersey plan, **1**. 244, (247, **2**. 157).

in Hamilton plan, **1**. 292, **3**. 626.

in notes of committee of detail, **2**. (147), 173, **4**. 48, **S**. 190.

in its report (XI. § 3), **2**. 186.

as referred to committee of style, **2**. 576.

in its report, **2**. 601.

in Constitution, **2**. 661.

See also Immigration; Naturalization.

Forts. *See* Federal sites.

Foster, Roger, acknowledgment to, **1**. ix.

Fourteenth amendment, text, **4**. 99.

Fourth amendment, text, **4**. 94.

France, references to government and foreign relations, **1**. 84, 448, (456, 458), **2**. 274, 289, 307.

United States debt, **1**. 262.

tobacco contract, **2**. 306.

slavery, **2**. 371.

rumor of interest in Convention, **3**. 305.

state violation of treaty, **3**. 548.

attitude, **4**. 22, **S**. 101.

See also Otto, Louis G.

Franklin, Benjamin, delegate from Pennsylvania, **3**. 558.

credentials, **3**. 566.

Pierce on, **3**. 91.

French character sketch, **3**. 235.

attendance, **1**. 7, (10), **3**. 33, 98, 270, 588.

and presidency of Convention, **1**. 4, [**4**. 3].

on veto of state laws contrary to treaties, **1**. 47, (54, 61), [**4**. 3].

opposes bicameral Congress, **1**. 48.

on importance of discussions, **1**. 65.

opposes payment of executive, **1**. (77), 81–85, (89, 91), **2**. 626.

favors plural executive, **1**. 85, 102 *n*., 103, (108).

on veto, **1**. 94, 98, (103, 106, 107, 109).

on appointment of judges, **1**. 119, (128).

counsels harmony, plan for representation and contributions, **1**. 197–200, [**4**. 3], **1**. (205).

on payment of congressmen, **1**. 216, 427.

proposes prayers, **1**. 450–452, (457).

compromise proposals on representation, **1**. 488, (498, 505), 507.

committee on representation, proposal in, **1**. 509, (516, 520), 523, (526 *n*., **2**. 12).

objects to piecemeal vote on report, **1**. 543.

on importance of control of money bills, **1**. 546, **2**. 233.

and secrecy, **1**. 606 *n*., **3**. 59.

on judges' salary, **2**. 44.

on impeachment of executive, **2**. 65, 67.

on reeligibility of executive, **2**. 120.

on suffrage, **2**. 204, (208, 210).

on qualification of congressmen, **2**. 236, 239, (243), 249.

on treason, **2**. 348.

favors a council, **2**. 542.

favors a second convention for amendments proposed by states, **2**. 564.

committee on economy, **2**. 607.

on canals, **2**. 615, (620).

on finished Constitution, plan for signing, **2**. 641–643, 646, 647, (649), **4**. 78–80, **S**. 279, 285, 289.

"rising sun" remark, **2**. 648.

signs Constitution, **2**. 664.

dines delegates, **3**. 20, 21.

letters: on assembling of Convention, **3**. 21(2);

(July) on hopes, **3**. 61;

(Sept.) on attendance and results, **3**. 98.

remark (June) on character of Convention, **3**. 33.

anecdote, **3**. 85.

and results, **3**. 98.

comment on final speech, garbled versions, **3**. 104, 168.

letters: (1787–88) on achievement, **3**. 131, 270, 296;

(1788) on bicameral Congress, **3**. 297;

(1788) on reeligibility of executive, **3**. 354.

as referred to committee of detail, **2**. 133.

in its notes, **2**. (144, 147), 168, 172, 173, **4**. 44, 47, 48, **S**. 188, 190.

in its report (VII. § 1, XI. § 1), **2**. 182, 186.

right of Congress to assign jurisdiction to, in report of committee (XI. § 3), **2**. 186.

report on establishment voted, **2**. (313), 315.

jurisdiction provisions, dropped, **2**. (425), 431, **4**. 53.

establishment as referred to committee of style, **2**. 570, 575.

in its report, **2**. 595, 600.

vote on reconsideration, **2**. 611.

in Constitution, **2**. 655, 660.

L. Martin (Nov.) on opposition, **3**. 206.

G. Morris (1802) on requirement, **3**. 391.

See also Judiciary.

Ingersoll, Charles J., letter from Madison, **3**. 495.

Ingersoll, Jared, delegate from Pennsylvania, **3**. 558, **S**. 7.

credentials, **3**. 565.

Pierce on, **3**. 91.

attendance, **1**. 7, (10), **3**. 588.

on signing of the Constitution, **2**. 647.

signs it, **2**. 664.

letter (April) on secretaryship, **3**. 18.

committee on Address, **4**. 83, **S**. 310.

speech, **S**. 100–105.

Inhabitance in the state, as qualification of congressmen, in notes of committee of detail, **2**. (139*n*.), 153, 155, 164, 165, **4**. 39*n*., **S**. 184*n*.

residence required in its report (IV. § 2, V. § 3), **2**. 178, 179.

"resident" changed to "inhabitant" and voted, term of inhabitance rejected, **2**. (213), 216–219, (225, 226, 228, 229), 239, (243).

as referred to committee of style, **2**. 565, 567.

in its report, **2**. 590, 591.

in Constitution, **2**. 651, 652.

in Hamilton's unpresented plan, **3**. 629.

McHenry's explanation (Nov.), **3**. 147.

See also Qualifications; Residence.

Inspection charges, permitted state export charges, discussed and voted, **2**. (583), 588, 589, 597*n*., (605), 607, 624.

import duties added, **2**. 624.

in Constitution, **2**. 657.

King (1788) on clause, **3**. 268.

Institutions, power of Congress to establish proposed, **2**. 322, (325).

Insurrection. *See* Domestic violence.

Interior, department of. *See* Domestic affairs.

Internal improvements, Randolph on, as needed power of Congress, **1**. 26.

See also Canals; Harbor; Post roads.

International law. *See* Law of nations.

Interstate agreements. *See* Agreements.

Interstate cases and state as party, jurisdiction in cases of citizens of different states, in Virginia plan, **1**. 22, (28).

Congress to decide disputes between states, in Pinckney plan, **2**. 135, **3**. 117, (607).

Virginia plan amended in committee of the whole, **1**. 211, (220).

general statement of jurisdiction substituted, **1**. 223, (232), 238.

territorial cases between state and federal government, in New Jersey plan, **3**. 611.

jurisdiction in notes of committee of detail, **2**. (147), 173, **4**. 48, **S**. 190.

and in its report (XI. § 3), **2**. 186.

trial by Senate of interstate land cases in its notes, **2**. 160–163, 170, 171.

and in its report (IX. §§ 2, 3), **2**. 183–185.

original jurisdiction of Supreme Court where state is party, in notes of committee, **2**. 173.

and in its report (XI. § 3), **2**. 186.

Senate trial dropped, **2**. (396), 400, 401, (406).

land cases added to court jurisdiction, **2**. (425), 431.

Mason papers on, **2**. (432), **4**. 54, **S**. 244.

as to cases involving western claims, **2**. (458, 459), 466, **3**. 627.

provisions as referred to committee of style, **2**. 576.

in its report, **2**. 600, 601.

in Constitution, **2**. 661.

McHenry, James (*continued*)
  reasons for signing Constitution, **2**. 649.
  signs it, **2**. 664.
  anecdotes on Convention, **3**. 85.
  address (Nov.) before Maryland House, **1**. xxv *n*., **3**. 144–150, **4**. 79, **S**. 285.
  on Randolph's presentation of Virginia plan, **3**. 145.
  on membership and organization of Congress, **3**. 146–148.
  on powers of Congress, **3**. 149.
  on prohibitions on Congress and states, **3**. 149, 150.
  on executive, **3**. 150.
  on judiciary, **3**. 150.
McKean, Thomas, pluralist, **1**. 320 *n*.
McLaughlin, Andrew C., acknowledgment to, **1**. ix.
McNeir, William, acknowledgment to, **1**. viii.
Madison, James, delegate from Virginia, **3**. 558.
  credentials, **3**. 559–562.
  Pierce on, **3**. 94.
  French character sketch, **3**. 237.
  lodgings, **3**. 58.
  attendance, **1**. 1, (3, 5), **3**. 589.
  on proportional representation in both Houses, opposes compromise, **1**. (31), 35, (36), 37, 206, (208), 321, (407), 415, 446, (455), 457, (458, 459), 463, (471), 475, (477–479), 485, 490, (496, 504, 505), 515, (519), 527, (535, 537), 543, 551, 554, (555), 562, **2**. 5, 8.
  on "national" government or mere amendment, **1**. 44, 134, (141, 146, 147), 219, 241, 246, 314, (325, 329, 333), 356, (363, 367), 499.
  on election of congressmen, **1**. 49, 52, (56, 57, 59), 134, (143, 146), 151, 154, 158, 364, (367), 416.
  on enumeration of powers of Congress, **1**. 53, (60).
  on coercion of states, **1**. 54.
  on preliminary establishment of general principles, **1**. 60.
  on powers of executive, **1**. (63), 66, 67, (70, 72).

on single executive and council, **1**. 70, 74, 97, **2**. 542.
on term of executive, **1**. 71, 74, **2**. 34, 35.
on removal and impeachment of executive, **1**. 86, (92), **2**. 65, 550, 551, 612.
on justices and veto, **1**. 94, (104), 108, 110, (131), 138, (144), **2**. 73, 74, 77, 298, (**4**. 81).
on provisional veto, **1**. 99, (106, 107, 109), **2**. 301, [**4**. 5], **2**. 586, 587, 608.
on appointment of justices, **1**. 120, (126, 128), 232, (238), **2**. 42, 44, 80, 82.
on ratification, **1**. 122, (126), **2**. 92, (96), 469, 475, 476.
on need of inferior courts, **1**. 124, 125, (128).
on veto of state laws, **1**. (162), 164, 168, 169, (170), 171, 318, 319, **2**. 27, 390, 440, 589.
on guarantee to states, **1**. (202), 206, 318, **2**. 47–49.
on term of representatives, **1**. 214, (220), 361, [**4**. 4].
on public opinion and action of Convention, **1**. 215, (220).
on payment of congressmen, **1**. 215, 373, (378), 427, (434), **2**. 291.
on term of senators and purpose of Senate, **1**. 218, (222), 421, (430).
on New Jersey plan, **S**. 95.
on federal jurisdiction, **1**. 223, (232), **2**. 46, 430, 431.
on control of money bills, **1**. 233, 527, (535), **2**. 224, 233, 276, 280.
on powers of Convention, **1**. 314, (325).
on compact, **1**. 314, (326), **2**. 93.
on violations of Confederation, **1**. 315–317, (326).
on interstate comity, **1**. 317, (327), **2**. 448, 489.
on ineligibility of congressman to office, **1**. 380, (383), 386, 388, (391–393), 429, 434.
on leaving matters for future amendment, **1**. 475, (478).
fears sectional (slavery) division, **1**. 476, 486, **2**. 10, 81.

committees: apportionment of representatives, **1**. 588, (562);

slave trade, **2**. 366, (375);

remaining matters, **2**. 473, (481);

style, **2**. 547, (553, 554).

on apportionment, original, basis, ratio, **1**. 568, 585, 601, **2**. 221, 553.

on equality of new states, **1**. 584, **2**. 454.

on period of census, **1**. 588.

on separation of powers, **2**. 34.

on salary of judges, **2**. 45, 429, 430.

on continuance of Confederation, **2**. 47.

on election of executive, **2**. 56, 63, 109, 114, 121, 403, 427, 500, 513–515, 526, 527, 535, 536, **S**. 301.

on qualifications of congressmen, **2**. 122, 123, 217, 235, (243), 249, 250, 268, 270.

on mutual negative of Houses of Congress, **2**. 197, (206).

on meeting of Congress, **2**. 197–199, (206).

on qualifications of electors of representatives, **2**. 203, 204 n., (208, 210).

on filling Senate vacancies, **2**. 232.

on regulation of congressional elections, **2**. 239, 240.

on compelling attendance in Congress, **2**. 253.

on expulsion of congressmen, **2**. 254.

on journals, **2**. (257), 259.

on location and stability of capital, **2**. 261, [**4**. 5].

on new Constitution and state pledges (naturalization), **2**. 270.

on export duties, **2**. 306, 361, 363.

on bills of credit, **2**. 309, 310 n.

on definition and punishment of crimes, **2**. 315, 316.

on power to subdue rebellion in state, **2**. 318.

on war power, **2**. 318.

proposes additional powers as to public lands, territorial government, Indians, federal district and sites, incorporations, copyright, university, encouraging knowledge, **2**. 324, [**4**. 52], **2**. 325, 615, 616, (620).

on control of militia, **2**. 332, 385, 386, 388.

on wording of implied powers, **2**. 345.

on definition of treason, **2**. 345–347, 349.

on taxation before first census, **2**. 358.

on assumption of Confederate obligations, **2**. 377.

on treaty-making power, **2**. 392, 394, (395), 540, 548, 549, **4**. 58, **S**. 262.

on appointive power, **2**. 405, 627.

on slave trade, **2**. 415, 417.

on treaties as supreme law, **2**. 417.

on oath of executive, **2**. 427.

on presidential succession, **2**. 427, 535.

on obligation of contracts, **2**. 440.

on state embargo, **2**. 440.

on state imposts and protection of manufactures, **2**. 441.

on revenue from state duties, **2**. 442.

on vote for commercial laws, **2**. 451.

on western claims, **2**. 465.

on restriction of ports of entry, **2**. 480.

on judging privileges of congressmen, **2**. 503.

on amendment, **2**. 558, 559, 629, 630.

on state inspection-charge duties, **2**. 588, 589.

on Senate rotation by lot, **2**. 612.

on suspension during impeachment, **2**. 612.

on standing army, **2**. 617.

on publication of expenditures, **2**. 618.

on exclusive control over commerce, **2**. 625.

on pardon for treason, **2**. 627.

signs Constitution, **2**. 664.

letters: to Jefferson (May) on assembling, **3**. 20;

from Grayson (May) on attitude of eastern delegates, **3**. 26, 30;

to Pendleton, father, and Jefferson (May, June) on organization, **3**. 27, 34;

to Short (June) on character and importance, **3**. 36;

to Jefferson and father (July, Aug.) on progress and notes, **3**. 60, 65, 69;

from McClurg (Aug.) on not returning, and on veto of state laws, **3**. 67, 73;

to father (Sept.) on probable adjournment, **3**. 76;

to Jefferson (Sept.) on outline, probable reception, and efficiency, **3**. 77;

from Jones (Sept.) on rumored discord, **3**. 80;

Madison, James (*continued*)

to Pendleton (Sept.) on framing plan,
3. 98;

from Carrington (Sept.) on return to
Congress, **3**. 98;

with Washington (1788) on Pinckney's
pamphlet, **3**. 123, 131;

to Washington (1788) on Mason's objections, **3**. 129;

and on Antifederalist tricks, **3**. 168;

to Jefferson and Short (1788), observations on Constitution, veto of state
laws, **3**. 131, 136;

to Pendleton (1788) on regulation of
commerce, **3**. 136.

in *Federalist:* on liberty and energetic
government, **3**. 243;

on divergent interests on Convention, **3**.
243, 244;

on Constitution as achievement, **3**. 244;

on ratification, **3**. 257;

on powers and action of Convention, **3**.
257–259;

on election of senators, **3**. 270.

letters: from Nicholas (1788) on Mason's antagonism, **3**. 296;

to Randolph (1788) on assumption and
religious tests, **3**. 297;

from Carroll (1788) on Antifederalist
stories, **3**. 305;

from Williamson (1788) on Mississippi
navigation, **3**. 306.

in Virginia convention: on publicity of
proceedings and accounts, **3**. 311,
326, 327;

on regulation of elections, **3**. 311, 319;

on adjournment of separate Houses, **3**.
312;

on congressional salaries and ineligibility
to office, **3**. 313–317;

on control of revenue bills, **3**. 317;

on militia, **3**. 318;

on slave trade, taxation, fugitives, **3**.
324–326;

on assumption, **3**. 327;

on state export duties, **3**. 328;

on election of President, **3**. 329, 331;

Mason's insinuations on consolidation,
3. 330;

on phraseology, **3**. 331;

on salary of judges, **3**. 332;

on jury trial, **3**. 332;

on mutual concessions, **3**. 335;

on regulation of commerce, **3**. 335.

letters: to Mazzei (1788) on supporting
Constitution, **3**. 353;

to Turberville (1788) on second convention, **3**. 354;

from C. Pinckney (1789) on election of
representatives, **3**. 355.

in House: (1789) on impost on slaves,
3. 355;

on origin of money bills, **3**. 356;

on power of removal, **3**. 356, 357;

on bill of rights, **3**. 357;

(1790) on assumption of state debts, **3**.
361, 366;

(1791) on bank charters, **3**. 362;

(1792) on strict construction, **3**. 366;

(1796) on proceedings of Convention
and interpretation (House and Jay
treaty), **3**. 371 *n*., 372–375.

letters: to Randolph (1789) on Virginia
plan speech, **3**. 358;

from Coxe (1790) on slave-trade memorial, **3**. 361;

to Jefferson (1799), Ritchie and Jackson
(1821), Smith (1827), Robertson
(1831) on publication of notes, **3**.
381, 447, 448, 475, 497;

to N. Webster (1809) and Grimké
(1834) on origin of Virginia plan, **3**.
409, 532.

Federalists (1803) on his views in Convention, **3**. 396, 398, 399.

Ellsworth on, as real framer, **3**. 397.

Genet's edition (1808) of Yates' notes on
same, **3**. 410–416.

and report of Hamilton's speech and
plan, **3**. 416–418, 426, 434, 480,
500, 533, 534.

aid in publication of *Journal,* correspondence with Adams (1817–20), **1**. xii,
3. 423, 426, 431, 434, 435, 445.

letters: to Monroe (1817) on judiciary
and veto, **3**. 424;

to Roane (1819), Lee (1824), Hurlbut
(1830) on broad (Marshall's) construction, **3**. 435, 464, 482;

to Walsh and Monroe (1819–20), on
slave-trade provision as applying only
to foreign trade (Missouri debate), **3**.
436, 438, 439.

71, 79), 88, 89, (90, 92, 93), 96, 97, (105, 106, 109), 110–114, **4**. 17–20, **S**. 50–51.

Franklin on multiple, **1**. 85.

in report of Virginia plan, **1**. (226), 230, (236).

multiple, in New Jersey plan, **1**. 244, (247).

Wilson on single, **1**. 254, (261, 266, 272).

single, in Hamilton plan, **1**. 292.

single voted in convention, **2**. (22), 29.

Williamson on multiple, **2**. 100.

as referred to committee of detail, **2**. (116, 121, 132), 134.

in its notes, **2**. (145), 171, **4**. 46, **S**. 189.

single, in its report (X. § 1), **2**. 185.

report voted, **2**. (396), 401.

as referred to committee of style, **2**. 572.

in its report, **2**. 597.

in Constitution, **2**. 657.

in Hamilton's unpresented plan, **3**. 619.

Davie (1788) on single, **3**. 347.

See also Council; Executive.

Number of representatives. *See* Apportionment.

Number of senators, discussed in committee of the whole, **1**. 51, 52, 150–155, (158), 163, (169).

proposed apportionment, **2**. (1), 5, 11, (12).

three for each state rejected, two voted, **2**. (85), 94, 95.

as referred to committee of detail, **2**. 133.

in its notes, **2**. (141), 154, 165, **4**. 41, **S**. 186.

two, in its report (V. § 1), **2**. 179.

report voted, **2**. (228), 233, (243).

as referred to committee of style, **2**. 566.

in its report, **2**. 591.

in Constitution, **2**. 652.

in Hamilton's unpresented plan, **2**. 621.

C. Pinckney on (1789), **2**. 355.

See also Senate.

Oath of senators in impeachment trials, requirement voted, **2**. (547), 552.

affirmation as alternative added, **2**. 610 *n*.

See also next titles.

Oath or affirmation of executive, in notes of committee of detail, **2**. (146), 172, **4**. 47, **S**. 190.

in its report (X. § 2), **2**. 185.

report amended and voted, **2**. (422), 427, (432).

as referred to committee of style, **2**. 575.

in its report, **2**. 599.

amended further, **2**. 621, 633 *n*.

in Constitution, **2**. 659.

See also next titles.

Oath to support the Constitution, by state legislators and officials, in Virginia plan, **1**. 22, (28).

postponed in committee of the whole, **1**. (117), 122.

discussed and voted in committee, **1**. (194), 203, (207).

in report of Virginia plan, **1**. (227), 231, (237).

discussed in convention, federal addition, **2**. (84), 87, 88.

as referred to committee of detail, **2**. 133.

in its notes, **2**. (146, 148), 151, 160, 174, **4**. 47, 49, **S**. 190, 191.

in its report (XX), **2**. 188.

prohibition of religious test committed, **2**. (335), 342.

affirmation added and oath voted, **2**. (461), 468.

prohibition of religious test voted, **2**. (461), 468.

as referred to committee of style, **2**. 579.

in its report, **2**. 603.

in Constitution, **2**. 663.

in Hamilton's unpresented plan, **3**. 630.

L. Martin on (Nov.), **3**. 227, 293.

Madison (1788) on interpretation of prohibition, **3**. 297.

Randolph (1788) on prohibition, **3**. 310.

See also preceding titles.

Obligation of contracts. *See* Contracts.

O'Brien, Michael M., letter from Carroll, **4**. 62, **S**. 21.

in its report, **2**. 595.

in Constitution, **2**. 655.

mail of delegates franked, **3**. 17.

Post roads, power of Congress to establish, voted, **2**. (303), 308.

    regulation of stages on, committed, **2**. (322), 326, 328.

    as referred to committee of style, **2**. 569.

    in its report, **2**. 595.

    in Constitution, **2**. 655.

Powell, John H., acknowledgment to, **4**. ix.

Powers. *See* next titles; Division of powers; Separation of powers.

Powers and duties of executive, in Virginia plan, **1**. 21.

    in Pinckney plan, **2**. 135, 158, **3**. 111, (606).

    discussion and vote in committee of the whole, **1**. (63, 64), 66, 67, 70, (73).

    in report of Virginia plan, **1**. (226), 230, (236).

    in New Jersey plan, **1**. 244, (247).

    in Hamilton plan, **1**. 292, (300).

    report voted, **2**. (23), 32, (116, 121).

    as referred to committee of detail, **2**. (132), 134.

    in its notes, **2**. (145, 146), 171, **4**. 46, 47, **S**. 189, 190.

    in its report (X. § 2), **2**. 185.

    council and cabinet, **2**. 285, 328, 329, 335–337, (342–344), 367, 427, (495), 499, (533), 537, 539, 541–543, (543).

    authority to require opinion of Supreme Court committed, **2**. 334, (341).

    report of committee of detail discussed and amended, **2**. (398), 404, (411), 419, 420, (422), 426, (547), 553.

    as referred to committee of style, **2**. 574.

    in its report, **2**. 599, 600.

    amendment of report, **2**. 621.

    exclusion of treason from pardoning power, rejected, **2**. 626, 627.

    C. Pinckney on weakness, **2**. 632.

    Mason's objections, **2**. 638, 639.

    in Constitution, **2**. 659, 660.

    in Hamilton's unpresented plan, **3**. 624.

    Randolph and L. Martin (Oct.) on pardon for treason, **3**. 127, (158), 218.

Butler on (1788), **3**. 302.

C. Pinckney (1818) on hasty increase at end of Convention, **3**. 427.

Madison's criticism of this statement (1831), **3**. 502.

See also Appointment; Executive; Treaty-making; Veto; and, for details, other subjects by name.

Powers of Congress, general expression in Virginia plan, **1**. 21, (28).

    exclusive, in Pinckney plan, **2**. 135, 136, 158, 159, **3**. 116–120, (607–609).

    discussion and vote of general powers in committee of the whole, **1**. (47), 52–54, (55, 56, 59–61).

    desire for enumeration, **1**. 53, (60), **2**. 17.

    proposals on power to remove executive, **1**. (78), 85–87, (92), 244, (247).

    to constitute inferior tribunals, **1**. (118), 125, (127), **2**. (38), 45, 46, 133, 144, 146, 168, 182, (313), 315, (320).

    in report of Virginia plan, **1**. (225), 229, 236.

    in New Jersey plan, **1**. 243, (247).

    in sketches of the plan and in Sherman's proposals, **3**. 612, 615.

    in Hamilton plan, **1**. 291, 292, (300).

    to change apportionment of representatives, **1**. (558), 559, 560, (599), 603, 606, **2**. 130, 178, (214), 223, 591, 644, 652.

    report of Virginia plan considered, all legislative powers of Confederation voted, **2**. (14), 16, 17.

    and basis of representation, **2**. 17, 25.

    in matters of "general interests" discussed and voted, **2**. (21), 25–27.

    general expression, as referred to committee of detail, **2**. 131.

    in its notes, **2**. (142–145), 151, 167, 168, **4**. 43–45.

    enumeration, in its report (VII. §§ 1, 2), **2**. 181, 182.

    regulation of jurisdiction of federal courts, **2**. 147, 173, 186, 424, 425, (431), 433, 576, 601, 661.

    to establish property qualifications for congressmen, reported, discussed, and

Qualifications of electors of representatives, in notes of committee of detail, **2**. (139), 151, 163, **4**. 40, **S**. 185.

control by states, in its report (IV. § 1), **2**. 178.

report discussed and voted, freehold requirement proposed and rejected, **2**. 201–206, (206–210, 213), 215, 216, (225).

as referred to committee of style, **2**. 565.

in its report, **2**. 590.

in Constitution, **2**. 651.

in Hamilton's unpresented plan, **3**. 619.

McHenry's explanation (Nov.), **3**. 146.

Qualification of executive, residence, in Pinckney plan, **2**. 158, (**3**. 600).

committee of detail to consider property and citizenship, to consider freehold rejected, **2**. (116, 117), 121–125, (134).

on religious test, **2**. (335), 342, (461), 468, 579, 603, 663.

committee to consider, **2**. (337), 344.

35 years, citizenship, and 21 years residence reported, **2**. 367.

nativity, or citizenship at adoption of Constitution, 14 years residence, and 35 years age reported and voted, **2**. (494), 498, (532), 536.

as referred to committee of style, **2**. 574.

in its report, **2**. 598.

in Constitution, **2**. 659.

Jay's suggestion (July) of native citizenship, **3**. 61.

Qualifications of presidential electors, ineligibility of congressmen or federal officers, **2**. 61, (517), 521, 572, 597, 658.

Qualifications of representatives, age in Virginia plan, **1**. 20.

age dropped in committee of the whole, **1**. (210), 215, (221).

25 years voted in convention, **1**. (370), 375, [**4**. 4], **1**. (379).

committee of detail to consider property and citizenship, to consider freehold and certain financial disqualifications rejected, **2**. (116, 117), 121–126.

as referred to that committee, **2**. 129, 134.

in its notes, **2**. (139), 153, 155, 156, 164–166, **4**. 39, **S**. 184.

25 years, 3 years citizenship, and residence in state, in its report (IV. § 2), **2**. 178.

power of Congress to establish property, in its report (VI, § 2), **2**. 179.

right of House to judge, in its report (VI. § 4), **2**. 180.

reported discussed and voted with 7 years citizenship and "inhabitant," **2**. (213), 216–219, (225, 226).

attempt to alter period of citizenship rejected, **2**. 230, (245), 251, (265, 266), 267–272, (281).

report as to property, discussed and rejected, **2**. (245), 248–251, (256).

report on judging, voted, **2**. (246), 254, (256).

prohibition of religious test, **2**. (335), 342, (461), 468, 579, 603, 663, **3**. 227, 297, 310.

as referred to committee of style, **2**. 565, 567.

in its report, **2**. 590, 592.

in Constitution, **2**. 651, 653.

in Hamilton's unpresented plan, **3**. 629.

McHenry's explanation (Nov.), **3**. 147.

King (1788) on lack of property, **3**. 255.

Qualifications of senators, age in Virginia plan, **1**. 20.

30 years, in committee of the whole, **1**. (211), 217, 218, (221, 228, 235).

affirmed in convention, **1**. (395), 408, (415, 435).

property, suggested, **1**. 428, (433).

committee of detail to consider property and citizenship, to consider freehold and certain financial disqualifications rejected, **1**. (116, 117), 121–126.

as referred to that committee, **1**. 129, 134.

in its notes, **1**. (141), 155, 156, 165, 166, **4**. 41, **S**. 186.

30 years, 4 years citizenship and residence in state, in its report (V. § 3), **2**. 179.

power of Congress to establish property, in its report (VI. § 2), **2**. 179.

right of Senate to judge, in its report (VI. § 4), **2**. 180.